Studies in the English Renaissance

John T. Shawcross, General Editor

Margaret Cavendish

AND THE

Exiles of the Mind

Anna Battigelli

The University Press of Kentucky

Publication of this volume was made possible in part by a grant from the National Endowment for the Humanities.

Scholarly publisher for the Commonwealth,
serving Bellarmine College, Berea College, Centre
College of Kentucky, Eastern Kentucky University,
The Filson Club Historical Society, Georgetown College,
Kentucky Historical Society, Kentucky State University,
Morehead State University, Murray State University,
Northern Kentucky University, Transylvania University,
University of Kentucky, University of Louisville,
and Western Kentucky University.

Editorial and Sales Offices: The University Press of Kentucky
663 South Limestone Street, Lexington, Kentucky 40508-4008

02 01 00 99 98   5 4 3 2 1

Library of Congress Cataloging-in-Publication Data

Battigelli, Anna, 1960-
    Margaret Cavendish and the exiles of the mind / Anna Battigelli.
      p.   cm. — (Studies in the English Renaissance)
    Includes bibliographical references (p.   ) and index
    ISBN 0-8131-2068-3 (cloth : alk. paper)
    1. Newcastle, Margaret Cavendish, Duchess of, 1624?-1674—Learning and
scholarship. 2. Women and literature—England—History—17th century.
3. Royalists—Great Britian—History—17th century. 4. Great Britain—
Intellectual life—17th century. 5. Exiles—Europe—History—17th century.
6. British—Europe—Intellectual life. 7. Exiles in literature. 8. Renaissance—
England. I. Title. II. Series.
PR3605.N2Z59   1998
828′.409—dc21   97-47261

Manufactured in the United States of America

This book is dedicated to my parents,
Mario and Giovanna Battigelli

Contents

Note on Dates, Spelling, Editions, and Titles   ix

Acknowledgments   xi

1   Introduction: The Writing Life
1

2   A Strange Enchantment:
"The Wooing of the Mind" at the Court of Henrietta Maria
11

3   World and Mind in Conflict:
Cavendish's Review of the New Atomism
39

4   "No House But My Mind":
Cavendish's Hobbesian Dilemma
62

5   Rationalism versus Experimentalism:
Cavendish's Satire of the Royal Society
85

6   Conclusion: The Exiles of the Mind
114

Appendix A
Problems in the Dating of Margaret Lucas's Birth
117

Appendix B
The Letters of Margaret Lucas Addressed to William Cavendish
119

Notes   133

Bibliography   159

Index   175

Note on Dates, Spelling, Editions, and Titles

Old Style dates are retained, but with the year beginning on 1 January. The Old Style Calendar was ten days behind the New Style Calendar used on the Continent. With the exception of the young Margaret Lucas's personal letters, spelling, capitalization, and punctuation have been left in their original state. The decision to modernize her personal letters within the text was based on the fact that their original spelling poses substantial difficulties to the reader and would interfere with the process of entering into the young Margaret Lucas's mind. The curious will find these letters transcribed with their original spelling in Appendix B.

Cavendish republished most of her volumes, sometimes more than once. Unless otherwise noted, I have used the first edition of each of her volumes in order to trace the proper sequence of the development of her ideas. Where pagination is faulty, I have tried to properly indicate the page number in the notes.

Some explanation is needed in order to account for the decision to refer to the subject of this book simply as Cavendish. She was born Margaret Lucas and discussions of her early life refer to her as such. In 1645 she married William Cavendish, marquess of Newcastle, and she became Lady Margaret, marchioness of Newcastle. In 1665, when her husband became the duke of Newcastle, she similarly became the duchess of Newcastle. She routinely signed her name as Margaret Newcastle; thus our modern habit of referring to her simply as Cavendish is admittedly anachronistic and will inevitably annoy both the reader whose historic sensibility notices the inaccuracy and the reader who believes, rightly, that we ought to refer to people by the names they choose for themselves. No objection can be made to these claims other than to suggest that for better or for worse she has become Margaret Cavendish. She transformed her life into a myth that has taken on a life of its own; I refer to her as Cavendish and to her husband as Newcastle, an admittedly lop-sided arrangement that has as its chief virtue some added clarity.

Acknowledgments

In the process of writing this book, I have incurred many debts. It is a pleasure now to acknowledge them. The research for the book began in 1992, during a National Endowment for the Humanities Summer Seminar, "The Uses of Biography and Biographical Evidence," directed by Paula R. Backscheider. Plattsburgh State University of New York facilitated further research in London and Oxford. A summer stipend from the National Endowment for the Humanities and a short-term fellowship from the Folger Shakespeare Library made it possible for me to complete the work.

Both Paula R. Backscheider and James A. Winn read and commented on chapters as they were written. I am grateful to both of them. Material from this volume was presented to members of the Folger Institute Conference on early modern women's political writings and to members of the Harvard Center for Literary and Cultural Studies, and I have benefited from comments from participants, particularly Gordon Schochet, Lois Schwoerer, Hilda Smith, and Susan Staves. Friends and colleagues have also been generous-spirited in both responding to queries and presenting them. Among these, I am especially grateful to Kim Barnes, Franca Betti, Kevin Cope, Lois Crum, Alan DeGooyer, Elizabeth Hageman, Frances Harris, Frances Huemer, Lisa and David Nurme, and Harriette L. Walker. Linda Barnard, Lorraine Moriarty, and Jeannine Zenge have my long-standing appreciation. My husband, Paul Johnston, read and commented on the manuscript as it evolved, keeping me company during the sometimes lonely work of writing.

Early versions of chapters 4 and 5 have already appeared in print. An article on Cavendish and the Royal Society appeared in *1650-1850: Ideas, Aesthetics, and Inquiries in the Early Modern Era* 2 (1996): 25-38. An article on Margaret Cavendish and Thomas Hobbes appeared in *Women Writers and the Early Modern British Political Tradition*, edited by Hilda Smith (Cambridge: Cambridge University Press, 1998). My thanks to Kevin Cope and to Cambridge University Press for permission to print extended versions of those pieces here. The British Library Board kindly granted permission to reprint Margaret Lucas's letters in Appendix B.

Special thanks go to the expert staff at the Folger Shakespeare Library, especially to Harold Batie, LuEllen DeHaven, Rosalind Larry, Camille Seerattan, Betsy Walsh, Laetitia Yeandle, and Georgianna Ziegler. The staff of the British Library, the Bodleian Library, the London Public Office, the Bailey/Howe Library at the University of Vermont, the Houghton Library at Harvard University, and the Hallward Library at the University of Nottingham graciously responded to a number of queries. I am grateful to Linda Shaw and Barbara A. Andrews for help with letters from Theodore Mayerne to William Cavendish. The Hon. Mrs. George Seymour has also been most kind. I am indebted to Nancy Grayson Holmes, to the expert staff at the University Press of Kentucky, and to the anonymous and attentive readers there for the final shape of this book. At Plattsburgh State University of New York, H.Z. Liu, dean of Arts and Sciences, and Tom Moran, provost, have steadily supported my work by facilitating travel for research. Mary Turner and the late Craig Koste graciously and efficiently obtained books and microfilm for me through interlibrary loan; without their help, this book would not now be complete.

My greatest debt is to my parents, Mario and Giovanna Battigelli. My father took an active interest in the project as it was being written, serving as a tireless, insightful, and much appreciated research assistant. It is to them that I dedicate this book.

Introduction

The Writing Life

To live over other people's lives is nothing unless we live over
their perceptions, live over the growth, the change, the varying intensities of the same—since it was by these things they
themselves lived.

—*Henry James*

No seventeenth-century English woman focused her energies more intensely on the life of the mind than did Margaret Cavendish. This characteristic more than any other distinguishes her work. She became a compulsive writer, so furiously driven that by her own account she could
not be bothered to revise for fear that doing so might "disturb [her]
following Conceptions."[1] That she considered her thoughts worthy of
recording for a future audience, one that might evaluate them with greater
equanimity than she credited her contemporaries with possessing, is
not surprising. She led a sensational life marked by public and historic
moments that brought her into close contact with kings, queens, and
the leading thinkers of her day. By marriage and by birth, she was con-
nected to families that paid huge sums, in money and in lives, to support
Charles I's losing cause during the English civil wars. For sixteen years
she lived in exile, first in Paris, then in Rotterdam, and finally in Antwerp, together with her husband, William Cavendish, marquess and later
duke of Newcastle. Their childless marriage provided her with secretar-
ies, books, tutors, time, and even encouragement to write. Because William
Cavendish was a known patron, officiating over a renowned literary
and scientific salon, her marriage also introduced her to a world of political, scientific, and literary ideas to which women were generally denied di-

rect access. In the twenty-three volumes she produced during her lifetime, she wavers between despair at the political chaos of her world and exhilaration at its new scientific discoveries; these volumes yield a rich and often prescient critique of the intellectual texture of seventeenth-century life.

The rough outlines of her life are well known. She was born Margaret Lucas, the youngest of eight children born to Elizabeth Leighton Lucas and Thomas Lucas of Colchester, Essex. The year of her birth is generally agreed to have been 1623. Her father died in September of 1625, leaving her mother to care for the family, a charge she seems to have handled capably with respect to family finances, though psychologically she created an insular family environment that had lasting and not entirely positive consequences for the formation of her daughter's character.[2] Lucas's early education was described by Lucas herself as minimal. She later wrote that

> as for tutors, although we had for all sorts of Vertues, as singing, dancing, playing on Musick, reading, writing, working, and the like, yet we were not kept strictly thereto, they were rather for formalitie than benefit, for my Mother cared not so much for our dancing and fidling, singing and prating of severall languages, as that we should be bred vertuously, modestly, civilly, honorably, and on honest principles.[3]

She nevertheless claims to have begun writing at an early age, though this work is lost. With her brothers and sisters, she attended plays in London, and she seems to have been attentive to court fashions, a characteristic in keeping with her family's royalism.

Hers might have been an unremarkable life were it not for the English civil wars, which, as she put it, "came like a Whirlwind," altering forever everything in its sweep. The Lucas family house was plundered on 22 August 1642 by parliamentary soldiers, who rightly suspected her brother John Lucas of storing arms and ammunition for the king's forces.[4] This event may well have encouraged Margaret Lucas to seek protection, mistakenly, by joining the court of Henrietta Maria at Oxford as a maid of honor. As a consequence, in the fall of 1644, when Henrietta Maria fled into exile in France, Lucas was part of her entourage. The next spring in Paris, she met William Cavendish, who had come to Paris after having abandoned his post as commander of the northern forces following his devastating defeat at Marston Moor. There, he doubtless hoped to repair his relations with the queen. Outside of the royal family itself, he was the most notorious exile in Paris. By mid-December he and Margaret Lucas were married; Margaret Lucas became Lady Margaret, marchioness of Newcastle. Together, they remained in exile until the restoration in 1660.

Though their marriage was in many senses a successful one, its early years were marked by her depression, undoubtedly intensified by the news in 1647 of the deaths of her niece, her sister, and her mother. She also learned in 1648 that her brother Sir Charles Lucas had been tried by court-martial and shot after defending their hometown of Colchester. Finally, with the news that Charles I had been executed on 30 January 1649, the exiled Royalists were forced to confront the fact that returning home was now indefinitely delayed, though they could not, even then, have foreseen the full duration of their exile. The seriousness of her husband's situation in England was made clear when on 14 March he and twelve others, including Charles Stuart and his brother James, were "proscribed and banished as enemies and traitors, and [would] die without mercy, wherever they shall be found within the limits of this nation."[5] By October the Newcastle household moved to Antwerp, which soon became a meeting ground for exiled Royalists; there they lived in the mansion formerly owned by the painter Peter Paul Rubens. For Margaret Cavendish, now secluded in Rubens's magnificent home, it must have come as something of a relief during those tumultuous years to turn away from the hostile external world to the worlds of philosophical and scientific ideas to which she had first been exposed at her husband's salon in Paris; there she had met and begun reading the works of some of the most illustrious thinkers in Europe, René Descartes, Thomas Hobbes, and Pierre Gassendi among them. She turned to studies of natural philosophy in part because, like many seventeenth-century thinkers, she read the new scientific systems as metaphors for the political chaos of her world.

She began her prolific publishing career in 1653, during a trip to England with her brother-in-law, Sir Charles Cavendish. They left for London in November of 1651 to try to compound for their sequestered estates. Her effort at compounding for her husband's estate was unsuccessful; with Charles II at large in Europe, Parliament was unlikely to compromise with the loyal duke or with his wife.[6] Charles Cavendish was more successful; he compounded for his estate and, at great cost, bought his brother's estates at Welbeck and Bolsover, saving the latter from destruction. Meanwhile, Margaret Cavendish published her first two volumes, *Poems and Fancies* and *Philosophicall Fancies*. These caused an immediate sensation. Hearing about the publication of *Poems and Fancies*, Dorothy Osborne wrote to Sir William Temple, asking him to procure a copy. Before he could do so, she had found and read a copy and had concluded "that there [were] many soberer People in Bedlam."[7]

From this point on, Cavendish wrote compulsively, thus entering public life officially and puzzling her readers as much by the sheer mass and variety of her literary production as by her strange social manner. Although her most frequently read works have been her biography of her husband and her brief autobiography, her twenty-three volumes also include volumes of plays, romances, poetry, letters, and natural philosophy. In them she explored the leading political, scientific, and philosophical ideas of her day. The diarist Samuel Pepys, like Osborne, eventually concluded that the duchess was a "mad, conceited, ridiculous woman." John Evelyn, who was initially charmed by the duchess, grew irritated by her scientific pretensions and noted that she "was a mighty pretender to Learning, Poetrie, and Philosophy, and had in both published divers books." But it is important to remember that others seemed to consider her something of an oracle. Bathsua Makin wrote that Cavendish "by her own Genius, rather than any timely Instruction, over-tops many grave Gown-Men." And even Mary Evelyn, who wrote a scathing description of Cavendish's social manner, unhappily acknowledged that Cavendish was considered by wise men to be the equal or better of Katherine Philips: "[M]en who are esteemed wise and learned, not only put them in equal balance, but suffer the greatness of the one to weigh down the certain real worth of the other."[8] The juxtaposition of Cavendish with the Royalist Philips, like her juxtaposition with the parliamentarian Lucy Hutchinson, has never benefited Cavendish; she lacks their poise and restraint. They understood how to use their status as women to their benefit in ways that she either did not understand or refused to follow.

With the restoration of Charles II to the throne of England in 1660, the couple returned to London, which they found to be a much changed and now alien environment. Though William Cavendish was created duke of Newcastle in 1665, he was profoundly disappointed to find himself excluded from the king's inner circle; and Margaret Cavendish, by now a cult phenomenon because of her prolific publishing record, was relieved when they retired to the Newcastle estate at Welbeck Abbey. They visited London occasionally, and she continued to be an item of intense public curiosity. Samuel Pepys wrote in 1667 that "all the town-talk is nowadays of her extravagancies." Never one to dismiss a fad, he joined the crowd chasing the duchess's coach in order to catch a glimpse of her. An early attempt was, he writes, frustrated by "a horrid dust and a number of coaches, without pleasure or order. That which we and almost all went for was to see my Lady Newcastle; which we could not, she being fallowed [*sic*] and crowded upon by coaches all the way she went, that nobody could come near her; only, I could see she was in a large black coach, adorned with silver instead of gold, and so with the curtains and everything black and white, and herself in her cap; but other parts I could not make." Nine days later, he was again prevented from seeing the duchess on account of the "100 boys and girls running looking upon her."[9] That spring she caused an even greater sensation when she arranged to be invited to a meeting in May of the Royal Society. Controversial, bewildering, and fascinating to her last day, the duchess died on 15 December 1673. She was buried in Westminster Abbey on 7 January 1674, where her husband had a magnificent monument built in her honor.

Those are the external facts of her life. They tell us surprisingly little about her life as a writer. When we look for evidence of her writing life, we are confronted with her extraordinary and flamboyant self-invention. One of the liabilities of leading a life so intricately bound to major historical events is that one's life so readily takes the form of a two-dimensional silhouette cast against a historically rich background; background becomes foreground as the life recedes into the distance.[10] No one appears to have been more aware of this possibility than Cavendish, who invented herself within her texts, writing herself into history. In her hands her life story and her husband's become iconic myths of the "exiled cavalier."

She choreographed her public appearances so as to appear in the role of the female cavalier, sometimes donning men's clothes or the cavalier hat or resorting to masculine gestures such as bows rather than curtsies.[11] According to John Evelyn, she arrived at her meeting with the Royal Society looking "so like a Cavalier / But that she had no beard." Sir Charles Lyttelton records meeting her in 1665 "dressed in a vest," noting that "insteed [*sic*] of courtesies, [she] made leggs and bows to the ground with her hand and head."[12] In her work and in her conversation she called attention repeatedly to her husband's financial losses, to his unrewarded loyalty and self-sacrifice, to their long banishment. Listeners like Mary Evelyn grew irritated by her catalog of greatness and loss:

I found Doctor Charlton with her, complimenting her wit and learning in a high manner; which she took to be so much her due that she swore if the schools did not banish Aristotle and read Margaret, Duchess of Newcastle, they did her wrong, and deserved to be utterly abolished. My part was not yet to speak, but admire; especially hearing her go on magnifying her own generous actions, stately buildings, noble fortune, her lord's prodigious losses in the war, his power, valour, wit, learning, and industry,—what did she not mention to his or her own advantage? . . . Never did I see a woman so full of herself, so amazingly vain and ambitious.[13]

The extravagance of Cavendish's self-fashioning before Walter Charleton and Mary Evelyn suggests the construction of a mask, and, like most writers, she hid behind the masks she created. We must turn to her work if we are ever to learn something about the elusive self behind the mask of the exiled cavalier to which she so frequently resorted. What we find, inevitably, are additional masks, but these may more closely approach what Leon Edel calls the "palpable projections of the impalpable and wholly personal inner experience."[14]

An intellectual life history is easier to explore and convey coherently when it is placed within a social context in which interactions with other people can be traced and explored. But Cavendish's social contacts, as opposed to her intellectual contacts, were minimal and problematic. As Mary Evelyn's description suggests, Cavendish never seemed able to come out from behind the mask of the "exiled cavalier" long enough to establish anything like an intimate friendship with people outside of her family circle. Thus, although everyone seems to have known about her and many recorded their observations of her, her only intimate female friend seems to have been her maid, Elizabeth Chaplain.[15] Similarly, the many letters written to her and collected for publication by her husband after her death reveal, with the possible exceptions of those from Walter Charleton, Sir Kenelm Digby, and Joseph Glanvill, respect for her family name and position more than an informed response to her work. Her own self-portraits, both those she wrote and those she had engraved as frontispieces for her volumes, typically project a woman alone with her thoughts.

And yet it seems to have been true in her case that when she was alone with her thoughts she felt least alone. Her public manner was not likely to encourage sociability. From childhood, she had been painfully bashful; she claims to have feared strangers and to have found more delight "with thoughts than in conversation." No contemporary description of her alters this characterization. Her eccentric fashions, her theatrical manners, her odd self-portraits—each of these gestures is calculated to engage people while keeping them at a comfortable distance. We might conclude that for Cavendish this distance was in some way convenient, and yet for someone as interested in the world of ideas as she was, it cannot have been wholly satisfactory. Although she met the leading thinkers of her day and read their works, she never seems to have felt comfortable speaking with them. They, in turn, seem to have felt awkward around her. When, for example, during her trip to London in 1651-53, she ran into her husband's intimate friend, Thomas Hobbes, and invited him to dinner, he refused. She records as his excuse that he claimed to have had "some businesse," which, she speculates, "I suppose required his absence."[16] One senses in this remark that she longed to talk with Hobbes and others with the kind of ease her husband and her brother-in-law found so natural. Prevented both by social conventions and by temperament from interacting fully with others in public, she turned to her writing. Writing provided her with a means of intellectual engagement that was not possible for her through ordinary conversation. Whatever other selves existed—wife, stepmother, sister-in-law, sister, daughter—became of secondary interest to her compared to the writing self she invented within her texts.

As a writer, she identifies herself consistently throughout her work as an exile, transforming her comparative social isolation into a rhetorical stance, a position of advantage from which to address her world. Her life story can be said to have consisted, in fact, of a series of exiles—first from her childhood in an insular Colchester family to the displaced court at Oxford, then to Henrietta Maria's exiled court in Paris, to her husband's banished households in Paris and Antwerp, to her study at Welbeck Abbey, and, ultimately, to the worlds within her texts. She turned this life story to use in her work, using her very real experience as an exile as a privileged rhetorical stance from which she might address and even critique her world authoritatively.

We need to be watchful, however, that her rhetorical stance as an exile not distract us from the very real fact that she was familiar with the work of the leading thinkers of her day. Her social isolation was not an intellectual isolation, though she frequently portrays herself as a lonely and isolated genius creating volumes of natural philosophy exclusively through the use of her imagination. In fact, however, she read Hobbes and Descartes and was introduced to the ideas of Gassendi; if she lacked the kind of discipline expected of a serious response to these writers, she nevertheless grasped—more presciently than many of her contemporaries—some of the major consequences of their work. Furthermore, the uses to which she put the new science and its systems are revealing; these systems seemed to her to promise to provide explanations for the political turbulence of mid–seventeenth-century England. For her and for others, the civil wars had, in large part, been caused by controversies that resulted from an incorrect understanding of the proper relation between mind and world. That relation is frequently her true subject; she used the new scientific systems, for example, to explore its delicate and potentially volatile nature. But while she viewed the relation between mind and world with anxiety, she was actively engaged with the world of ideas to which her life exposed her. If she retreated from the external world to the inner worlds of her mind, she did so in the company of the thoughts and ideas of others.

It is characteristic of exiles to criticize their culture, and Cavendish's work is a sustained and sometimes passionate criticism of hers. But here we arrive at a central paradox governing her work and her life and complicating the mask of the exiled cavalier that she seems to have found so useful. Her compulsion to write was matched by a contradictory concern, an anxiety expressed throughout her work regarding her public engagement in controversies. One of the brutal lessons of the English civil wars had been their demonstration of the ease with which written controversy could escalate into physical violence. For Cavendish, ideas had a material reality: "Notions of Nothing," she explains, "cannot be, for we cannot Think, but it hath some Thing, or Matter, or Substance, as a Ground to move on." In the same volume she claims that "to say Nothing, as that No Substance can, may, or hath a Beeing, is against Sense and Reason, for there is not any Motion, or Notion, Thought, Imagination, or Idea, but is of a Corporeal Substance." Elsewhere she claims that "fancy is not an imitation of nature, but a naturall Creation . . . so that there is as much difference between fancy, and imitation, as between a Creature, and a Creator."[17] Like others writing after the wars, Cavendish reveals a heightened sensitivity to the potentially aggressive and disputatious nature of the human mind. She was, in short, a compulsive writer deeply suspicious, even fearful, of the printed word. In this, too, she was emblematic of her time.

⌐Compelled to write and yet fearful of the consequences of writing, she was forced to develop complex rhetorical strategies that met her paradoxical needs.⌐Here, too, her self-created role as an isolated exile became useful to her. She turned to highlighting the subjective nature of her writing, choosing genres and rhetorical stances accordingly. Thus, she reviewed Gassendi's revival of Epicurean atomism in a series of poems; she cast her response to Hobbes, Descartes, Henry More, and Jan Baptista Van Helmont in the form of private letters to a friend; she attacked the Royal Society's empiricism in a romance; and she explored the emerging philosophy of mind in plays and fiction. When she chose more apparently objective genres, as she did in *Observations Upon Experimental Philosophy* (1666), she framed her discussions by highlighting their origin in the subjective realm of her mind; *Observations,* she explains, originated in a "war in [her] Mind" between old thoughts and new thoughts.[18] By choosing genres carefully or by highlighting their apparently subjective nature, she could address matters of public interest while appearing to be engaged in private and subjective discourse. She was perhaps too successful in calling attention to her subjectivity, and her satirical reviews have been traditionally dismissed as the uninformed if sometimes charming ramblings of an isolated, eccentric, or even mad woman.

This intellectual biography focuses on Cavendish's mature writing life from her experience at the court of Henrietta Maria to her death in 1673. It thus looks back only fleetingly at her early life. Cavendish's writing life has been surprisingly neglected; it seems to have been central to her sense of self, and, despite and perhaps even as a result of her eccentricity, it reveals a great deal about the nature of the thinking life in seventeenth-century England. It is time to acknowledge and explore her thought by tracing her responses to the figures she encountered throughout her spectacular life. Separate chapters explore her responses to Henrietta Maria, Pierre Gassendi, Thomas Hobbes, and finally to Robert Hooke and the members of the Royal Society. Although this is not in any sense an exhaustive list of the contemporaries to whom she responded, it serves to trace her developing sense of herself as an exile, as a thinking self consciously and willfully detached from a chaotic and at times frightening external world.

Finally, her sense of herself as an exile of the external world has a place in the emerging philosophy of mind.⌐She was, more than most of her contemporaries, unguarded and open in acknowledging and exploring the fluid, elusive, and erratic shapings and reshapings of the self.]Her unwillingness to revise much helped her to record, more immediately than most writers dare, the subjective nature of the mind. This interest in subjectivity is in itself significant, since she wrote at the very moment when concepts of inwardness, interiority, and selfhood were reaching full development in Hobbes's and Descartes's philosophies of mind.[19] Because she grasped the significance of their project, and in fact might be said to have tried to domesticate it, her work is a revealing document, displaying a thinking life aware of its role as a thinking life. Placed in this context, the very characteristics that have caused scholars to dismiss Cavendish—her lack of method, her willingness to embrace contradictions, her confidence in deductive thinking, her eccentricity and self-absorption—become historically significant. Tracing her interest in interiority throughout her mature life—evident in her very real retreat to the exiles of the mind—makes possible a fuller and more accurate understanding of the self behind the mask of the exiled cavalier.

2

A Strange Enchantment

"The Wooing of the Mind"
at the Court of Henrietta Maria

Margaret Cavendish—then Margaret Lucas—first encountered Platonism when she joined the court of Henrietta Maria at Oxford in 1643. She became a maid of honor at a moment of crisis, as the hostilities of the English civil war intensified, focusing in large part on the Catholic queen, whom the House of Commons had that summer accused of high treason.[1] Lucas's brief attendance on the queen would have profound consequences for her later writing career as Margaret Cavendish. She accompanied Henrietta Maria into exile in France, and though she could not have foreseen it at the time, she spent most of the next sixteen years in exile. There in April of 1645 she met one of the queen's favorites, William Cavendish, then marquess of Newcastle. By mid-December, after a whirlwind courtship that apparently occupied the gossipy exiled court at Saint Germain, they were married.[2] Both lived out the rest of their lives as conscious symbols of a past order, one that existed chiefly in the communal realms of the mind.

By attending the queen, Lucas was exposed to one of the most well-connected and intellectually driven women of her day. Charged by her godfather, Pope Urban VIII, with the mission of improving conditions for Catholics in England, Henrietta pursued that charge actively—even, her subjects might have added, disastrously.[3] Lucas herself never became interested in Catholicism, though she was surely exposed to it at court; in fact, she was all her life critical of plans for any sort of religious campaign, in part, we might guess, because she had witnessed the unhappy results of Henrietta's attempts at proselytizing, but also because of her deep skepticism about what could be known about the nature of God. She was nevertheless profoundly influenced by the queen's character. In particular, she appropriated the language of the Platonic love doctrines that Henrietta had imported into court culture. By 1643 Henrietta's pastoral Platonism was admittedly in retreat; nevertheless, Lucas's letters to William during their courtship in 1645 reveal a profound interest in the language of Platonic love, used in ways that parallel directly the language employed in the masques of Henrietta's court. As the first written records of Lucas's thought and as the only actual and sustained correspondence of her career, these letters reveal Cavendish's character more immediately, if not more directly, than her printed work. In her letters to William Cavendish, the language of Platonic love seems to provide her with welcome relief from the turmoil and pettiness of court life by opening up the worlds of the mind as a refuge. Furthermore, the politically explosive uses to which Henrietta and her Roman Catholic coterie put these doctrines underscored what became for Lucas a lifelong theme: the inevitable conflict between competing sensibilities.[4]

Although Lucas joined the court too late to participate in court masques, she and her brothers and sisters were acquainted with Caroline drama, having been used "in Winter time to go sometimes to Plays."[5] Like Mary Rich, countess of Warwick, who confessed remorsefully to having spent her time "in seeing and reading plays and romances, and in exquisite and curious dressing," Margaret Lucas may well have spent time at her Colchester home reading plays, copies of which circulated broadly.[6] She may even have read printed descriptions of masques which, as Martin Butler notes, "were commonly sent into the country." Once she joined the court, Platonic love doctrines would have been available to her in romances, circulating manuscripts such as Walter Montagu's *The Shepheard's Paradise* (a pastoral comedy that served as a code book of the queen's fashions), and as part of the general code of polite manners any minister needed to master if he were to gain the queen's ear.[7] Finally, by marrying a courtier thirty years her senior, steeped in the manners and theatrical traditions of the court, Lucas continued to learn about the details of Platonic love fashion even after she left the queen's immediate circle. She absorbed these doctrines, putting them to use in exaggerated form throughout her work. Their significance for Lucas's intellectual development is crucial: Platonism focused Lucas's attention on the worlds of the mind. Although later influences—atomism, Cartesian rationalism, Hobbesian political theory, empiricism—proved instrumental in modifying Lucas's extreme Platonic idealism, the source of that idealism can be traced directly to the striking queen and to the court's Platonic interests in the "wooing of the mind."

HENRIETTA MARIA AND HER COURT

Central to court culture throughout the 1630s and particularly after 1635, when she and her faction acquired a new authority because of her assurance of having "the king's ear," was the lively French queen.[8] Far from being the pleasure seeker she has often been called, Henrietta was a formidable presence, refashioning herself as necessary, shedding her early role as a glamorous if somewhat frivolous court beauty when an Amazonian role proved more suitable for leading troops from Bridlington Bay to her husband at Oxford. Her attention to dress, her sometimes whimsical use of costume, her redecoration of palaces, her interest in portraits, her piety and religious practices, and her presentation of and performance in theatrical entertainments—each of these practices reflects an active interest in the ways in which she might construct a public image of herself and her court. Her protean self-fashioning was governed by two passionate and frequently contradictory interests: the first was her devotion to her religion; the second, her devotion to her husband. Theatrical activity seems to have provided her with an outlet through which she could reconcile these two competing concerns by both pleasing her husband with her performances and obliquely addressing religious issues through the language of Platonic love.

Like Henrietta, Charles was alive to the degree to which he might control his public image. His temperament differed from hers, however, in being more retired. His biographer, Kevin Sharpe, observes that

> in his personal conduct and morality, Charles was an ascetic figure of great personal control. He dressed unostentatiously, he ate moderately, he drank little alcohol. The king organized his day carefully around duties and devotions; he adopted the rigid routine of the controlled personality, from his early rising when he donned his badge of St. George to winding his watch last thing at night.... The king set an example of decorum, upright behaviour and self-control which he expected to see emulated by others.... It may be that such self-regulation had been learned rather than naturally inherited. His impulsive behaviour in going to Spain, and while he was there,

do not suggest a complete absence of passion. As Charles was to tell his son in his last hours, 'we have learnt to own ourself by retiring into ourself.'... He placed such an emphasis upon morality because, as the iconography of paintings and masques evidences, he believed the regulation of the passions to be the foundation of order.[9]

Charles's interest in learning "to own [himself] by retiring into [himself]" matched Henrietta's religious interest in regulating her own mind; if she proved more willing to proselytize while he proved more interested in regulating his courtiers' morality, they nevertheless shared an interest in the regulation of the mind.

The *Calendars of State Papers, Domestic* are littered with references to Henrietta's interest and active participation in pastorals and plays, activities described with some anxiety, as having once "been thought a strange sight" for a queen. Her innate vivacity led her to shift roles frequently both onstage and offstage, often through the use of costume. She is recorded, for example, as having impulsively taken up a fork and rake and joined haymakers in a field: "The Queen is much delighted with the River of the Thames and doth love to walk in the meadows and look upon the haymakers, and will sometimes take a rake and fork and sportingly make hay with them," wrote Sir John Davys to Henry, earl of Huntingdon, in 1625. In 1626 she is described as having "acted in a beautiful pastoral of her own composition, assisted by twelve of her ladies whom she had trained since Christmas. The pastoral succeeded admirably; not only the decorations and changes of scenery, but also in the acting and recitation of the ladies—Her Majesty surpassing all the others. The performance was conducted as privately as possible, inasmuch as it is an unusual thing in this country to see the Queen upon a stage; the audience consequently was limited to a few of the nobility, expressly invited, no others being admitted."[10] And although at first efforts were made to hide her theatrical activities because they were out of keeping with the code of royal behavior, by 1636 Henrietta could make a public gesture of "putting off majesty" by dressing in citizens' clothes to attend a masque presented by the Middle Temple.[11]

Henrietta's theatrical tastes, like her religious tastes, did little to promote her popularity among her subjects. In the words of one critic, Henrietta arrived at court accustomed "to court entertainments in which royalty and nobility took a more histrionic role than was thought decorous at the Stuart court." Largely at issue was Henrietta's use of Platonic love doctrines, which, as another critic explains, antagonized Henrietta's subjects: "French in origin, artificial in manners, casuistic in ethics, [they] naturally aroused Puritan ire, which flamed even hotter as the Queen and her party displayed increasing allegiance to Rome."[12] Particularly vexing was the proselytizing nature of these Platonic love doctrines. Henrietta's Catholicism was inspired by Saint Francis de Sales, whose brand of devout humanism lent itself to the précieuse Platonic love traditions with which Henrietta entertained her court.[13] At the heart of Sales's religion was a celebration of spiritualized love, evident in the following passage, that blended easily with those traditions: "How good is it to love upon earth, as they love in heaven: to learne to cherish one another in this world, as we shall doe eternallie in the next. I speak not heere of the simple love of charitie, for that must be borne unto all men, but of spirituall frindshippe, by which two, or three, or manie soules, do comunicate their devotion, their spirituall affections, & make themselves to be but one spirit in diverse bodies." Furthermore, Sales's instructions on the virtues of friendship could be interpreted as encouraging the kind of exclusivity and elitism at work at court: "Love everie one ... according as charitie commandeth ... but have frindship onely with those, with whome thou maist comunicate in good and virtuous things." Like Thomas à Kempis, whose sterner *Imitation of Christ* Henrietta read daily later in life, Sales encouraged a sort of spiritual elitism, one inevitably intensified by the tensions between Charles's Anglican court and the courtiers and Catholic priests with whom Henrietta surrounded herself.[14] The degree to which Henrietta's religious practices shaped court fashions is evident in the fact that John Cosin's *Collection of Private Devotions* (1627) was written in response to the request of court ladies who hoped, according to John Evelyn, to "appear as devout, and be so too, as the new-come-over French Ladys."[15] Henry Cavendish, second duke of Newcastle, carefully signed his copy of an English translation of Sales's *Delicious Entertainments of the Soule* (1626), dating it 1676, the year of his father's death. The book may well have belonged to the Newcastle library and perhaps even to Margaret Cavendish and passed on to Henry after he inherited his father's title and his books in 1676.[16]

Platonism was, of course, not new to the English court when Henrietta arrived in 1625 at the age of fifteen. But the young queen, motivated by firm religious and artistic beliefs, systematically incorporated into court life the précieuse cult of Platonic love to which she had been introduced through her mother, Marie de Medici, and through the Hôtel Rambouillet.[17] Book 3 of Henrietta's favorite book, Honoré D'Urfé's *L'Astrée,* was dedicated to Marie de Medici. D'Urfé's pastoral romance served as the source book of the Platonic system, providing a code of manners for polite society in France and England.[18] An English translation is dated 1620, and by 1627 its Platonic theories circulated widely at court through *The Private Memoirs of Sir Kenelm Digby.* Under Henrietta's influence, the impact of D'Urfé's book for the English court was to create a stylized and integrated court culture in which, in pointed contrast to the Jacobean court, the relationship between men and women was both idealized and celebrated. As Erica Veevers notes, "contemporaries credited [*L'Astrée*'s] elegant form of expression with being able to teach manners to men, and philosophy even to women."[19]

The Platonic elements of Caroline theater are well documented; by 1634 the Platonic love cult governed both the themes of the Caroline theater and the fashions of court culture. The moment of its arrival is generally documented by James Howell's letter of 1634: "The Court affords little News at present, but there is a Love call'd Platonick Love, which much sways there of late; it is a Love abstracted from all corporeal gross Impressions and sensual Appetite, but consists in Contemplations and Ideas of the Mind, not in any carnal Fruition. This Love sets the Wits of the Town on work; and they say there will be a Mask shortly of it, whereof Her Majesty and her Maids of Honour will be part."[20] Howell's amusement with this new love fashion, which consisted "in Contemplations and Ideas of the Mind, not in any carnal Fruition" calls attention to the degree to which the Platonic love craze had infiltrated court culture. It also prefigures Cavendish's dramatic characters such as Lady Contemplation, who "makes but little use of her Body, living always within her Minde," or the Princess in *The Presence,* who falls in love not with a corporeal lover but with an idea in her mind. Ridiculed as the Platonic love craze was, even William Cavendish, an anti-Platonist, looked back nostalgically, after five years of exile, to the masques in which he and other courtiers participated, recommending them to the young Charles as a suitable "divertisement" for a king and noting in particular that "Etaliens make the Seanes best."[21]

That Henrietta's interest in play-acting went beyond mere pleasure seeking is evident in the kind of influence she exerted over court writers such as Inigo Jones and Walter Montagu, whose productions very often served to disseminate her Platonic love doctrines. Noting the vacuum in which Jones found himself after his break in 1630 with Ben Jonson, John Peacock suggests that both Henrietta and Charles became "Jones's chief collaborators." Erica Veevers has suggested that the "interminable debates on the religion of love" presented in Henrietta's masques could "in a changed atmosphere, become debates on and expositions of religion itself."[22] As evidence, Veevers cites William Davenant and Inigo Jones's *The Temple of Love.* In that masque Henrietta played Queen Indamora, whose beauty was to reestablish the temple of chaste love in Britain. Indamora and "the beauties of her train"

> . . . raise strange doctrines and new sects of love,
> Which must not woo or court the person, but
> The mind, and practice generation not
> Of bodies, but of souls.[23]

Veevers notes that the masque coincided with the near completion of the queen's chapel at Somerset House. The chapel offered what Malcolm Smuts refers to as "the most spectacular example of the queen's efforts to proselytize through art." As Veevers suggests, the queen may well have hoped that the considerable splendor of the chapel, which was illuminated by four hundred candles, might inspire "generation not / of bodies but of souls" through conversion.[24] The celebration of Indamora's beauty as exerting power to enforce the "wooing of the mind" signals one of the key attractions of Platonic love doctrine: it offered a way of transforming feminine beauty into intellectual power. By joining the court, Margaret Lucas was introduced to a young queen who understood how to use both aesthetic and feminine beauty to gain access to the life of the mind and whose example may well have encouraged Lucas as a young woman to begin perceiving herself as a thinking self.[25]

Unpopular from the start because of her open and aggressive Catholicism, the queen became increasingly disliked as her efforts at conversion became known and exaggerated through rumor. With the publication of William Prynne's *Histriomastix* (1633) and his subsequent sentencing by the Star Chamber for his alleged attack on the queen, the court culture Henrietta Maria helped shape had become, as Peter William Thomas and others have shown, "a potentially explosive political issue."[26] At issue was Prynne's violent denunciation of actresses, which appeared (coming as it did on the heels of Henrietta Maria's marathon eight-hour all-female presentation of Walter Montagu's *The Shepheard's*

Paradise) to attack the queen's visible role in shaping court culture. The fact that *The Shepheard's Paradise* was a thinly veiled and idealized account of the royal couple's romance and that it presented a set of codified rules for the queen's household only aggravated matters further. It had the status of a cult piece even before Prynne's attack, and though it was not published until 1659, it had circulated broadly in manuscript form before that.[27]

The proselytizing interests behind Henrietta's use of Platonic love doctrine irritated her subjects, but the acting role that led to her being charged with treason occurred offstage. In February of 1642, she assumed a military role reminiscent of her role as an Amazon in the last masque produced by Inigo Jones, *Salmacida Spolia* (1640): taking with her the crown jewels, Henrietta left for Holland to pawn or sell them in order to raise money for arms and ammunition for the Royalist army. She had been in Holland roughly a year, when Parliament discussed forcibly taking her hostage on her return.[28] Her negotiations in Holland had been difficult; her voyage home, stormy; and her return to Bridlington Bay on 22 February 1643 was greeted the next morning with cannon fire from parliamentary ships firing on her anchored ships. Her biographer describes the early morning attack: "[Henrietta] was forced to rise from her bed and to flee in such clothes as she could hastily gather about her to the dubious safety of a ditch behind the nearby village. As she hurried for shelter, cannon shot striking the ground sprayed dirt over her, and a soldier about twenty paces away was shot dead. When the receding tide forced the large Parliamentary ships to withdraw seaward, the attack ended without having inflicted damage on the munitions contained in the holds of the vessels moored in the harbor."[29] Far from collapsing in fear, however, Henrietta seems to have been stimulated by the excitement and danger of military confrontation. For instance, despite the danger of the situation, she claimed cheerfully in a letter to Charles that in case of an invasion she was prepared to "act the captain, though a little low in stature."[30]

Henrietta's letters to Charles during this period confirm that she found her new military responsibilities exhilarating and that she enthusiastically created a military identity for herself. When her march across England at the head of an army to meet the king at Oxford was delayed, she had an opportunity to develop her military role further. Her hunger for still more power over her troops is evident in her complaint, for example, that "this army is called the queen's army, but I have little power over it, and I assure you that if I had, all would go on better than it does" (200). Elsewhere, she describes herself as a "she-majesty generalissima" and refers proudly to "*our* army" and to "*my* regiment" (222, 179, 191). Her forecast that "our army marches tomorrow to put an end to Fairfax's excellency," like her report that one of her troops had "made" six of theirs "fly," reveals the pleasure she took in martial engagements (179, 223). She must have talked about this experience with her courtiers at Oxford as she did later with Madame de Motteville, who recorded Henrietta's account of the march across England: "Having mustered a gallant Army, she put her self at the Head of it, and marched on directly towards the King her Husband, always riding on Horseback without the Effeminacy of a Woman, and living with her Soldiers in the Manner that it may be imagined Alexander did with his. She [ate] with them in the open Field without any Ceremonies. She treated them as Brethren, and they all loved her entirely."[31] The many similarities between this passage and Cavendish's tales about cross-dressed heroines who engage in military encounters and capture the hearts of their subordinates suggest Henrietta's lifelong impact on her young maid of honor. In writing the biography of her husband, Cavendish described Henrietta's behavior at York as "shew[ing] as much Courage as ever any person could do."[32]

For her military role and Parliament's efforts to capture her, Henrietta was portrayed in newsbooks and pamphlets either as a dangerous invading she-general or as a pursued heroine.[33] Alternately horrified or admiring, reports circulated of Henrietta's military recruitment in Holland and of her Amazonian march across England at the head of an army to join her husband at the displaced court at Oxford. There, Charles and Henrietta once again held court, though soon enough they would be separated for good.

A DEFAMILIARIZED WORLD: WAR AND EXILE

It was at this critical junction—after the court moved to Oxford, after the queen's march across England, after the House of Commons charged the queen with high treason—that the young Margaret Lucas joined Henrietta Maria's court. As she describes it, she was taken with "a great desire to be one of [the queen's] Maids of Honour, hearing [that she] had not the same number she was used to have." The romantic image of a martial queen leading troops across England to the king may well have prompted Lucas to join the court. But there were also other reasons for Lucas's "great desire" to join the court. Her home in an insular and unpopular Royalist Colchester family had become increasingly uncomfortable. A year earlier, the Lucas home had been plundered by parliamentary sympathizers who rightly suspected her brother, John Lucas, of collecting arms and horses and of intending to bring them to the king.[34] According to *Mercurius Rusticus,* a supplement to the Royalist newsbook *Mercurius Aulicus,* a mob beset the Lucas house and twenty men

> rusht into the Ladies Chamber, laid hands upon [John Lucas's wife], set a sword to her breast, requiring her to tell where the Arms and Cavaliers were. . . . The People lay[ed] hands on Sir John Lucas his Sister, and carr[ied] them attended with swords, guns, and halberts to the common Goal. Last of all they [brought] forth his Mother with the like or greater insolency, who being faint and breathless, hardly obtained leave to rest herself in a shop by the way; yet this leave was no sooner obtained, but the rest of that rude rabble threatened to pull down the house, unless they thrust her out, being by this meanes forced to depart from thence. A Countryman (whom the Alarme had summoned to his work) espye[d] her, and pressing with his Horse through the Crowd, struc[k] at her head with his sword so heartily, that if an Halbert had not crossed the blow, both her sorrowes and her journey had there found an end.[35]

Even allowing for the partisan sentiment of the source of this report, the experience of having her house plundered must have had deep emotional consequences for Lucas. According to this report, the houses and gardens were defaced, and deer in the park were killed along with cattle. Finally, the intruders broke into the family vault "where [Lucas] Ancestours were buryed, and with Pistols, Swords, and Halberts, transfix[ed] the Coffins of the dead."[36] Four days later, the women were released from the common jail and allowed to return to their ransacked home. The event would become a permanent part of Royalist martyrology, first in 1643, when it was the lead story in *Mercurius Rusticus,* and again in 1646, when it was represented on the title page of the collected edition of *Mercurius Rusticus* in one of the ten compartments detailing parliamentary atrocities.[37] Though it is not clear whether it was Margaret or her sister Anne who accompanied their mother, it is clear that even as Henrietta Maria marched to Oxford at the head of an army, Margaret Lucas found herself inextricably aligned with the Royalist cause and with the queen.

By joining the court, Lucas stepped out of an insular family into an insular court. The court's move to Oxford had, of course, disrupted court life. Lucas seems to have found Oxford a strange and frightening place, and in this she was hardly alone. Anne Fanshawe's description of Oxford reveals the defamiliarized world in which courtiers now found themselves:

> My father commanded my sisters and myself to come to him to Oxford where the Court then was but we that had till that hour liv'd in great plenty and great order found ourselves like fishes out of the water and the sene so changed that we knew not at all how to act any part but obedience, for from as good houses as any Gentleman of England had we come to a Bakers house in an obscure Street and from roomes well furnished, to lye in a very bad bed in a Garrett to one dish of meat and that not the best ordered, no mony for we were as poor as Job, nor clothes more than a man or two brought in their cloak bags, we had the perpetuall discourse of losing and gaining Towns and men; at the windows the sad spectacle of war.[38]

Lucas would willingly have left the court soon after she arrived. By her account, she was simply unequipped for the contradictions inherent in the court's social life. Henrietta Maria's personal piety, for instance, did not prevent the queen from tolerating a much looser standard of behavior among her courtiers, many of whom viewed the court as a sort of sexual playground. This Lucas found difficult. As she explains, leaving the comfort of her brothers and sisters meant that she "had no Foundation [on which] to stand, or Guide to direct me, which made me afraid; lest I should wander with Ignorance out of the waies of Honour, so that I knew not how to behave my self. Besides, I had heard the World was apt to lay aspersions even on the innocent, for which I durst neither look up with my eyes, nor speak, nor be any way sociable, insomuch as I was thought a Natural Fool." Despite her discomfort with court life and her desire to leave the court, her mother urged her to stay:

> In truth, my bashfulness and fears made me repent my going

from home to see the World abroad, and much I did desire to return to my Mother again, or to my sister Pye, with whom I often lived when she was in London, and loved with a supernatural affection: but my Mother advised me there to stay, although I put her to more charges than if she had kept me at home, and the more, by reason she and my Brothers were sequestred from their Estates, and plundered of all their Goods, yet she maintained me so, that I was in a condition rather to lend than to borrow, which Courtiers usually are not.[39]

Her decision to stay proved decisive. In April of 1644, Henrietta took her retinue first to Exeter, where she gave birth to a daughter, whom she was forced to leave behind her, then to Bath, and finally to France. Her health suffered, and when she arrived in France she was described as looking "more like a miserable heroine of a romance than a true queen." She finally arrived in Paris in November, where she was given apartments and a pension by the French government. Lucas fled with Henrietta Maria into France, and she never saw most of her family members again. As she explained, "this unnatural War came like a Whirlwind," destroying her family and the life with which she had been familiar.[40]

All the exiled courtiers found the experience of living in a penurious and exiled court uncomfortable. For Lucas, who claimed never fully to command French, exile was even more uncomfortable. The queen's spirits were no longer buoyed by military engagement, and she seems to have been frustrated by her inability to help her husband's cause further; moreover, her recovery from illness was slow, and it was "beginning to affect her spirits, so that she became sensitive to imagined slight or injury."[41] Part of the queen's dejection must have resulted from the increasingly precarious status of her husband's forces. On 2 July 1644 the Royalists had effectively lost the war in the north with the battle of Marston Moor, after which William Cavendish, commander of the king's northern forces, had fled abroad, first to Hamburg, then on April 10 to Paris.[42] He had headed for Paris hoping to reestablish, despite his military failure, his longtime relationship with Henrietta and with the court; instead, he fell in love with the queen's unusual maid of honor.

Lucas's letters, written during her courtship, reveal her discomfort with court life. Like the queen, though for different reasons, the young Lucas had become dejected, and although she avoided the queen's Catholicism, she adopted its Neoplatonic rejection of the external world. She described her state of mind, for instance, as "a very melancholy humor . . . most of my contemplations are fixed on nothing but dissolutions, for I look upon this world as on a death's head for mortification, for I see all things subject to alteration and change, and our hopes as if they had taken opium; therefore I will despise all things of this world, I will not say all things in it, and love nothing but you that is above it." Part of this melancholy can be attributed to the malice of court gossip. Courtiers, apparently shocked by the match, circulated rumors regarding the illegitimacy of Lucas's oldest brother, who was born before his parents married, while his father was banished to France for killing a man in a duel. When Newcastle wrote to Lucas about this, she dismissed the charge, claiming that "they that told you of my mother [had] better intelligence than I."[43] That she was stung by the attempts to break the match is evident, however, in her repeated warnings throughout her letters of her "many enemies" and of the court's "idle discourse," "frivolous talk," and "malice."[44] When in addition to the court's gossip, the queen revealed her displeasure at not being consulted in the match, Lucas collapsed under the pressure and became ill. She wished "life only to be still" and came to depend on Newcastle as providing the only happiness available in an otherwise morally decayed world: "[M]y lord, I have not had much experience of the world, yet I have found it such as I could willingly part with it, but since I knew you, I fear I shall love it too well, because you are in it, and yet, methinks, you are not in it, because you are not of it; so I am both in it and out of it, a strange enchantment."[45] This "strange enchantment" of being both in the world and out of it characterizes Margaret Cavendish's mature work. Like the queen, whose unpopular Catholicism provoked her retreat—first into an elite court coterie in London and Oxford, then into physical exile in France, and ultimately into monastic life—Lucas's unhappiness with court culture led her to position herself intellectually as a willing exile from a corrupt world.

Perhaps it was in reaction to this hostile environment that she began in her letters to Newcastle to portray herself as something of a voluntary exile who shuns the morally corrupt world by articulating sentiments fully in keeping with the Platonic love doctrines popularized by Henrietta. She claimed, for example, that she was "not easily drawn to be in love, for I did never see any man but yourself that I could have married." Later, when she wrote *A True Relation*, she recalled her love for her husband at that time:

My Lord the Marquis of Newcastle did approve of those bashfull fears which many condemn'd, and would choose such a Wife as he might bring to his own humours, and not such an one as was wedded to self-conceit, or one that had been temper'd to the humours of another, for which he wooed me for his Wife; and though I did dread Marriage, and shunn'd Mens companies, as much as I could, yet I could not, nor had not the power to refuse him, by reason my Affections were fix'd on him, and he was the onely Person I ever was in love with: Neither was I ashamed to own it, but gloried therein, for it was not Amorous Love, I never was infected therewith, it is a Disease, or a Passion, or both, I onely know by relation, not by experience; neither could Title, Wealth, Power or Person entice me to love; but my Love was honest and honourable, being placed upon Merit.[46]

In her behavior and in her writing, the mature Margaret Cavendish devoted herself to memorializing the values of Henrietta's household, even as she criticized both the kind of proselytizing zeal Henrietta herself embodied and the frivolous nature of court life. Her frequent recourse throughout her life to claims of being chaste can be understood as a remnant of the Platonic love craze that had flourished in Henrietta's household.[47] Her plays and fiction document her interest in Platonic love doctrine. And even when she returned from exile after the Restoration, she continued to refer to her life with her husband in terms of a pastoral retirement.

THE COURT RECALLED:
THE PLATONIC ELEMENT IN CAVENDISH'S PLAYS

When in subsequent years Margaret Cavendish recalled court life and its cult of Platonic love, as she did throughout her sixteen plays, it was to explore what she saw as the disturbing incongruity between the inner world of the mind and the external world. That her experience at court had been profoundly disappointing is evident in the many passages condemning it, such as the following one from *The World's Olio* (1655): "Courts should be a pattern and an example of vertue to all the rest of the kingdom, being the ruler and chief head, to direct the body of state; but most commonly instead of clemency, justice, modesty, friendship, temperance, humility, and unity, there is faction, pride, ambition, luxury[,] covetousness, hate, envy, slander, treachery, flattery, impudence, and many the like; yet they are oft-times covered with a vaile of smooth professions and protestations, which glisters like gold, when it is copper'd tinsel; but to study Court-ship, is rather to study dissembling formality, then noble reality" (48). The comparison drawn here between the ideal court, which "should be a pattern and an example of vertue" and the actual courtier, who too often studies "dissembling formality," reflects Cavendish's lifelong attention to the incongruity between ideals and reality, between the worlds of her mind and the conflicting external world.

There are reasons to believe that Cavendish composed her plays earlier than their publication dates suggest. She published two volumes of plays: *Playes* (1662) and *Plays, Never Before Printed* (1668). We know that they were not written before her marriage because she tells us that she began writing them only after reading her husband's plays: "I should never have writ them, nor have had the Capacity nor Ingenuity to have writ Playes, had not you read to me some Playes which your Lordship had writ."[48] That many of her plays were well under way by 1656, however, is suggested by the title of a poem William Cavendish prefixed to *Nature's Pictures* (1656), which reads as follows: "A Copy of Verses to the Lady Marchioness of Newcastle, of all her Works, which are now all printed, except her Tragedies and Comedies, which will shortly come out" (sig. B2r). Eight years passed before the first volume of plays was published. In *Sociable Letters* (1664), Cavendish explains that the ship carrying the manuscript of a volume of plays from Antwerp to London was lost at sea, leaving her with a copy of the volume, which she had fortunately retained. This would place the date of the completion of her first volume of plays somewhere between 1656 and 1660, at the latest. Their attention to court life suggests that they may even have been written during the early years of her marriage. Once the first volume was lost at sea, the couple's habit of living on credit may well have further delayed its publication; William Cavendish's lavish *La Methode Nouvelle et Invention Extraordinaire de Dresser les Chevaux* (1658) was so costly that he complained of being "tormented about my book of horsemanship" by the process of financing its publication.[49]

The writing of plays was a Newcastle family activity, as is evident in the plays of William Cavendish's daughters, Lady Elizabeth Brackley (1623-63) and Lady Jane Cavendish (1621-69). Margaret Ezell notes that the family's interest in the Cavendish sisters' plays is evident in the care taken to preserve the plays in "a handsomely calligraphed volume."[50] Similarly, the carefully acknowledged scenes that William Cavendish contributed to his wife's plays reveal that her plays were also a matter of family interest; as such, their recurring theme—the contrast between active and contemplative lives—suggests that Cavendish took into consideration her husband's active military career and subsequent banishment as she reviewed her own experience of the queen.

Cavendish's plays reveal that Henrietta proved to be a problematic role model, a figure Cavendish studied and restudied throughout her writing career. Like Henrietta, Cavendish found the inner life rewarding; she absorbed the queen's Platonic love doctrines, using them as a language for the inner life of the mind. Yet, fascinated as she must have been by the queen's active interest in the inner life, she had experienced firsthand the disastrous results of Henrietta's attempts at imposing her ideals on her world. Cavendish's exile, her husband's wartime losses, and her family's tragic civil war experience had forced her to see, perhaps more clearly than Henrietta allowed herself to see, the disastrous consequences of trying to enforce religious and political change on an unyielding world. Thus, when she began writing plays, sometime after leaving the court, she put Platonic love doctrine to different uses than had Henrietta. Whereas the queen used the "wooing of the mind" to encourage religious conversion, Cavendish used it more broadly to explore the troubled negotiations between the mind and its world.

Like Henrietta and like their author, Cavendish's heroines are always at odds with their world. Frequently, Cavendish juxtaposes heroines who differ from one another in the philosophical stance they take to their world; faced with similar problems, they respond very differently to those troubles. In many of her plays, two types of heroine emerge: the "active cavalier," who engages with her world, using language and action to change it; and the "contemplative cavalier," who retreats from her world altogether. Each provides an obverse take on Henrietta's character, the first idealizing her cavalier bravado, the second questioning her proselytizing zeal. To the first category belong bold and enterprising women like Lady Orphant in *Love's Adventures*; these heroines set out to reshape the unsatisfactory external world, bringing it more closely into accordance with the ideal world in their minds. By cross-dressing, by taking on male roles, or, most significantly, by speaking eloquently, these heroines impose change on their world, thereby improving their lot in life. They suggest, in exaggerated form, what Henrietta—the indefatigable letter writer and sometime general—might have been had her consider-able efforts on behalf of her husband met with success. The second cat-egory of heroine altogether rejects the utopian optimism behind such activity; this heroine proves unable or unwilling to engage with the world altogether. Like Lady Contemplation in the play of that name or Lady Bashful in *Love's Adventures,* these heroines retreat into silent contem-plation out of a sort of hopelessness of effecting useful change in the real world or because they understand the dangers of trying to impose change on others.[51] Cavendish typically includes versions of both types of hero-ine within the same play; their dialogic relationship frequently pulls at whatever formal unity the play might have had, revealing Cavendish's profound ambivalence about the proper relation between mind and world. In depicting these two types of heroine, Cavendish seems less in-terested in taking sides than she is in examining their competing phi-losophies of mind.

THE LADY CONTEMPLATION

The three heroines of *The Lady Contemplation* exemplify Cavendish's ac-tive and contemplative cavaliers: Lady Ward is an active cavalier, whereas Lady Contemplation and Poor Virtue are versions of the contemplative cavalier. Each is faced with either an unsatisfactory courtship or the pros-pect of one. By exploring how each heroine approaches courtship, which here threatens jealousy, betrayal, or psychological and at times physical harm, Cavendish explores the problem that engages her: given an unsatis-factory world, what ought to be our response? Silence? Vocal objection? Militant action? As these heroines respond to unsatisfactory courtships, they present different answers to this question, each using language very differently from the others.

Lady Contemplation, for example, serves as an extreme example of the contemplative cavalier; she chooses to avoid actual courtship alto-gether, avoiding conversation in order to retreat to the ideal worlds of her active imagination. There, she explains, lovers "never make me jealouse, nor never disturb me; come to me, and goe from me; speak or are silent as I will have them, and they are behaved, qualified, and adorned to my humour, also of what Birth, Age, Complexion, or Stature I like best" (184). Her remarkable fantasy life leads her to envision streets "strew[n]" with lovers who have died upon hearing that she has chosen to marry an imaginary monarch (183). She defends her self-absorption by highlighting, somewhat extravagantly, the pleasures of the imaginative life: "The greatest pleasure is in the imagination not in fruition; for it is more pleasure for any person to imagin themselvs Emperour of the whole world, than to be so, for in imagination they reign & Rule, without the troublesome and weighty cares belonging thereto" (183). She spends much of the play either in silent contemplation or complaining about the distressing frequency with which her contemplations are interrupted; in one such instance, she remarks that, uninterrupted, "I should have govern'd all the world before I had left off Contemplating" (183). Her devotion to the pleasures of the imagination, like the similar celebration of those pleasures in *The Blazing World* (1666), leads Lady Contemplation to protect herself from the vexations of the external world by retreating to the inner worlds of the mind.

A second plot calls into question Lady Contemplation's praise for the pleasures of the imagination by exploring the dangers of solipsistic silence. This second plot examines the mismatched courtship between Lord Courtship and Lady Ward. Lord Courtship openly claims to hate women's talk, and he is brutally dismissive of Lady Ward, whom he is supposed to marry. When she warns him that his frequent infidelities will soon teach her to follow his ways, he charges her to "keep silence" (214). When she refuses to deliver his love letter to his mistress, he threatens to torture her, warning ominously "I will have you drawn up high by the two thumbs, which is a pain will force you to submit" (215). With this threat, she openly rebels, articulating her resentment of his behavior by promising to "take a Thunderbolt, and strike you dead, and with such strength I'll fling it on you, as it shall press your soul down to the everlasting shades of death" (215). At first, Lord Courtship interprets her verbal revolt as madness, sending for a doctor and noting that she is "transformed from a silent young Maid to a raging Fury" (215). She dismisses the doctor's advice by diagnosing her problem herself: "[W]hat noble minde," she asks, "can suffer a base servitude without rebellious passions?" (219). Mistreated, threatened with torture, and accused of madness, Lady Ward gives voice to her "rebellious passions," renouncing her engagement to Lord Courtship: "I perceive you are one that loves Pleasure more than Honour, and Life more than Fame; and I hate to be in that mans company, or to make a Husband, whose courage lies in Voluptuousness, and his life in Infamy: I will sooner marry Death, than such a man" (227). Ironically, this speech renouncing their engagement converts Lord Courtship. He is surprised by the effect her words have on him: "Her words have shot through my soul, and have made a sensible wound therein. How wisely she did speak! how beautiful appear'd! Her minde is full of honour, and the actions of her life are built upon noble principles; so young, so wise, so fair, so chaste, and I to use her so basely as I have done! O how I hate my self for doing so unworthily!" (227). Lady Ward's speech has powerful effects: it reveals her beauty and wisdom to an unappreciative suitor, causing him to fall in love with her; it allows him to recognize the mental experience of the woman he has spurned; and, finally, it reveals to him his poor behavior, which leads to his reformation. The last of these is perhaps the most significant; her outburst—her attempt at modifying the external world through language—reforms Lord Courtship, transforming their relationship into a meeting of true minds. Thus, whereas Lady Contemplation's plot celebrated the silent pleasures of the imagination, Lady Ward's plot, with its threats of torture and brutality, warns against the dangers of solipsism and silence. Lady Ward might thus be classified as an active cavalier.

A third plot further qualifies both Lady Contemplation's claims about the pleasures of the imagination and Lady Ward's lesson about the power of language. Like Lady Contemplation, though less excessively, Poor Virtue enjoys contemplation and silence, thus conforming to the model of the contemplative cavalier. She has reason to be melancholy, having lost her father and a considerable estate to war. She retires into the country, accommodating her reduced circumstances by taking a place as a shepherdess in a farmer's house and satisfying her melancholy temperament by surrounding herself with silence: "I love melancholy so well, as I would have all as silent without me, as my thoughts are within me; and I am so well pleased with thoughts, as noise begets a grief, when it disturbs them" (206). Yet her retreat to a pastoral life, unlike Lady Contemplation's retreat to the worlds of her mind, has the unexpected consequence of putting her at risk. She becomes the target of a number of noblemen whose progresses through the country lead them to her. Unaware that she is a member of the nobility disguised as a shepherdess, they read her role as a shepherdess as a metonymy for an easy target for seduction. In one passage her chief suitor, Lord Title, uses the language of pastoral romance to try to seduce her, even as she uses the same language to try to protect herself from him:

Lord Title. Fair Maid, may I be your Shepheard to attend you.
Poor Virtue. I am but a single Sheep that needs no great atten-

> dance, and a harmless one, that strayes not forth the ground I
> am put to feed.
>
> *Lord Title.* Mistake me not fair Maid, I desire to be your
> Shepheard, and you my fair Shepheardess, attending loving
> thoughts, that feed on kisses sweet, folded in amorous arms.
>
> *Poor Virtue.* My mind never harbors wanton thoughts, nor sends
> immodest glances forth, nor will infold unlawful love, for
> chastity sticks as fast unto my Soul, as light unto the Sun, or
> heat unto the fire, or motion unto life . . . for I am as free, and
> pure from all unchastity as Angels are of sin. [196]

Poor Virtue may well be as "free and pure from all unchastity as Angels are of sin," but she is nevertheless at real risk. Although her language has attracted Lord Title's admiration, it also confuses him by leading him to perceive the apparent conflation of "so noble a soul" and a "mean-born body" (215). He acknowledges that he is in love with her, but he cannot bring himself to marry "one I am asham'd to make . . . known," and he does not recognize that the "Beauties and Graces" to which he is attracted are, in the tradition of Platonic love doctrine, indications of actual nobility (218). Her language cannot save her as long as Lord Title believes that her disguise accurately signifies her station in life. What saves her, ultimately, is not her language, which is here revealed to be powerless, but the revelation that she is a member of the nobility.[52] Once her identity is revealed, their courtship can proceed properly, and the language of pastoral romance once again becomes functional and safe. In fact, their plot is concluded when Lord Title again employs the language of pastoral love to explain that he and his bride "will live a Country-life, I as a Shepherd, and this Lady as my Fair Shepherdess" (241).

By exploring the difficulties Poor Virtue encounters trying to transform her world, Cavendish further explores the relation between mind and world. Whereas Poor Virtue's language succeeded in attracting Lord Title's admiration, it could not transform what he perceived to be the reality of her "mean-born body." Just as Lady Ward's plot problematized Lady Contemplation's contemplative stance, Poor Virtue's plot questions Lady Ward's lesson by challenging the optimistic view that change can be imposed on the world by the mind. None of these plots provide a universal truth about the relation between mind and world, and none embody an authorial point of view; rather, their interplay reflects

Cavendish's ambivalence about the proper relation between the mind and its world.

Cavendish remained all her life profoundly ambivalent about the respective merits of the active life and the contemplative life, at times taking on the militancy of her active cavaliers, at others embodying the quietism of her contemplative cavaliers. More typically, she seems to have been attracted to both philosophical stances simultaneously, and this led her to difficulties that are evident within her work. This is nowhere better illustrated than in her struggle not to name names in her husband's biography. The struggle emerges visibly, both in her prose and in the inked-out revisions of her printed pages. In the preface to *The Life of . . . William Cavendishe* (1667), she complains that her husband commanded her "not to mention any thing or passage to the prejudice or disgrace of any Family or particular person (although they might be of great truth, and would illustrate much the actions of your Life)" (sig. a1v). She adds that "this Book would however, have been a great Volume, if his Grace would have given me leave to publish his Enemies Actions" (sig. C2v). The active cavalier within her clearly wanted to publish the names of men who in her mind were responsible for her husband's misfortunes; the contemplative cavalier within her knew to obey her husband's wishes in refraining from such public controversies. A look at the inked-out names suggests that this struggle was never fully resolved. After the book's publication, two passages had to be deleted, one mentioning the king's failure to provide pay, another identifying Lord Goring and Sir Francis Mackworth as being guilty of "invigilancy and carelessness" (26).[53] James Fitzmaurice notes that the revisions are "not uniformly conducted" and that in some copies the covered words are easily legible. The inevitable result is that "the inked-out words are supplied in contemporary hands. Rather than eliminating the embarrassing references to Charles I's parsimony and to the 'invigilancy and carelessness' of Goring and Mackworth, the attempted eradication calls attention to them." As Fitzmaurice goes on to note, John Rushworth was able to detect the names sufficiently to use "material from the inked-out portions in his account of the various commanders in the Bishops' Wars."[54]

That she tried, unsuccessfully, to smooth over her own difficulty in choosing between active and contemplative lives is also evident in her dedication of *The Life of . . . William Cavendishe*. There she compares her husband's active life with her own contemplative life: "I matter not the Censures of this Age, but am rather proud of them; for it shews that my

Actions are more then ordinary. . . . they'l make no doubt to stain even Your Lordships Loyal, Noble and Heroick Actions, as well as they do mine, though yours have been of War and Fighting, mine of Contemplating and Writing: Yours were performed publickly in the Field, mine privately in my Closet: yours had many thousand Eye-witnesses, mine none but my Waiting-maids" (sig. b1r-b1v). The self-portrait she draws here of a woman leading a contemplative life within the private confines of her closet is belied by her extraodinary publication record, which officially introduced her to a reading public beyond her closet. And the portrait she draws of William Cavendish in the *Life* depicts a strange mixture of the active and the contemplative cavalier. As a military commander, for example, he had assigned John Cosin the task of "view[ing] all Sermons that were to be Preached, and suffer[ing] nothing in them that in the least reflected against His Majesty's Person and Government" because he knew that "Schism and Faction in Religion is the Mother of all or most Rebelliouns, Wars and Disturbances in a State or Government" (14). And yet his role as a military commander was paradoxically the most extreme example of engaging in those very "schism[s] and faction[s] in religion" he most hoped to avoid. Cavendish's inked-out revisions in the *Life*, like her ambivalence toward her active and contemplative cavaliers in her plays, further suggest her unwillingness to conform exclusively either to the active or to the contemplative life.

Understanding Cavendish's ambivalence toward choosing between the active and the contemplative life helps to make sense of the formal flaws of her plays. Short on dramatic action, her plays quickly disintegrate into extended dialogues or monologues reminiscent of Alfred Harbage's description of Caroline plays: "Drama lapses and action comes to full stop while the characters weave their fine spun disquisitions, and split hairs already of gossamer thinness. Sometimes to be sure these discourses are imbued with a tone of hauteur, pathos, or moral urgency, so that a slight effort will remind us that we are reading a play, but just as often we might think we were reading pages from a conduct book in dialogue." That she was aware of these flaws is evident in her description of her composition process: "Having pleased my Fancy in writing many Dialogues upon several Subjects, and having afterwards order'd them into Acts and Scenes, I will venture, in spight of the Criticks, to call them Plays."[55]

Cavendish's interest in dialogue has been underestimated. The common practice of lifting striking statements from her works and presenting those statements as somehow representative of her thought has hindered a full understanding of her work. Her governing interest lies in the relational interplay and tension between multiple voices. Read as philosophical dialogues rather than as plays, her plays become more interesting. Far from expounding a particular ideology or ideal, they reflect her ambivalence in positioning herself philosophically with regard to her world; unable or unwilling to engage with it or retreat from it, to choose between the active or the contemplative life, she occupies an indeterminate position, one that occasioned what she described to Newcastle during their courtship as the "strange enchantment" of being both in the world and out of it.[56]

Thus, in *Love's Adventures,* for instance, Lady Orphant, an active cavalier, boldly cross-dresses and takes on military roles in order to pursue and successfully capture the heart of the lover who has spurned her, Lord Singularity. But when, in the same play, Lady Ignorance similarly tries to enter the sociable world, her efforts lead to domestic disaster; she quickly retreats, learning instead "to study how to order my house without noise" in order to restore domestic peace. And lest we conclude that the contemplative life is being held up as an ideal, we are presented with Lady Bashful, who hopes to shun both marriage and society in order to avoid being "disturbed with noise and company."[57] She becomes so mortified by her social ineptitude, however, that she wishes she could take opium to kill herself. Although each heroine eventually attains a more or less satisfactory conclusion, none provides an extractable lesson that can be read without being challenged by another heroine's plot.

Frequently Cavendish's heroines are themselves torn between active and contemplative lives. This tension is often expressed as an ambivalence between desiring to retire from the world and desiring to engage in it. In *Youth's Glory and Death's Banquet,* Lady Innocence leads a reserved life unlikely to bring her fame; even she wavers, however, between actively wishing on the one hand to "be buried in the grave with dust, and [to] feast the worms, rather than [to] live amongst mankind" while on the other hand fearing "Oblivions grave."[58] Later, a similar tension becomes fatal for Lady Sanspareille, who shuns the private world of marriage in order to pursue a public philosophical life.[59] Like Lady Innocence, Lady Sanspareille desires fame and fears being "buried in Oblivions grave" (130). The life course she plots is designed to achieve fame: she commits herself to a single life, promises to avoid private visits, to speak only in public, to commit her ideas to the printed page so as to protect them, and to adjust the topics of her speeches to a variety of audiences. In her devotion to pursuing the life of the mind in this public manner, she conflates the active and contemplative lives, but this conflation becomes a problematic internal struggle. In her last speech before her suitors, she publicly rejects the many marriage offers she has received, characterizing the state of marriage as "a ship, which alwayes lyes on the roughest Bilows of the Sea, rouling from side to side with discontents, sailing uncertainly, with inconstancy, and various winds" (161). She vows never to marry but consoles her suitors by promising to "dye every mans Maid" (161). The public nature of this private outpouring proves fatal. Conflating the active life and the contemplative life simply will not work. The active life's confident pursuit of fame and its imposition of one's ideals on the external life cannot be reconciled with the contemplative life's modest withdrawal from the condition of marriage and, more generally, from the world. Lady Sanspareille concludes her speech by noting that the assembly "hath occasioned a quarrel here; for bashfulnesse, and confidence hath fought a Duel in my Cheeks, and left the staines of bloud there" (161). Her unexplained death soon after this internal conflict suggests the intensity of the struggle she experiences negotiating between active and contemplative lives. The blush that leads to Lady Sanspareille's death suggests too that the uncertain sailing of rough seas was not confined to the experience of marriage but was, more generally, a question of confronting opposing philosophies of mind. Like her characters, Cavendish also weathered this internal storm.

The Presence

In *The Presence*—Cavendish's most aesthetically flawed play—Cavendish's struggle with her two heroines seems to have overwhelmed her; the play collapses into two segregated units. Cavendish wrote many of her plays in two parts, labeling each "part I" or "part II," but the two parts of *The Presence* are not so labeled. Instead, she appended to *The Presence* sixty-three pages labeled "Scenes," which, she explains, "were design'd to be put into *The Presence*; but by reason I found they would make that Play too long, I thought it requisite to Print them by themselves" (93). At ninety-two pages, *The Presence* is her second-longest play, but there are reasons other than length that disrupt the play's formal unity. The two plots revolve respectively around a princess and her new maid of honor, Lady Bashful. As we might expect, the Princess is a type of active cavalier, and Lady Bashful is a type of contemplative cavalier. The play proper is set at court, where the Princess determines court fashions; the "scenes" take place away from court, largely at Mademoiselle Civility's house, where Lady Bashful rejects not only court fashions but also, with them, the court's active cavalier mode.

The parallels between the two worlds of the play and the two worlds inhabited by the young Margaret Lucas at the exiled court in Paris are compelling: as a maid of honor, Lucas had relied on the civility of John Evelyn's parents-in-law, Sir Richard and Lady Browne. Lucas and William Cavendish were married in Richard Browne's private chapel, where English Protestant services were conducted.[60] We might reasonably deduce that the Brownes' Protestant chapel served as a welcome refuge for Protestant courtiers now exiled in Henrietta's Catholic court culture. In *The Presence* Cavendish transforms these two sites of court culture into the implicit debate between the active princess and her contemplative maid of honor. Their debate is over the proper relation between mind and world, and it is a debate that originated in Lucas's complex attitude toward the queen she had served as maid of honor.

In the first plot, the princess and heir to the throne faces a psychological and political crisis when she falls in love "with an Idea she met with in a Dream in a Region of her Brain" (7). The Princess's Platonic love fashion soon becomes a court craze; all the maids of honor imitate her by taking to their beds to dream of Platonic lovers, as is evident by the following stage direction: "Enter the young Princess Melancholy, and some Ladies, whereof one rubs her eyes, the other gapes, the third stretches her self; all passing over the Stage" (13). That the Princess is not a contemplative cavalier is evident when, unlike Lady Contemplation, whose celebration of the pleasures of the imagination was discussed earlier, the Princess reveals her dissatisfaction with the immaterial nature of her Platonic lover. Her governess tries to comfort her by encouraging her to consider the pleasures of the mind, where, she argues, "Souls may meet and converse," but the Princess responds by foregrounding the transitory and whimsical nature of dreams (10). Having glimpsed her dream lover once, with little chance of seeing him again, the Princess falls into a depression. The problem the Princess faces is the problem all of Cavendish's active cavaliers face: having identified an ideal, she must make it materialize, imposing it on her world. Her dissatisfaction with her lover's immaterial nature underscores this fact. By hinging the succession on this dream lover, Cavendish politicizes this problem; the Princess's indulgence in her imaginative life poses a potential threat to political stability. Although this dream lover does, within the context of the play, conveniently materialize, his arrival at court sets in motion a number of political difficulties before his true identity is revealed and he and the Princess can marry.

In a comic scene Cavendish underscores the unreliability of the imagination by having the court fool run on stage, claiming to have seen "monstrous strange sights" (23). When asked, he explains that he has been dreaming, and he describes his dream as follows:

> I saw Men with strange Heads, and as strange Bodies; for they had the speech of Men, and the upright shape of Men, and yet were partly like as other Creatures; for one Man had an Asses head, and his body was like a Goose; another Man had a Jack-a-napes-head, but all his body was like a Baboon. . . . Then I saw a Woman that was not like a Mare-Maid, for Mare-Maids are like Women from the head to the waste, and from the waste like a Fish; but this Woman was like a Fish from the head to the waste, and from the waste like a Beast. [23-24]

The extravagant mismatching within the Fool's dream echoes the opening paragraph of Horace's *Ars Poetica,* in which Horace describes a painter joining "a human head to the neck of a horse" and other acts of poetic license.[61] By highlighting the wildness of an imagination untamed by judgment, the Fool criticizes the Princess's uncritical devotion to a product of her imagination. In the process he emphasizes the dangers of insisting that the product of an unbridled imagination be imposed upon the real world.

Lady Bashful's plot begins in *The Presence* but is developed fully only in the "scenes" appended to the play; there it extends the Fool's critique of the Princess's faith in the imagination. As a new maid of honor, Lady Bashful is ill at ease with the court and "loth to be made much of, after the Court-fashion" (36). She soon leaves the court to marry Lord Loyalty, a ruined nobleman. Her courtship takes place outside of the court in Mademoiselle Civility's house. Unlike the Princess, who indulges her imaginative life, Lady Bashful criticizes her own wit for its extravagance, confessing that it is "so Fantastical, and changes into so many shapes, and various Dresses, as it will tire your Ears to listen after it, and your Patience will not endure to keep it Company; for Wit without Judgment to order it, is more offensive, then pleasing or delightful" (110). Her unwillingness to indulge the "Fantastical" productions of the mind so popular at court places her in clear opposition to her princess.

The conversations between Lord Loyalty and Lady Bashful serve as a further review of the proper relation between mind and world. Lord Loyalty instructs her, for example, not to engage in controversies over religious issues: "No questions concerning the gods can be resolved, nor any Arguments proved. . . . Therefore Lady, let me advise you, never to hearken after Controversies concerning the gods, nor to enter into any Controversies; for all sorts of Controversies will disquiet your mind, trouble your head, tire your thoughts, disturb your rest, divide your affairs, disorder your Family, distract your life, and torment your Soul" (131-32). Unlike the Princess, who "disquiet[s]" her mind by falling in love with an idea, Lady Bashful learns the dangers of the ideas produced by an unbridled imagination.

Like the Princess in *The Presence*, Henrietta, whose devotion to Catholicism seems never to have wavered despite the grief it brought her and her husband, had in this sense also fallen in love with "an Idea she met with in a . . . region of her brain." And like Lord Loyalty, William Cavendish warned his wife repeatedly about the dangers of entering into controversy. One might conclude that the two plots of *The Presence* represent Henrietta's and Margaret Cavendish's respective philosophies of mind. Read this way, the play becomes a satire on Henrietta's Platonically driven court culture. Yet such a reading seems partial in that it overlooks the complexities of Cavendish's internal conflict regarding the proper relation between mind and world. She could hardly satirize Platonic love doctrine or Henrietta's stubborn determination to impose her religious ideals on an unyielding world without herself engaging in a similar sort of imposition. Married to a man who prided himself on his loyalty and who "commanded" her to refrain from naming names in his biography, she seems to have shied away from direct satire. This may explain the strange decision to add the "Scenes" to *The Presence* without working to integrate them in a more aesthetically satisfactory manner. If the Princess and Lady Bashful represent Henrietta and Margaret Cavendish, they also reflect two sides of Cavendish's own character.

But satire may not have been her chief goal. If this play has an authorial stance, it may be that of the court fool who occupies a position on the boundary between the court and the external world and on the boundary between the two heroines' competing philosophies of mind.

The Fool criticizes the Princess's indulgence in her imagination, for example, but he is also the mechanism through which the true identity of the Princess's materialized lover is eventually revealed. Like the young Margaret Lucas in an exiled court, the court fool seems to experience the "strange enchantment" of being both in the world and out of it.

We see in *The Presence* the difficulty this strange enchantment posed for Cavendish. If Henrietta had taught her the dangers of engaging with the world and particularly of imposing one's ideas on it, she had also awakened her to the considerable pleasures of the life of the mind. Cavendish's plays thus explore her ambivalence toward the relation between mind and world. She explored this ambivalence further through her application of the scientific ideas discussed at her husband's salon in Paris in the late 1640s. There she was acquiring a new scientific vocabulary, which allowed her to further examine the relation between mind and world. Her first published works reflect her emerging interest in science, and in order to see more clearly the relation between her scientific work and her literary work, we must turn to the context in which she was introduced to the leading scientific ideas of her day. We turn, then, to her husband's salon in Paris, where intense discussion focused on Pierre Gassendi's controversial revival of an ancient theory of matter: atomism.

3

World and Mind
in Conflict

Cavendish's Review of the New Atomism

Some factious Atomes will agree; combine,
They strive some form'd Body to unjoyne.
The Round beate out the Sharpe: the long
The Flat do fight withall, thus all go wrong.
        —*Margaret Cavendish,* Poems and Fancies

As a new bride in Paris, Cavendish experienced a bewildering concurrence of intellectual exhilaration and deep emotional pain. From her privileged place at the center of her husband's salon, she had the rare opportunity of learning about the leading scientific and philosophic ideas of her day directly from their expositors and indirectly from her husband and her brother-in-law, both of whom tutored her. She became particularly fascinated with atomism, which was then the rage in Paris. As members of her husband's salon pieced together competing atomist systems, she too began to explore the world as an atomist system, one that, to her mind at least, seemed to be on the brink of dissolution. The physical universe, the political world, the mind—each of these could be envisioned as an atomist system. Cavendish was finally less interested in atomism as a theory of matter than as an explanatory discourse for the political and emotional turmoil that surrounded her. Atomism helped to account for the political and psychological conflict that shaped her life by depicting a system in which stability of any kind—material, political, or emotional—was ultimately elusive. Although she dropped atomism as a theory of matter in 1655, she retained it as a metaphor for the body politic and for the mind throughout the course of her life.

Her interest in atomism was inextricably linked to the storm of tragic personal and political news that arrived from England during the early years of her marriage. During those years she faced the uncertainty of exile and great personal loss. Atomism's Greek expositor, Epicurus, also more interested in atomism as a useful philosophical stance than as a theory of matter, provided a philosophy that must have resonated with the experience of exile, which doomed both Margaret and William Cavendish to watch helplessly as the events of the civil war and the interregnum unfolded. The Epicurean stance at the opening of book 2 of Lucretius's *De Rerum Natura* summarized both the futility and the inevitability of conflict:

> But this is the greatest joy of all: to stand aloof in a quiet citadel, stoutly fortified by the teaching of the wise, and to gaze down from that elevation on others wandering aimlessly in a vain search for the way of life, pitting their wits one against another, disputing for precedence, struggling night and day with unstinted effort to scale the pinnacles of wealth and power. O joyless hearts of men! O minds without vision! How dark and dangerous the life in which this tiny span is lived away! Do you not see that nature is clamouring for two things only, a body free from pain, a mind released from worry and fear for the enjoyment of pleasurable sensations?[1]

Like Epicurus and his Latin expositor Lucretius, Cavendish seems to have initially hoped to find some measure of tranquility from the world view that atomism offered: it seemed to account for the political and emotional conflict she now faced. To understand the intensity with which she was drawn to atomism, we must turn to the context in which she first encountered it.

WORLD AND MIND IN CONFLICT

The early years of Cavendish's marriage were markedly strained; she was suddenly confronted with exile, financial insecurity, and personal tragedy. Her marriage seems to have provided her with affection, and it certainly introduced her to a stimulating intellectual life, but she now found herself banished to a foreign country, the language of which she claims

never to have learned.[2] And although Newcastle seems to have been re-
markably successful at living on credit, his repeated negotiations with
creditors cannot have been pleasant. Furthermore, she knew that her
family in Colchester was also experiencing financial difficulties. Her
mother had written to Newcastle in December 1645 to bless their marriage and to apologize for being unable to send her daughter's portion.
The letter reveals a thoughtful woman in a troubled state of mind:

> Most Honorable,
> You have been pleased to honor me by your letters, my
> daughter much more by marriage. And thereby made her
> extremely happy: for oftentimes these come not together,
> but by yourself she hath attained to both. The state of the
> kingdom is such yet that I confess her Brother cannot give
> unto her that which is hers, neither can I show my love and
> affection towards my Daughter as I would, in respect of the
> great burdens we groan under. God deliver us, and send us
> a happy end of these troubles which we ought with patience
> to bear till almighty God in his due time shall be pleased to
> deliver us.[3]

For the former maid of honor who had prided herself on being "in a
condition rather to lend than to borrow," the experience of living on
credit and of knowing that her family in England was in financial distress could only have confirmed her growing sense of the world as a
hostile environment.[4]

It must have been especially difficult, then, to bear the news in 1647
that her niece, her sister Mary Killigrew, and her mother had died within
months of one another. She had clearly idolized her mother; in *A True
Relation,* she later described her as having been "of a grave Behaviour,
and ha[ving] such a Majestick Grandeur, as it were continually hung
about her, that it would strike a kind of an awe to the beholders, and
command respect from the rudest, I mean the rudest of civiliz'd people,
I mean not such Barbarous people, as plundered her, and used her cru-
elly, for they would have pulled God out of Heaven, had they had power,
as they did Royaltie out of his Throne."[5] The implied comparison between the rough treatment of her mother at the hands of parliamentar-
ians and the beheading of Charles I suggests the degree to which
Cavendish fused personal and political history, linking her personal pain

to political events. With the death of her mother, as with the execution of Charles I, there was now no longer any real possibility of returning home.

Her sense of alienation was confirmed beyond all possible doubt the following year. Since 1645, her brother Sir Charles Lucas had served as lieutenant-general of the king's cavalry. Between 14 June and 27 August of 1648, he found himself defending his hometown of Colchester, which was under siege by parliamentary forces led by Gen. Thomas Fairfax. The siege was brutal and Lucas's defense uncompromising. By the beginning of August, famine had reduced the inhabitants to eating dogs and horses; soon even those became scarce.[6] Colchester surrendered on 27 August; on 28 August Charles Lucas and his fellow soldier George Lisle were tried by court-martial and summarily shot. Royalists perceived their execution to be one more piece of evidence of parliamentary severity, and the story of Lucas and Lisle was woven into Royalist martyrology. The rumor spread, for example, that on the spot where Lucas and Lisle were shot no grass would grow. Six years later, when John Evelyn visited the "wretchedly demolished" town, he was shown the spot: "But what was showed us as a kind of miracle, at the outside of the Castle, the wall where Sir Charles Lucas and Sir George Lisle, those valiant and noble persons who so bravely behaved themselves in the last siege, were barbarously shot, murdered by Ireton in cold blood, after surrendering on articles ... The place was bare of grass for a large space, all the rest of it abounding with herbage."[7]

In the printed accounts of the siege, the defeat of Colchester is bound with the Lucas family history. Charles Lucas was a local boy; the Lucas house had itself served as a useful Royalist outpost until it was seized on 14 July 1648 by parliamentary soldiers.[8] One version of the siege accuses parliamentary soldiers of having entered the Lucas family vault, "not only to cut away the led wherein those Bodies were infolded, but to pull off the very haire (O matchless impiety!) which grew upon their Scalps; whereof diverse among them, made them *Hat-bands* and *Bracelets,* which they no lesse contemptibly then disgracefully wore; glorying (as it seemes) in their pilage of those native remains and Ornaments of the dead. This they did in a despite and grounded hate to his *Family,* after such time as they had acted their cruell tragedy." Another report specifies that "officers and souldiers entered, and broake open the tombs of their ancestors, amongst whom the Lady Lucas and Lady Killigrew, the mother and sister of the present Lord Lucas, were so lately buried, that their sinues and haire were unconsumed. Then they scattered the bones about with profane jests, and cut off the hair and wore it in their hats." The motive provided in the first of these accounts for the desecration of the Lucas family graves—"a despite and grounded hate to [Lucas's] Family"—may well have mirrored the truth; the second civil war was marked by exasperation toward those, like Charles Lucas, perceived to be stubbornly and uselessly prolonging it. Thomas Fairfax attempted to justify his execution of the two men, for example, by explaining to Parliament that he and his chief officers decided on the execution so as to provide "some satisfaction to military Justice, and in part of Avenge for the innocent Blood they have Caused to be spilt, and the Trouble, Damage, and Mischief, they have brought upon the Town, this Country, and the Kingdom."[9] The shooting of Lucas and Lisle remained controversial despite the justifications provided by Fairfax and by others. To Cavendish, this rationale of blaming Lucas for prolonging the bloodshed could only have made a tragic event more incomprehensible and more distressing.

These gruesome events, combined with the earlier deaths of her mother, her sister, and her niece, undoubtedly contributed to her continuing melancholy, which had so concerned Newcastle that spring that he consulted Sir Theodore Mayerne. Mayerne's reply indicates that, like his wife, Newcastle himself suffered from melancholy and hypochondria, for which Mayerne noted, "the tymes" furnished "subiect Enough." He acknowledged that Newcastle's suffering was aggravated by his having been "brought into a condition of . . . fortune, neither to heare, nor doe, any thinge that pleases you," and he tried to encourage him by suggesting that "God will give an End to these [political troubles]."[10] In addition, Newcastle seems to have been concerned about the fact that his new wife had not become pregnant. Mayerne's sober reply to Newcastle advised putting off childbearing temporarily and perhaps permanently, and it reveals that Mayerne himself was more concerned about Margaret Cavendish's profoundly troubled state of mind than he was about her failure to become pregnant: "Touching Conception, I know not, if in the estate she's in, you ought Earnestly to desire it, It is hard to get Children with good Corage, when One is Melancholy, and after they are gott and come into the World, they bring a great deale of Payne with them, And after that very often one Looses them, as I have try'd to my great greefe and am sory to have had them. Be in good health & then you may till your ground, otherwise it will be but tyme Lost if you Enter that race frowningly." Mayerne's psychological analysis is significant in that it confirms Cavendish's depictions of her melancholy and bashfulness as being so extreme as to inhibit her sociability with anyone outside of her family circle. His concern that her mental health was not sufficiently robust to withstand the burden of raising children suggests that the news of her brother's execution and the desecration of her mother's and sister's graves must have been debilitating. Her health deteriorated, and a year later, in response to further queries from Newcastle, Mayerne wrote again, expressing concern not so much about "the nature of the Disease, which is Rebellious, as for the disposition of the Patient."[11]

In fact, Cavendish seems never to have fully recovered; melancholy marks her work, emerging throughout her career with disturbing frequency in morbid passages like the following:

> I do not much Care, nor Trouble my Thoughts to think where I shall be Buried, when Dead, or into what part of the Earth I shall be Thrown.... for I did observe, that in this last War the Urns of the Dead were Digged up, their Dust Dispersed, and their Bones Thrown about, and I suppose that in all Civil or Home-wars such Inhuman Acts are Committed; wherefore it is but a Folly to be Troubled and Concerned, where they shall be Buried, or for their Graves, or to Bestow much Cost on their Tombes, since not only Time, but Wars will Ruin them.
> [*Sociable Letters*, 238-39]

That she was traumatized by the experience of civil war and exile is evident in her summations of the war, which generally intertwine personal and national tragedy. In her autobiography, for example, she personalizes national history, seeing the war as an unmitigated personal and political disaster:

> But not onely the Family I am linkt to is ruin'd, but the Family from which I sprung, by these unhappy Wars, which ruine my Mother lived to see, and then died, having lived a Widow many years. . . . She made her house her Cloyster, inclosing her self, as it were therein, for she seldom went abroad, unless to Church, but these unhappy Warrs forc't her out, by reason she and her children were loyall to the King; for which they plundered her and my Brothers of all their Goods, Plate,

Jewells, Money, Corn, Cattle, and the like, cut down their Woods, pull'd down their Houses, and sequestred them from their Lands and Livings; but in such misfortunes my Mother was of an Heroick Spirit, in suffering patiently where there is no remedy, or to be industrious where she thought she could help.[12]

A few pages later she recapitulates this theme, again focusing on her mother's tragic history: "But as I said, my Mother lived to see the ruin of her Children, in which was her ruin, and then dyed." Like many Royalists, she turned to the Book of Job, finding in it a tragic sensibility that matched her personal experience; looking back on her childhood life in the company of her brothers and sisters, she described them meeting daily "feasting each other like Job's Children."[13] And like Job, she must have felt that the test she and the members of her family were undergoing was utterly incomprehensible.

Atomist Systems in the Newcastle Salon

Henrietta's example had given Cavendish the confidence to explore the relation between mind and world; the civil wars had provided a strong motive; the atomist systems to which she was now introduced in Paris yielded a rich and surprising vocabulary with which to further explore that relation. That she would turn to science, and to atomism in particular, was entirely predictable, given her temperament, her interests, and the extraordinary cultural context of the early years of her marriage. In Paris in 1645, she found herself at the center of a scientific salon in which some of the leading thinkers of her day, including the great expositors of mechanism René Descartes and Pierre Gassendi, circulated, reviewed, and discussed their ideas. The salon itself became "an unofficial 'university' of the mechanical philosophy." This is not to suggest that a monolithic "atomism" governed the Newcastle circle; rather, atomisms varied. As Nina Gelbart explains, there were at least three types of atomisms available to seventeenth-century modernizers: "the animistic monad theory of Augustine, Bruno and Helmont; the Aristotelian theory of 'natural minima'; and the strictly mechanistic, quantitative atomism of Epicurus."[14] The Newcastle salon provided a fruitful place for the debate over varied atomisms.

Looking back on Newcastle's Parisian salon, the political economist William Petty recalled its exhilarating environment: "For about that time in Paris, Mersennus, Gassendy, Mr. Hobs, Monsieur DesCartes, Monsieur Roberval, Monsieur Mydorge and other famous men, all frequenting and caressed by your Grace and your memorable brother Sir Charles Cavendish, did countenance and influence my studies as well by their conversation as their Public Lectures and Writings."[15] Hobbes had been in France since 1641; Gassendi had been appointed professor of mathematics at the Collège Royal in 1645; Descartes both visited Paris and corresponded with members of the circle. John Aubrey records that Edmund Waller said he "had dined with them all three at the Marquiss's table, at Paris."[16] Although the relationships among Hobbes, Gassendi, and Descartes were occasionally strained by professional jealousies, the Newcastle salon seems to have provided a fertile environment for the review and dissemination of their ideas. Many of the exiled Royalists who corresponded with Margaret Cavendish—Sir Kenelm Digby, Walter Charleton, and later John Evelyn—shared her scientific interests; in particular, they shared her interest in atomism.

Despite the illustrious traffic through her husband's salon, Cavendish's scientific work has traditionally been dismissed as the product of an isolated and uneducated thinker. And yet she was emphatically not an isolated thinker.[17] Though she frequently portrays herself as an original and thus unlearned thinker, she acknowledged unequivocally that both her husband and her brother-in-law Sir Charles Cavendish tutored her. Her marriage, she explains, was particularly happy in that she had married a man who "instructed me, reading several lectures thereof to me, and expounding the hard and obscure passages therein." She also acknowledges that had she been denied the company of her husband's salon, had she been "inclosed from the world, in some obscure place, and had been an anchoret from my infancy, having not the liberty to see the World, nor conversation to hear of it, I should never have writ of so many things." Before marriage, she continues, she could "onely read the letters, and joyn the words, but understood nothing of the sense of the World."[18] As this echo of Lucretius's analogy between words and worlds suggests, marriage provided an exhilarating intellectual transition by allowing her access to a new world of ideas.[19]

The most important influence on her education was exerted by the overlooked figure of Charles Cavendish. Newcastle himself proudly acknowledged in print that his wife had been tutored "since she was married, with my worthy and learned Brother."[20] Less flamboyant and more intellectually rigorous than William Cavendish, Charles Cavendish was widely admired in his day. Like his brother, he hosted a scientific salon of sorts, although his was an epistolary salon through which he acquired, reviewed, and circulated new ideas, including those of Hobbes and Gassendi.[21] He was such an active and engaged correspondent that Miriam Reik appropriately calls him one of the seventeenth century's "philosophical merchants."[22] In one letter alone, for example, Charles Cavendish asks his good friend, the mathematician John Pell, for his reaction to Descartes's book on the soul (*Les passions de L'Ame,* 1649), looks forward to reading Gassendi's book on Epicurean philosophy, asks about Hobbes, whose *Leviathan* he awaits, and reports that Sir William Davenant has "lately sent my Brother a Preface to an intended Poem *[Gondibert]* of his not yet printed" with Hobbes's additions. Charles Cavendish took as one of his chief goals the arrangement of a meeting between Hobbes and Descartes, which he hoped, somewhat optimistically, would have the effect of leading both philosophers to "highlie esteeme one of the other."[23]

Psychologically, too, Charles Cavendish had all the characteristics of an ideal tutor, despite his disadvantageous physical stature—he was hunchbacked and dwarfish. Clarendon singles out his "gentleness of disposition, the humility and meekness of his nature, and the vivacity of his wit." He was, Clarendon continues, "so modest that he could hardly be prevailed with to enlarge himself on subjects he understood better than other men, except he were pressed by his very familiar friends; as if he thought it presumption to know more than handsomer men use to do."[24] The penultimate poem in *Poems and Fancies,* Cavendish's first published volume, includes a reference to Charles Cavendish that suggests that he took an active and at times playful interest in her writing:

> Sir Charles into my chamber coming in,
> When I was writing of my *Fairy Queen*;
> I pray, said he, when *Queen Mab* you doe see,
> Present my service to her Majesty:
> And tell her, I have heard *Fames* loud report,
> Both of her Beauty, and her stately Court.
> When I *Queen Mab* within my Fancy view'd,
> My Thoughts bow'd low, fearing I should be rude;
> Kissing her Garment thin, which Fancy made,
> Kneeling upon a Thought, like one that pray'd;

In whispers soft I did present
His humble service, which in mirth was sent.
Thus by imagination I have been
In *Fairy Court*, and seen the *Fairy Queen*.
For why, imagination runs about
In every place, yet none can trace it out.
[213-14]

The evidence suggests that Charles Cavendish's disposition and learning made him a congenial, if indulgent, tutor for his sister-in-law.

In November 1651 she and Charles Cavendish left for London to try to recover some of their estates. It was during this trip with Charles in 1651 that Margaret first set about publishing her work. In London, where she found herself rebuffed by the Committee on Compounding, ill at ease in an alien environment, and her rest "broke[n] with discontented Thoughts," she turned to atomism, finding in it a way of explaining the political and psychological conflict that surrounded her.[25] Cavendish's first three published volumes reveal the uses to which she put atomism. Her first published volume was a collection of poems and meditations titled *Poems and Fancies,* published in London in 1653. Within a week of its publication, she also completed and shortly thereafter published another volume called *Philosophicall Fancies.*[26] Both of these volumes are dedicated not to her husband but to Charles Cavendish. In 1650 she had begun an earlier volume, which would be published in 1655 as *The World's Olio.*[27] *Poems and Fancies* expounds an atomist theory of matter; all three volumes explore atomism's consequences for the problem of sensory perception.

Her active interest in science has generally been regarded as unfortunate by literary critics and irrelevant by historians of science.[28] For Virginia Woolf, for example, Cavendish's turn to science distorted her considerable poetic talent: "Under the pressure of such vast structures, her natural gift, the fresh and delicate fancy which had led her in her first volume to write charmingly of Queen Mab and fairyland, was crushed out of existence."[29] For historians of science, Cavendish appears as a participant in the history of atomism, mentioned only to be dismissed, having no lasting contribution to make to atomism itself. These points of view are not entirely invalid. By turning to science, Cavendish neglected her poetic talent without visibly changing the course of the scientific systems she discussed. But this conclusion misses the point by overlooking the fact that Cavendish's interest in atomism was less an interest in physical theories of matter than a fascination with a metaphor that served to explain political and psychological conflict; by questioning the validity of sensory perception, atomism helped caution against the kind of dogmatic certainty that to Cavendish's mind had fueled the English civil wars. Furthermore, Cavendish was one of the first to transmit Gassendi's revival of Epicurean atomism into England. Her early exploration of atomism in her first three published volumes tells us a great deal about how atomism was read and, significantly, about the cultural concerns it awakened. Perhaps more importantly, she examined atomism and its consequences more boldly than her contemporaries dared. Their puzzled reaction to her early work ought to be read, in part, as a reaction to atomism itself, which as a theory of matter posed political and religious implications that few writers and fewer readers felt comfortable exploring fully.

Cavendish's Review of the New Atomism

Atomism had already been put to use in print in France by Descartes and Gassendi, of course, and it was discussed at length by the members of William Cavendish's scientific salon in Paris in the 1640s. In the early 1650s in England, however, atomism was still either disregarded or entertained with considerable apprehension. As late as 1656, when John Evelyn published his fragmentary translation of Lucretius, he recorded the date of publication and added that "little of the Epicurean philosophy was then known amongst us." Except for university discussions, isolated scientific circles, and spotty and generally disapproving allusions in poems to Lucretius's *De Rerum Natura,* atomism was known in England primarily as a threat to Christianity.[30] In 1652 Walter Charleton touched on atomism in *The Darknes of Atheism Dispelled by the Light of Nature,* where he excoriated Epicurus for his "detestable opinion that Fortune was the Author" of the universe. He conceded, however, that "in this heap of dross lies raked up so much pure and rich metall," which if extracted by an "industrious hand" might be worth reviewing.[31] Charleton's glance at atomism here is brief and cautious. He provided a bolder and more complete account of atomism two years later in his *Physiologia Epicuro-Gassendo-Charltoniana* (1654) and defended it further in *Epicurus's Morals,* in 1656, the same year that Evelyn published his partial translation of Lucretius. The third volume of Thomas Stanley's three-volume *History of Philosophy*—in which a large section was devoted to Epicurus—was published in 1660.

Appearing as they did in 1653, Cavendish's *Poems and Fancies* and *Philosophicall Fancies* played a significant role in the importation of Epicurean atomism; although her volumes were not in any sense faithful expositions of any particular atomist system, they were far bolder in exploring the consequences of atomism than the expositions provided by other modernizers. They should be credited with being among the very first texts to import Gassendi's revival of Epicurean atomism from France into England, and they were the first texts to discuss the philosophical implications of atomism directly and unapologetically.

The chief difficulty historians of atomism encounter while trying to evaluate Cavendish's role in the importation of atomism from France into England is her radical departure from the kinds of concerns her contemporaries voiced about atomism. All of the other modern versions of these atomisms had one thing in common: they were studied efforts at purging atomism of its atheistic implications. Atomism was considered atheistic because it seemed to eliminate the matter/spirit dualism central to Christianity and because in the Epicurean version all things were explained by chance rather than divine plan. Gassendi, the principal proponent of Epicurean atomism, had carefully Christianized his atomism by positing God as the creator of all matter, thereby imposing a "sea-change" on classical Epicureanism.[32] His follower, Walter Charleton, correspondingly eliminated "the poisonous part of Epicurus's opinion" by positing God as the First Cause. René Descartes similarly revised atomism by replacing atoms with what he called "corpuscles," by stipulating that all natural phenomena could be explained by matter and motion, and by specifying that "God is the primary cause of motion."[33] Lucy Hutchinson translated, probably in the late 1640s or early 1650s, all of Lucretius's poem, making her his first known English translator.[34] She was careful, however, never to publish her work, and she even attached a lengthy and detailed apology to her manuscript, attacking the "lunatic" Lucretius for his interest in the "casual, irrational dance of atoms." John Evelyn pointed nervously to the fact that all ancients were pagan, asked why we should single out Lucretius for his atheism, and proposed that for every instance of Lucretius's failing "he has a thousand more, where amongst the rest of his most excellent *Precepts,* and rare discourses, he perswades to a life the most exact and *Moral;* and no man, I hope, comes hither as a *Spider,* to swell up his bag with *poyson* only, when with half that pains, he may with the industrious *Bee,* store and furnish his *Hive* with so much wholesome and delicious Honey." John Milton Christian-ized atomism when he used it in his description of Chaos in *Paradise Lost:* there, Chaos is an atomistic repository of matter "which thus must ever fight, / Unless th' Almighty Maker them ordain / His dark materials to create more Worlds" (bk. 2, ll. 914-17).[35] The tradition of Christianiz-ing atomism by purging it of its atheistic "poison" continued through-out the seventeenth and early eighteenth centuries, most notably through the efforts of Robert Boyle and Isaac Newton.[36]

The concern for Christianizing atomism simply does not appear in Cavendish's first three volumes. In stark contrast to other modernizers, she reveals no interest in securing a place for God in the new atomist systems under discussion. Instead, she reveals her own speculative de-light with what appeared to be the infinite number of possibilities and permutations of a natural order governed by atoms. Her atomic theory posits only one substance: matter, which consists of four types of atoms. The atoms' shapes determine their physical properties. Thus, fire con-sists of sharp atoms; air consists of long atoms; water consists of round atoms; and earth consists of square atoms.

Cavendish's disregard for making a place for God in her system is revealed in the first poem in *Poems and Fancies.* There she re-envisions the Creation with Nature rather than God as its creator. The immediate problem that Nature confronts is that she needs to create a perceptive being capable of appreciating her creation. The problem is defined in the following lines spoken by Nature as she considers the problem of creation before her.

> All paines I can take,
> Will do no good, *Matter* a *Braine* must make;
> *Figure* must draw a *Circle,* round, and small,
> Where in the midst must stand a *Glassy Ball,*
> Without *Convexe,* the inside a *Concave,*
> And in the midst a round small hole must have,
> That *Species* may passe, and repasse through,
> *Life* the *Prospective* every thing to view.
> [2]

The solution to the need for a perceiving being is to create man, a crea-ture "though not in Body, like a God in minde" (4). Cavendish's interest in the problem of perception is evident throughout the volume as in her consideration of the idea, for example, that "no *Light* would be without the *Eye*" (38). Having opened the volume with the problem of perception, she prepares the reader for what she would explore throughout it as one of the chief consequences of atomism: a heightened awareness of the fallibility of sensory perception.

Questioning the reliability of sensory perception was the inevitable result of the very nature of atoms: small units of matter invisible to the eye, their existence called into question the reliability of the senses. One of the startling characteristics of *Poems and Fancies* is her exploration of the epistemological consequences of atomism. She calls attention to the microscopic texture of the physical world, conjecturing that "small *Atomes* of themselves a *World* may make" (5). Repeatedly, she considers the fact that atoms escape the detection of the "dull" senses. "Severall Worlds" might, she conjectures, exist in a lady's earring:

> An *Eare-ring round* may well a *Zodiacke* bee,
> Where in a *Sun* goeth round, and we not see.
> And *Planets seven* about that *Sun* may move,
> And *Hee* stand still, as *some wise men* would prove.
> And *fixed Stars*, like *twinkling Diamonds*, plac'd
> About this *Eare-ring*, which a *World* is vast.
> That same which doth the *Eare-ring* hold, the *hole*,
> Is that, which we do call the *Pole*.
> There *nipping Frosts* may be, and *Winter* cold,
> Yet never on the *Ladies Eare* take hold.
> And *Lightnings*, *Thunder*, and great *Winds* may blow
> Within this *Eare-ring*, yet the *Eare* not know.
> [45]

The significance of this image can easily be overlooked, even though Cavendish takes pains to make her point clear:

> There *Governours* do rule, and *Kings* do Reigne,
> And *Battels* fought, where many may be slaine.
> And all within the *Compasse* of this *Ring*,
> And yet not tidings to the *Wearer* bring.
> [46]

The battles and even wars of the miniature worlds she imagines within the compass of the earring occur without the lady's perceiving them despite their contiguity to her ear.

Similarly, she points to physical laws, such as magnetism, that cannot be clearly understood exclusively through the senses:

> For *Sense* is *grosse*, not every thing can *Shape*.
> So in this *World* another *World* may bee,
> That we do neither *touch, tast, smell, heare, see*.
> What *Eye* so *cleere* is, yet did ever see
> Those *little Hookes*, that in the *Load-Stone* bee,
> Which draw *hard Iron*? or give *Reasons*, why
> The *Needles point* still in the *North* will lye.
> [43]

Her interest in the limitations of sensory perception governs the volume. Why, she asks, should we assume that something we cannot see or hear does not exist when our senses have so consistently been proven wrong? She points to what she sees as a logical contradiction inherent in those who deny the existence of fairies "and yet verily beleeve there are spirits." "We may as well," she concludes, "thinke there is no Aire, because we doe not see it."[37]

For Cavendish and others, atomism—like the discoveries of the microscope and the telescope (with which she was also familiar)—led to conjectures about a possible plurality of worlds and about the habitation of planets or of the moon. Imaginary travel to the moon had a long-standing literary tradition independent of the atomist revival, reaching back as far as Lucian. As Marjorie Nicolson notes, "with Kepler [imaginary travel to the moon] became science, as a great mathematician and physicist reported graphically the grim and austere world in the moon beheld through the telescope." More fancifully, Francis Godwin's *The Man in the Moone* (1638) envisioned a voyage to the moon made possible by means of swans that migrated to the moon. John Wilkins's *Discovery of a World in the Moone, or, A Discourse Tending to Prove, That 'tis Probable There May Be another Habitable World in That Planet,* also published in 1638, presents a more serious envisioning of such a voyage. In the late 1650s, Robert Hooke "contriv'd and made many trials about the Art of Flying in the Air," which failed, but he shared his designs with Wilkins.[38]

Thus, Cavendish's interest in a plurality of worlds is not as odd as it might at first appear. What has generally gone unnoticed, however, is her interest in exploring the reliability of the senses, evident in passages like the following one, in which she imagines a plurality of worlds nested within one another like so many Chinese boxes:

> Just like unto a *Nest* of *Boxes* round,
> *Degrees* of *sizes* within each *Boxe* are found.
> So in this *World*, may many *Worlds* more be,
> Thinner, and lesse, and lesse still by degree;
> Although they are not subject to our *Sense*,
> A *World* may be no bigger then *two-pence*.
> [*Poems and Fancies*, 44]

By questioning the reliability of the senses, Cavendish opened the door to epistemological skepticism. If, she seems to have thought, anything is possible, then nothing can be entertained with certainty. Despite her evident delight in speculating about new worlds, she insisted that comprehensive or certain knowledge of the natural order was not attainable. In "Of Stars," she observes of the night sky that

> The more we search, the lesse we know,
> Because we finde our *Worke* doth endlesse grow.
> For who doth know, But *Stars* we see by *Night*,
> Are *Suns* wich to some other *Worlds* give *Light*?
> But could our outward *Senses* pace the *Skie*,
> As well as can *Imaginations* high;
> If we were there, as little may we know,
> As those which stay, and never do up go.
> Then let not *Man*, in fruitless paines *Life* spend,
> The most we know, is, *Nature Death* will send.
> [*Poems and Fancies*, 36]

We notice, reading this poem, that even were our senses "to pace the Skie," we would know as little as we do now. For Cavendish, speculative labor does not result in any sort of certainty; in fact, she specifies rather gloomily in these lines that the only thing about which we can be certain is the prospect of death.

Cavendish extended her epistemological skepticism unapologetically to religious matters. She both insists that God is unknowable and articulates religious doubt, two claims that must have alarmed her readers. As Lisa Sarasohn has noted, Cavendish's "theology is completely negative; we can only know that God is not at all like us." Cavendish articulated this skepticism boldly, claiming that God, "being an Infinite, Incomprehensible, Supernatural, and Immaterial Essence, void of all Parts, can no ways be subject to Perception."[39] In *Orations* (1662) she included a Lucretian oration in which she speculated that "the most Valiant minds are somewhat Disturbed with the thoughts of Death, by reason the Terrors of Death are Natural to all mankind, not so much to Feel, as to Think of, not only for the Parting of Soul and Body, and the dark Oblivion in Death, but for the Uncertain condition after Death" (149). The writer who opened her first written volume with the thought that "the Desire of Fame proceeds from a doubt of an after being" was more willing than most of her contemporaries to consider openly the religious skepticism to which atomism seemed to lead.[40]

These articulations of religious skepticism had strong political and personal origins. Remembering the religious certainty that fueled the bloodshed of the civil wars, she openly speculates that "it is better, to be an Atheist, then a superstitious man; for in Atheisme there is humanitie, and civility, towards man to man; but superstition regards no humanity, but begets cruelty to all things."[41] If we assume that by "superstitious man" she means someone who clings dogmatically to unverifiable religious claims, we see that her religious skepticism was motivated, in part, by her personal experience of war. Because God was finally unknowable, it was thus useless in Cavendish's mind to speculate about the nature of God or to worry about his place in the natural order. Yet as Cavendish knew, such speculation was not only inevitable; it was often supported by an unwarranted sense of certainty. She knew that people are willing to kill for beliefs that often cannot be verified. On some level, she must have hoped that her exploration of epistemological skepticism might help warn against the dangers of dogmatic certainty.

Although her skepticism was not, finally, atheism, it was articulated too unapologetically and too unguardedly to avoid misunderstandings. Even friends, such as Walter Charleton, were made uncomfortable by such open and unqualified considerations of religious skepticism. In a private letter to her, Charleton tried, as tactfully as he could manage, to convey to her that their approaches to natural philosophy differed. Behind the following lines, one senses his need to distance himself from her heretical ideas: "For your Natural Philosophy; it is ingenious and free, and may be, for ought I know, Excellent: but give me leave, Madam, to confess, I have not yet been so happy, as to discover much therein that's Apodictical, or wherein I think my self much obliged to acquiesce." He tried to soften his criticism by highlighting his own skeptical method, claiming that "Men may, indeed enquire and determine what is most probable, but God alone knows what's true, in the things of Nature." He was supported in his cautious approach to natural philosophy, he explained, by the collective strength of the Royal Society, which was itself "of a constitution exceedingly strict and rigid in the examination of Theories concerning Nature . . . and that's the Reason why it made choice of these three Words for its Motto, *Nullius in verba*."[42] Charleton's caution was, we might guess, the result of the closeness of their enterprise; she and Charleton were the very first to introduce Gassendi's Epicurean atomism to England, and their atomist systems bore similarities. As Robert Kargon notes, "she laid the atomists open to attack on the charge of impiety," if only through the openness with which she explores epistemological and even religious skepticism.[43] It was the charge of atheism that Charleton was eager to elude, and he knew that his association with Margaret Cavendish, like his association with Thomas Hobbes, was a liability.

What Charleton and most other readers missed was the fact that what appeared to be religious skepticism in Cavendish's work was motivated primarily by political and psychological interests. Her interest in exploring epistemological uncertainty was aimed at those who embraced certainty unreflectively. She was all her life a harsh critic of unwarranted self-confidence, impatient with those who

> think not onely to learn Natures Waies, but to know her Means and Abilities, and become Lord of Nature, as to rule her, and bring her under his Subjection. But in this Man seems rather to play than work, to seek rather than to find; for Nature hath infinite Varieties of Motions to form Matters with, that Man knows not, nor can guess at; and such Materials and Ingredients, as Mans gross Sense cannot find out; insomuch that we scarce see the Shadow of Natures Works, but live in Twilight, and have not alwaies that; but sometimes we are in Utter Darkness.
>
> [*World's Olio*, 177]

The echo of Lucretius's claim that "all life is a struggle in the dark," like the many other echoes of Lucretius throughout these three volumes, suggests her familiarity with his Epicurean poem and with his philosophy. While the endless permutations allowed by atomism seemed to have fascinated Cavendish, they also led to a sober epistemological skepticism. By exploring skepticism openly, she hoped to help avoid conflicts over competing but unverifiable beliefs.

The civil war lent itself to being conceived of in terms of a troubled atomist system, a Hobbesian state of nature in which man was pitted against man. Cavendish used atomism throughout her career as a metaphor for the brutal and frightening clash of conflicting certainties, and she clearly viewed the political world as an atomistic system. For her the civil war was, however, merely a symptom of an eternal condition. She read a Hobbesian state of nature into the very fabric of the universe by using the language of war to describe the actions of atoms. An early poem in *Poems and Fancies* titled "A Warr with Atomes" depicts the equivalent of Hobbes's state of nature at the microcosmic level of matter:

> Some factious *Atomes* will agree; combine,
> They strive some *form'd Body* to unjoyne.
> The *Round* beate out the *Sharpe*: the *Long*
> The *Flat* do fight withall, thus all go wrong.
> [16]

This unsettling cosmological underpinning served as the basis for her understanding of the instability of political institutions, even after she dropped atomism as a theory of matter. She marvels, for instance, at the relative infrequency of war, writing, "It seems to me a thing above Nature, that Men are not alwaies in War one against the other, and that some Estates live in Peace, somtimes forty or an hundred years . . . without Civil Warrs; for the old saying is, '*So many Men so many Minds*'" (*World's Olio*, 162-63).[44] The villain of her world view was "the factious man" who clung dogmatically to unverifiable beliefs: "factious persons . . . are not onely the cause of the taking away our goods . . . and our lives, but our religion, our frends, our laws, our liberties, and peace; For a factious man makes a commotion, which commotion raiseth civil wars . . . . a factious man is a humane Devil" (*World's Olio*, 42). If she was sure of anything, she seems to have been sure of the ease with which society could dissolve into social and political chaos.

Just as atomism forced her to question the reliability of the senses, it and the conflict of certainties that fueled the civil war suggested that the operations of the mind were disturbingly erratic. If the political realm was a troubled atomistic system, so too was the mind. Both were, to use her language, vulnerable to rebellion. Her candor in displaying the chaotic activity of the thinking life is no doubt one of the most striking and unsettling characteristics of her work. It suggests how profoundly scarred she was by the experience of war. As if to warn others of the changeable nature of the human mind, her work is a consciously constructed catalog of its erratic and unpredictable nature. The mind, she argued, was in a constant state of flux: "Nature hath not onely made Bodies changeable, but Minds; so to have a Constant Mind, is to be Unnatural; for our Body changeth from the first beginning to the last end, every Minute adds or takes away: so by Nature, we should change every Minute, since Nature hath made nothing to stand at a stay, but to alter as fast as Time runs; wherefore it is Natural to be in one Mind one minute, and in another in the next" (*The World's Olio,* 162).[45] Her concern with changeableness focuses largely on the fact that despite the notoriously unstable texture of the self, men and women clung to unverifiable beliefs. Echoing Francis Godwin's introduction to *The Man in the Moone,* she points to the frequency and tenacity with which erroneous opinions are held: "How strong did men believe against the *Antipodes,* as one man believing such a thing to be, was put out of his Liveing, when in after Ages it was found a Truth? ... and many believ'd that the Earth was flat and not round, but Cavendish, Drake, and others, rectified that Error" (116).[46] Reason, she concludes, is not so much "born with a Man" as it is "bred with a Man" (139). "We may say," she explains, that "Man is born with Reason, because in time he is capable of Reason."[47] But being capable of reason was not, as Jonathan Swift illustrated more than seventy-five years later, the same thing as being a reasonable creature.

The surprising metaphors she uses for the mind reveal her sensitivity to and familiarity with internal conflict. Some of her stranger metaphors are variations on the concept of an atomistic system. She compares the head to a church, for example, in order to illustrate the need to control the acquisitive nature of curiosity:

The *Head* of *Man's* a *Church,* where *Reason* preaches,
Directs the *Life,* and every *Thought* it teaches.
Perswades the *Mind* to live in *Peace,* and *quiet,*

And not in fruitlesse *Contemplation Riot.*
For why, saies *Reason*, you shall damned be
From all *Content*, for your *Curiosity.*
To seek about for that you cannot finde,
Shall be a *Torment* to a restlesse *Mind.*
[*Poems and Fancies*, 153]

These lines are of psychological interest because they suggest her own strange personal combination of intellectual restlessness and epistemological despair. Elsewhere she elaborates on the burden that accompanies intellectual inquiry:

Reason doth stretch *Mans mind* upon the Rack,
With *Hopes*, with *Joyes*, pull'd up, with *Feare* pull'd back.
Desire whips him forward, makes him run,
Despaire doth wound, and pulls him back agen.
For *Nature*, thou mad'st *Man* betwixt *Extreames*,
Wants *perfect Knowledge*, yet thereof he dreames.
[*Poems and Fancies*, 59]

Like Samuel Johnson's Rasselas, who is troubled to discover that animals find contentment and satiety in ways not possible for him, Cavendish notes that were man "like a *Beast*, to live with *Sense* alone, / Then might he eate, or drink, or lye *stone*-still" (59). Later she would argue that humans are not alone in having the capability to reason and that they ought not, therefore, to be considered above all other animals.[48] But in 1653 she, like Johnson, seems to have felt that although the human mind lifts humanity above the beasts, it also delivers substantial burdens.

Her favorite metaphor links her interests in the mind and society. She compares the mind to a commonwealth and individual thoughts to citizens; at its best, the mind succeeds in governing its citizens/thoughts: "The Mind is like a Commonwealth, and the Thoughts as the Citizens therein; or the Thoughts like Household-servants, who are busily imployed about the Minds Affairs, who is the Master" (*The World's Olio*, 95). Different temperaments could therefore be explained by their differing internal governments: "Some brains that are well tempered, are like those Common-wealths, that are justly and peaceably governed, and live in their own bounds: other braines that are hotly tempered, are like those common-wealths that make wars upon their neighbours; others again that are unevenly tempered, are like those that are incombred with civil wars amongst themselves" (21). By comparing the mind to a commonwealth or the body politic, which she feared was always on the brink of dissolution, she was indicating the ease with which the mind could itself fall into anarchy. Pointing to the unstable texture of the self was, in turn, a way of highlighting the fragility of a political entity composed of so many unpredictable minds.

Her interest in atomism is significant for its early and enterprising role in transmitting Gassendi's Epicurean atomism to England. But its chief value may lie in the window it opens into the state of her mind during the strained early years of her marriage. She found in atomism a metaphor that proved useful in explaining political and psychological conflict, and she used it to explore her thoughts publicly as she struggled to cope with a world that seemed to be forever at odds with her and with her family. Like the "Register of Mournfull Verses" that appears toward the end of *Poems and Fancies,* presenting elegies for the many people she had lost to the English civil wars, her first three volumes served both as protests and as attempts to come to terms, as best she could, with her calamitous experience of war. The epistemological skepticism she embraced as a result of her inquiry into atomistic systems presented one response to the crisis of authority that catapulted England into civil war; by warning her readers of the unreliability of the senses, she must have hoped to help ward off the kind of conflict that led to war.

Unlike natural philosophers such as Charleton and Evelyn, she was less interested in a theory of matter than she was in using atomism as a metaphor that might account for the conflict that governed her mind and her world. Atomism became, through the efforts of Descartes, Boyle, Newton, and others, the foundation of modern physics, but Epicurean atomism was as much a moral philosophy as it was a natural philosophy. It might thus be argued that Cavendish represented the spirit of Epicurus more faithfully—if more whimsically—than the other modernizers, who found themselves unable to translate Epicurus without Christianizing him and thus altering his philosophy.

By 1655 she had rejected atomism altogether as a theory of matter, chiefly because the democratic implications of a universe governed by individual atoms seem to have troubled her. But while she rejected atomism as a theory of matter, she retained it as a metaphor for society and for the mind.[49] Her traumatic experience of war and exile found in

atomism an explanatory discourse for psychological and political conflict. Atomism provided her with a vocabulary to explore something that
had become terribly clear: mind and world were in conflict.

4

"No House But
My Mind"

Cavendish's Hobbesian Dilemma

When Cavendish rejected atomism as a theory of matter in 1655, she did so because such a system would result in "an infinite and eternal disorder."[1] With this statement a new political anxiety enters her writing. In 1663 she was still elucidating her reasons for having rejected atomism: "As for Atoms, after I had Reasoned with my Self, I conceived that it was not probable, that the Universe and all the Creatures therein could be Created and Disposed by the Dancing and Wandering and Dusty motion of Atoms."[2] The dance of atoms was unlikely, in her mind, to result in a stable universe governed by definable laws; furthermore, by positing a material system in which any given atom had power equal to that of any other atom, atomism threatened to level the hierarchical order that Cavendish felt was necessary if anarchy was to be avoided in both material and political systems:

> if Every and Each Atome were of a Living Substance, and had Equal Power, Life and Knowledge, and Consequently a Free-will and Liberty, and so Each and Every one were as Absolute as an other, they would hardly Agree in one Government, and as unlikely as Several Kings would Agree in one Kingdom, or rather as Men, if every one should have an Equal Power, would make a Good Government; and if it should Rest upon Consent and Agreement, like Human Governments, there would be as many Alterations and Confusions of Worlds, as in Human States and Governments by Disagreement.[3]

In short, as a theory of matter, atomism posed disturbing democratic implications. But although she rejected atomism as a theory of matter in 1655, she retained it throughout her life as a metaphor for the body politic and for the mind, exploring both as troubled atomistic systems. Her writing after 1655 reveals the tension she seems to have felt between her belief in hierarchy as an ordering political principal and her vision of the body politic as an atomistic system that by its nature resisted the imposition of hierarchical order.

Cavendish's energies were soon devoted to exploring more fully the profoundly troubling political consequences of envisioning the state as an atomistic system. Seen this way, the state appeared to be challenged by the very task that defined it: uniting the many in the one. Competing ideologies among citizens within the state were bound to clash, causing dissension and threatening the integrity of the state itself. With the 1651 publication of *Leviathan,* this problem had received a striking visual articulation in Wenceslas Hollar's now-famous engraving for *Leviathan*'s title page.[4] The engraving portrayed the sovereign's body emerging from the landscape, his body composed of his subjects' bodies. It perfectly encapsulated the concern Hobbes and Cavendish shared with Newcastle, Sir William Davenant, and the other members of the exiled Newcastle circle: "the problem of public order, and, in particular, the appropriate way to maintain it."[5]

The figure of Thomas Hobbes looms behind Cavendish's work, making it all the more remarkable that his influence on her thought has remained unexplored.[6] They shared an alarmingly pessimistic view of human nature: her frequent wonder at the relative infrequency of war was, after all, not all that different from Hobbes's description in *Leviathan* of life in the state of nature as "solitary, poor, nasty, brutish, and short" (pt. 1, chap. 13).[7] Like Hobbes, she seems to have been haunted by the problem of ethical relativism, a problem Hobbes articulated in *Leviathan:*

> But whatsoever is the object of any man's appetite or desire, that is it which he for his part calleth good: and the object of his hate and aversion, evil; and of his contempt, vile and inconsiderable. For these words of good, evil, and contemptible, are ever used with relation to the person that useth them: there being nothing simply and absolutely so; nor any common rule of good and evil, to be taken from the nature of the

objects themselves; but from the person of the man, where there is no commonwealth; or, in a commonwealth, from the person that representeth it; or from an arbitrator or judge, whom men disagreeing shall by consent set up, and make his sentence the rule thereof.

[pt. 1, chap. 6][8]

For Hobbes and Cavendish, conflict over contested definitions of words such as "good" and "evil" seemed inevitable without the ordering power of an absolute monarch.[9] Both writers devoted their energies to articulating the proper relation between subject and sovereign, and Cavendish absorbed many of Hobbes's ideas. That she did not merely echo Hobbes, however, will be evident in her response to and even revision of Hobbes's political theory. His influence both inspired her and directed her further inward to the worlds of the mind.

HOBBES'S ROLE IN THE NEWCASTLE HOUSEHOLD

It is worth remembering that whereas Hobbes was viewed with suspicion in England, he "seems to have been widely accepted abroad."[10] Cavendish thus met Hobbes in a context in which she might have felt freer to pursue his ideas than most English men or women back home. He was an intimate though unofficial member of her household, having been for years a deeply valued friend of her husband, William Cavendish, then marquess of Newcastle (referred to hereafter as Newcastle). Five years older than Newcastle, Hobbes had been hired in 1608 to tutor Newcastle's cousin, another William Cavendish, later second earl of Devonshire; except for a two-year period between 1628 and 1630, he remained part of the Devonshire household for the rest of his life.[11] The Newcastle-Hobbes correspondence dates to 1630, and by 1634 Hobbes was writing from London to apologize for not being able to find Newcastle a copy of Galileo's *Dialogue concerning the Two Chief World Systems* because, so Hobbes explained, "it is not possible to get it for mony."[12] Newcastle valued Hobbes enough to invite him to join his household in 1636, an invitation Hobbes considered carefully and was inclined at one point to accept. He remained with the Devonshires, but his friendship with Newcastle and with Newcastle's brother, Charles Cavendish, intensified during the late 1630s.[13] Shortly after the meeting of the Long Parliament in November 1640, Hobbes fled into exile, in part because of his concern over potentially hostile reaction to *Elements of Law,* which had been dedicated that year to Newcastle and had circulated widely in manuscript. By 1645 Hobbes joined the exiled Newcastle salon in Paris, and it was partly through his membership in this salon that he was introduced to the circle of scientific figures both in England and in France that made possible his later boast of being "numbered among the philosophers."[14] In 1646 he dedicated *Of Liberty and Necessity* to Newcastle along with the manuscript of *A Minute or First Draught of the Optiques.*[15] Thus, when Margaret Cavendish met Thomas Hobbes and began hearing about his work in Paris sometime after her marriage in 1645, she was learning of the work of her husband's intimate and valued friend. Much of Hobbes's writing was in Latin, but she was in an environment in which exposure to the general outline of his political and scientific thought was unavoidable. Furthermore, in 1650 Hobbes began to publish some of his works in English. By the time he published *Leviathan* in 1651, Cavendish could begin reading Hobbes's English works for herself.[16]

Despite the intimacy between Newcastle and Hobbes, however, Margaret Cavendish soon saw that Hobbes kept her at a comfortable distance despite and perhaps even because of her active interest in his philosophy. We have only two pieces of evidence regarding their personal relations; both reflect Hobbes's frosty civility toward his patron's wife. By her own account, during her trip to London in 1653, she ran into Hobbes, who was no stranger to her by that time, and invited him to dinner: "[F]or when I was in London I me[t] him, and told him as truly I was very glad to see him, and asked if he would please to do me the honour to stay at dinner, but he with great civility refused me, as having some businesse, which I suppose required his absence" (*Philosophical and Physical Opinions* [1655], sig. B3v). That Cavendish wondered whether Hobbes's absence from her table was actually required suggests that she perceived his civil refusal to be a mere excuse. Even her choice of the word "refused" hints that she perceived his response as a rejection.

We also have a 1662 letter from Hobbes thanking Cavendish for having sent him a copy of the volume of plays she published that year. The letter reveals that he preferred to keep a distance between himself and his would-be disciple:

> I have received, from your Excellence, the Book you sent me
> ... which obliges me to trouble you with a short expression of
> my thanks, and of the sense I have of your extraordinary

Favour. For tokens of this kind are not ordinarily sent but to such as pretend to the title as well as to the mind of Friends. I have already read so much of it (in that Book which my Lord of Devonshire has) as to give your Excellence an accou[n]t of it thus far, That it is filled throughout with more and truer Idea's of Virtue and Honour than any Book of morality I have read.[17]

His refusal to join her for dinner in 1653, and his alleged surprise in 1662 that she might consider him a friend, suggest a determined effort on his part to distance himself from her. Even the attempted compliments he makes by claiming already to have begun reading Devonshire's copy of the volume and by describing her plays as "filled throughout with more and truer Idea's of Virtue and Honour than any Book of morality I have read" are ways of fulfilling the politeness required of him toward his patron's wife without substantively discussing or, as his letter makes clear, even reading the volume all the way through. His coolness did not dissuade Cavendish from responding in print to his work. Nor, as we shall see, was a personal relationship necessary in order for Hobbes to influence her; by 1653, when she began to publish her work, he was well known to her and she was already deeply engaged with his work.

In exploring Hobbes's ideas, she joined other exiled Royalists. Sir William Davenant had made a public display of his interest in applying Hobbes's political theory to literature when he published his *Preface to Gondibert* together with Hobbes's "Answer to the Preface" and Edmund Waller's and Abraham Cowley's commendatory poems in 1650, one year in advance of the publication of his fragmentary epic.[18] The *Preface* was a personal address to Hobbes, thanking him for having done him "the honour to allow this Poem a daylie examination as it was writing."[19] One of the first territories Davenant lays claim to in the *Preface* is the mind: poetry, he explains, should be about psychological truth rather than historical fact, "for wise Poets think it more worthy to seeke out truth in the passions, then to record the truth of actions" (5). Davenant's interest in the passions had clear political motives; in the *Preface* he chastises the "Foure Cheef aides of Government (Religion, Armes, Policy, and Law)" for overlooking the power of poetry to influence the mind. By "prevail[ing] upon [subjects'] bodys [rather] then their mindes," government had "faild in the effects of authority" (evidenced, he might have added, by the English subjects' recent execution of their king) (37). In short, he was advancing an argument for the political utility of poetry: "The subject on which they [the powers of government] should worke is the Minde; and the Minde can never be constrain'd, though it may be gain'd by Persuasion: And since Persuasion is the principall Instrument which can bring to fashion the brittle and misshapen metall of the Minde, none are so fitt aides to this important worke as Poets: whose art is more then any enabled with a voluntary, and cheerfull assistance of Nature; and whose operations are as resistlesse, secret, easy, and subtle, as is the influence of Planetts" (38). Davenant offered the "secret, easy, and subtle" influence of poetry as a means by which government might effectively maintain public order.

Newcastle also formulated a response to the problem of maintaining political order in his *Advice* addressed to Charles II. The *Advice* reveals that he shared with Hobbes an anxiety regarding "the dangers of the public word."[20] Unlike Newcastle's work on horsemanship, the *Advice* remained unpublished until the twentieth century, perhaps because of its elite audience but also because of Newcastle's own qualms about the dangers of the public word. These qualms become evident as he advances the argument that maintaining political stability requires keeping the populace in ignorance: "[T]hat which hath [d]one most hurte, is the Aboundance of Gramer Scooles, & Ins of Courtes. . . . ther are so many scooles now, as moste read, so Indeed there should bee but such a proportion, as to serve the Church, & moderatly the Law, & the merchants, & the reste for the Labor, for Else they run out to Idle, & Unnecesary People that becomes a factious burthen to the Comon wealth, for when Moste was Unletterd, it was much a better world, both for Peace & warr."[21] Cavendish's biography of Newcastle documents his fear of the printed word, and it is clear that Cavendish shared that fear both with him and with Hobbes. But her response to Hobbes's political thought and to the problem of maintaining political order was finally less optimistic than that of either Davenant or Newcastle.

THE POLITICS OF THE HOBBESIAN DILEMMA

Surrounded by literati, equipped with translations and texts, and instructed by her husband and brother-in-law, both of whom were intensely engaged with Hobbes's thought, Cavendish was thus, at least at first, well positioned to experience Hobbes's work directly as a powerfully enabling influence. In particular, Hobbes's assault on authority must have exercised a strong appeal: his gleeful and ruthlessly logical assaults on the universities, the schoolmen, Aristotle, parliaments, Popes, and Protestant archbishops and bishops must have pleased Cavendish, who all her life both envied and criticized the institutions of power and learning. That Hobbes delighted in working his assaults on authority into everyday conversation seems evident in John Aubrey's now-famous passage recording Hobbes's boast that "if he had read as much as other men, he should have knowne no more than other men." Coming from one of the most outstanding thinkers of the day, an offhand remark of this sort was bound to encourage, however unwittingly, Cavendish's confidence in her own enterprise. The corollary to Hobbes's assault on authority—his deductive method—also influenced Cavendish; like him, she not only rejected authority but also sought, as he put it, "to prove everything in my own way."[22] We might guess that both the deductive method and the assault on authority were of particular interest to a woman who no doubt regretted deeply her lack of a formal education. Although Cavendish would take deductive reasoning to unsystematic extremes of which Hobbes no doubt disapproved, she found in Hobbes an eminent thinker whose method validated her participation in the life of the mind.

In the realm of speculative activity, then, Hobbes proved to be a powerfully liberating influence: his assault on the schoolmen, his deductive method, and his focus on the man-made nature of the polity equipped Cavendish with the tools of her own intellectual enterprise. His focus on the creative mental work behind the "artificial man" or "Leviathan" helps explain Cavendish's more extreme claims for the power of the imagination. Her claim, for instance, in *Nature's Pictures* that "fancy is not an imitation of nature, but a naturall Creation" is congruent with Hobbes's insistence on seeing the exclusively human design of the body politic. Nowhere does she reveal her awareness of the degree to which the mind shaped society more than when she considers the lives of women. She understood how much custom determined and confined the lives of women, forcing them to be "kept like birds in cages to hop up and down in our houses, not sufferd to fly abroad to see the several changes of fortune, and the various humors, ordained and created by nature. . . . thus by an opinion, which I hope is but an erronious one in men, we are shut out of all power, and Authority by reason we are never imployed either in civil nor marshall affaires."[23] She explored many aspects of women's lives, but she was particularly attentive to the arbitrary constraints that prevented women from engaging publicly in intellectual life.

Liberating as Hobbes proved to be in the realm of speculative activity, however, in the realm of political activity, he exerted a powerfully restraining influence, evident in her own adaptation of Hobbesian political theory. Although his political theory had the effect of encouraging her to engage in political thought, even feminist political thought, his Erastian fear of factionalism imposed extreme limits on her faith in political action. She was drawn to his political thought because it was motivated by anxieties she shared, and these counteracted for her (as they had for Hobbes) the more liberating elements of the assault on authority. His exaggerated sense of caution is well known: it is illustrated by his precipitous flight into France over his fear of the reaction to *Elements of Law;* more generally, it can be sensed governing his dark view of human nature. In his autobiography he attributed his timorousness to the rumor circulating at his birth regarding the possible invasion of the Spanish Armada: "Thus my mother was big with such fear that she brought twins to birth, myself and fear at the same time." As Alan Ryan has noted, Hobbes treated fear or caution as "one of the primary political virtues." Fear, Ryan continues, helps to explain "the causes and character of the 'war of all against all' in the state of nature, in motivating persons in the state of nature to contract with one another to set up an authority to 'overawe them all' and make peace possible, and in persuading them to obey that authority once it has been established."[24] Cavendish was also fearful by nature. Her repeated confessions to being bashful and unsure of herself in social situations are well known. More important, though less noted, is the fact that fear dominates her political thought. Like many Royalists, Cavendish and Hobbes were both struck by what they saw as the war's senseless brutality. The earl of Berkshire articulated this general sense of futility and loss when toward the end of the war he remarked, "Nobody can tell what we have fought about all this while."[25] In particular, her work documents her lifelong anxiety regarding the disputatious nature of the human mind and the threat that disputatiousness posed to the integrity of both the mind and the body politic.

When she considered the polity, she frequently applied atomism as a metaphor. She viewed society as a Hobbist-atomistic system perpetually on the brink of war, in which mind confronts mind, and moral certainty, moral certainty. She was acutely aware, for example, of the instability of political entities, or, as she put it, of the inevitability that "Self-love seeks and strives for Preheminency & Command, which all cannot have." Her plays and romances explore characters whose conflicting value systems pose irreconcilable differences. Similarly, her interest in natural philosophy returned obsessively to the problem of subjectivity.[26] Changeable and unpredictable, the very nature of the self posed a potential threat to political order, particularly as each self argued for competing definitions of key terms such as "justice." She considered the disputatious nature of the human mind with deep pessimism.

It is thus not entirely surprising that Hobbes's tragic sensibility, evident in his liberal allusions to the Book of Job, resonated with Cavendish.[27] Job's friends try inadequately to explain his suffering in human terms, but it is only when Job abandons that line of thought and realizes the limits of human understanding that he is spiritually transformed. Like Job, Hobbes was aware that concepts like "justice," for example, are human rather than divine concerns, that meaning is man-made, and that polities are, finally, the result of human convention rather than divine order. Given these conditions, it was of the utmost importance to agree on certain definitions, such as on the meanings of "good" and "evil." Similarly, it was crucial to avoid controversy over unverifiable claims like those purporting to depict the nature of God. And yet for Hobbes, men were neither likely to agree on definitions nor to avoid controversy over contested and unverifiable claims. He responded to this problem by embracing "the thoroughgoing Erastian principle that the state must be supreme in all matters affecting religion, else the power of the sovereign to protect the security of his subjects would be eroded by religious factionalism." In fact, he went beyond the normal definition of Erastianism by deferring all definitions to an absolute sovereign; this shocked his English readers, most of whom believed in the concept of an "absolute and immutable" natural law whose "final arbiter is God, not man."[28]

Unlike her English contemporaries, Cavendish unapologetically shared Hobbes's concern regarding the problem of competing definitions. She understood that the polity was the product of human reason rather than divine fiat: "[N]atural reason did first compose Common-Wealths, invented arts, and sciences," she explains in *Philosophical and Physical Opinions.* Like Hobbes, she knew that "natural reason" did not necessarily lead to shared definitions, especially when competing interests were at stake: The "dispositions of men," she notes, "are governed more by passion, then by reason, as the body is governed more by appetite, then by conveniences."[29] That she, like Hobbes, reached for ultra-Erastianism as a solution to this problem, at least at first, is evident in passages such as the following:

> But it is Time and Occasion that makes most things Good or Bad: For example, it were a horrid thing, and against Nature, and all Civil Laws, for Children and Parents, Brethren and Neighbours, and Acquaintance, to kill one another, although their Offences to each other were very hainous; but when the King or chief Magistrate in a Commonwealth commands it, as they do to those that are of their side in a Civil War, then it is not onely Warrantable, but it is accounted Sacred and Divine; because nothing pleaseth Divinity more than Obedience to Magistrates, and Nature loves Peace, although she hath made all things to War upon one another; so that Custome and the Law make the same thing Civil or Pious, Just or Unjust.
>
> [*The World's Olio* (1655), 81]

Similarly, she returns repeatedly to the timeworn image of the body politic, through which she depicts the ideal form of government as one in which the individual submits to an absolute authority. Such a commonwealth would be "governed by one Head or Governour, as a King, for one Head is sufficient for one Body: for several Heads breed several Opinions, and several Opinions breed Disputations, and Disputations Factions, and Factions breed Wars, and Wars bring Ruin and Desolation: for it is more safe to be governed, though by a Foolish Head, than a Factious Heart" (205-6). A great monarch, Newcastle told her, had "a Soveraign Command over Church, Laws, and Armes."[30]

In her biography of Newcastle, she presents her husband's sustained and unambiguously Erastian view of government. There, she commends her husband's decision to regulate the content of sermons during the war, noting in particular his belief that "Schism and Faction in Religion is the Mother of all or most Rebellions, Wars and Disturbances in a State or Government."[31] She quotes him as saying that there should "be more Praying, and less Preaching for much Preaching breeds Faction, but much Praying causes Devotion" (166). "The more divisions there are in Church and State," he had remarked, "the more trouble and confusion is apt to ensue" (167). Earlier, Newcastle had warned the Prince of Wales regarding the dangers of the "Bible Madd" who were equally invulnerable to kingly displays of love and to kingly attempts at generating fear.[32] *The Life of . . . William Cavendishe* can be read as a Hobbesian warning of the dangers of the printed word.

Like Hobbes and like her husband, then, Cavendish worried about conflict over unverifiable beliefs such as those attempting to identify the nature of God. Fearing the destructive power of religious conflict, she urged repeatedly that God was unknowable. We have seen how her exploration of atomism led her from questioning the reliability of the senses to cautioning against outspoken dogmatic religious certainty. She generally regarded religious certainty as intellectual presumption; in *Sociable Letters* she suggests that "Man was so Ignorant, as he Knew not himself, yet would Pretend to Know God, and his Attributes, Counsels, Laws, Rules, and Decrees . . . but if God be Absolute, and Incomprehensible, it is an High Presumption to Assimilize God to any Creature."[33] It was best, Cavendish resolved, to submit publicly to the sovereign's definitions while holding silently to one's own beliefs; a monarchist by nature, she had seen firsthand what happened when subjects took it upon themselves to engage in disputes with their king.

Cavendish's Erastianism, though, led her to difficulties when she considered her own writing, which, she worried, might be misunderstood as inciting political antagonisms that threatened political stability.[34] This anxiety intensified after the Restoration, when she began reading more broadly and responding in print to specific authors.[35] She expresses concern, for example, that her husband, who otherwise always encouraged her to write, might be displeased with *Philosophical Letters* (1664), which critiqued Hobbes, Descartes, Henry More, and Van Helmont. She worried that he might "be angry with me for Writing and Publishing this Book, by reason it is a Book of Controversies, of which I have heard your Lordship say, That Controversies and Disputations make Enemies of Friends."[36] Her husband had told her that "disputations and Controversies are a kind of Civil War, maintained by the Pen, and often draw out the sword soon after." For this reason all controversies should be written in Latin "that none but the Learned may read them."[37] In *Orations* she explores the argument that writing itself poses a danger to the state, especially when it takes politics as its subject: "[I]t is to be Observed, that much Writing of that [political] Nature makes much Trouble, wherein the Pen doth more mischief than the Sword, witness Controversies, that make Atheism; for the more Ignorant a people are, the more

Devout and Obedient they are to God and his Deputies, which are Magistrates; Wherefore it were very Requisite, that all such Books should be Burnt, and all such Writers Silenced, or at least none should write of States-affairs, but those the State allows or Authorises."[38] She was willing to allow subjects "Liberty of Conscience, Conditionally, that they do not meddle with Civil Government or Governours" (69). Even eloquence worried her because of its power to "make Men like Gods or Devils, as having a Power beyond Nature, Custom and Force."[39] Her prolific literary career is thus characterized by the tension between her compulsion to write herself into history and her anxiety regarding the power of the printed word to spark controversies.

CAVENDISH'S NARRATIVE FRAMES

Her anxiety regarding the power of the written word could not keep her from her compulsive writing, but it did determine the generic shape of her work. In the works she wrote after 1655, she focused on the conflicts that arose from multiple and conflicting sensibilities. Repeatedly, she turned to narrative frames that contained multiple and competing perspectives, no one of which can be identified unproblematically with Cavendish's own perspective. Through these narrative frames, she was able to explore the disputatious nature of the human mind. She had also found a rhetorical strategy that allowed her to explore heterodox ideas boldly without necessarily presenting them polemically.

Book 1 of *Nature's Pictures* (1656), for example, provides an example of the kind of narrative frame Cavendish liked to create. We are introduced to a group of storytellers, not unlike Chaucer's pilgrims, each of whom tells a story.

> In Winter cold, a Company was met
> Both Men and Women by the Fire set;
> At last they did agree to pass the time,
> That every one should tell a Tale in Rhime.
> [sig. B1r, ll. 13-16]

What follows is a collection of tales in verse that highlights the human penchant for controversy. Many of the tales provide a moral that departs from or directly contradicts the previous storyteller's moral. Thus, a tale illustrating male inconstancy sparks a tale about female inconstancy. Similarly, a tale about the burdensome nature of wives is followed by a tale about the burdensome nature of husbands. Brief interpretive commentary is interspersed between the tales, serving as the transition from one tale to the next. The storyteller who responds with the tale about burdensome husbands, for example, introduces her story as a direct and pointed response to the previous tale about oppressive wives:

> if Women had but Wit,
> Men neither Wives nor Mistresses should get;
> No cause should have to murmure and complain,
> If Women their kinde Freedome would restrain.
> But Marriage is to Women far more worse
> Than 'tis to Men, and proves the greater Curse;
> And I, said she, for proof a Tale will tell
> What to a virtuous marryed Wife befell.
> [57]

Rather than putting forth an authorial point of view, each tale functions as an atomistic unit; taken as a whole, they illustrate the inevitability of disagreement over any number of issues pertaining to the internal world of the emotions or to the external codes of social behavior. The meta-narrative that results might be likened to a sort of troubled atomistic system. Tale answers tale, not in order to reach a conclusion, but rather to highlight the inevitable problem of competing points of view and the controversy they cause.

Thus, when the fourth tale, a romance called "A Description of Constancy," presents a tale of true love overcoming all obstacles and ending in a happy marriage, the following discussion ensues:

> A Lady said such constant love was dead,
> And all Fidelity to Heaven fled.
> Another Lady said she fain would know,
> When married were, if continued so.
> O, said a Man, such Love (as this was) sure
> Doth never in a Married Pair endure.
> But lovers cross'd use not to end so well,
> Which for to shew, a Tale I mean to tell.
> [26-27]

The tale that follows, "The Description of the Violence of Love," ends, predictably, not with the lovers overcoming obstacles and marrying happily but with their tragic deaths. Although some storytellers are commended for telling their stories well, most find their tales refuted or revised. In one instance, when a long-winded preface tires a listener's patience, she simply interrupts:

> Now saies a Lady which was sitting by,
> Pray let your rusty tongue with silence lie,
> And lissen to the Tale that I shall tell,
> Mark the misfortunes, that to them befell.
> [37]

In another instance, a tale sparks an even more heated reaction; after a bitter rant by an "old" and "spiteful" bachelor, the women storytellers become so angry that they threaten to leave. They are convinced to stay only after the men fall on their knees and beg the ladies to forgive the bachelor.

Book 1 reaches its highest pitch of controversy when a woman tells a tale about the need to govern the passions. In her tale a man finds a lady weeping. He learns from her that she is suffering from unrequited love for which there is no remedy; having been struck by physical desire for a man as beautiful as Narcissus, she feels hopeless in the face of his disregard for her. Further discussion reveals that she believes that desire enslaves the soul, making her incapable of remedying her situation. The traveler corrects her by explaining that the soul is not a slave to the senses:

> If that the Soul should give consent
> In every thing the Senses to content,
> No Peace, but War amongst Mankinde will be,
> Ruine and Desolation would have Victory;
> Few Men can call or challenge what's his own,
> For he would Master be that was most strong.
> Lady, love Virtue, and let Beauty dye,
> And in the Grave of Ruins let it lye.
> [86]

Hearing this advice, the lady abandons her despair and feels great joy.

The men listening to this tale, however, feel considerably less joy since they recognize that the lesson's insistence on governing the passions involves a curb on their own sexual license. They reply that to love many is natural; "for of one Dish we glut our palat, / Although it be but of a Salat." "Inconstancy," they explain, is "nature's play, / And we, her various Works, must her obey" (87). The debate over this topic intensifies until a storyteller interrupts, asking everyone to be silent so that the tales can continue.

Thus, the real story of book 1 of *Nature's Pictures* is the interaction among the storytellers as they argue over central elements of human behavior. No particular story can be identified with Cavendish's authorial point of view until the end of book 1, where a series of lugubrious and melancholy tales depicting the calamities of civil war sound very much like Cavendish's accounts elsewhere of the English civil wars. This autobiographical note becomes particularly clear when in the third of these tales a woman tells of her brother's cold-blooded murder. The man is described as a valiant soldier who finds himself surrounded by enemies and shot:

> Vollyes of Shot did all his Body tear,
> Where his Blood's spilt, the Earth no Grass will bear.
> As if for to revenge his Death, the Earth
> Was curs'd with Barrenness even from her Birth.
> And though his Body in the Grave doth lye,
> His Fame doth live, and will eternally.
> His Soul's Immortal, and so is his Fame,
> His Soul in Heaven doth live, and here his Name.
> [91-92]

The soldier's name appears, however, only by implication. The myth that no grass would grow on the spot where Charles Lucas was executed identifies him as the soldier in this story, though Cavendish never provides his name directly. Similarly, when in another brief story Cavendish provides an account of her encounter with the Committee for Compounding, the name of the country "Happland" disguises the real name of England:

> I over Sea to happ'land went,
> My Husband being then in Banishment;

His estate gone, and being very poor,
I thought some means Compassion might restore:
But when I ask'd, no pity could I finde,
Hard were their Hearts, and cruel every Minde.
[99]

With the introduction of these thinly disguised autobiographical stories, the controversial subject matter threatens to spill out of the textual
world of book 1 of *Nature's Pictures* into the real world. Cavendish knew
very well that other interpretations of the circumstances leading to her
brother's execution and to her husband's wartime losses existed. It is
thus not a coincidence that the tales are interrupted here by a man who
accuses the storyteller of breaking "all orders" by speaking "so long on
Melancholy Subjects" (99).

Significantly, the next two tales, the final ones in book 1, are clearly
identified as being by Newcastle. The first of these tales, "The Beggars'
Marriage," is a bawdy tale that successfully changes the tone of the volume from melancholy to the kind of levity one might expect from a tale
of aged and beggarly lovers. The second, "The Philosopher's Complaint,"
presents a satire on mankind. In particular, it explores the problem of
language. Noting that "mute" beasts find contentment because they are
not "litigious" or vulnerable to the deceptive power of "flow'ry Rhet'rick,"
or misled by the "multiplicity of Books," the philosopher concludes that
the "quiet silent li[f]e" of beasts is preferable to a human life governed by
"vain gossipings" (98, 101).

But the philosopher's conclusions ought not to be identified too
closely with those of Newcastle, since in the final stanza Newcastle in-
vokes the authorial "I" in order to comment on the philosopher:

I pity'd him, and his sad case,
Wishing our Vicar him to teach,
For to infuse a saving Grace,
By his tongues rhet'rick for to preach.
[102]

Thus, book 1 concludes with a tribute to authority in religious and, by
implication, political realms. By hoping that the philosopher might be
"infused" with "saving Grace" by the vicar's rhetoric, Newcastle suggests
that the solution to the problem of competing sensibilities lies in obedi-

ence to the proper authority. And by surrendering the power of concluding book 1 to her husband, Margaret Cavendish might also be seen to be demonstrating the need to obey the proper patriarchal authority.

But having "broken all orders" earlier with her civil war tales, she had already made clear the difficulty, perhaps even impossibility, of adhering to her husband's advice to avoid controversy. More generally, she demonstrates the inevitability of controversy through her depiction of contentious storytellers throughout book 1. In the implicit dialogue between husband and wife, Cavendish reveals her ambiguity toward the printed word: on the one hand, she yearned to tell her story; on the other, she understood the reason for her husband's "orders." She was, finally, unable to choose either option unproblematically. Just as her ambiguity toward the spoken word governs her plays, manifesting itself in her inability to choose between the active life and the contemplative life, so her ambiguity toward the printed word informs book 1 of *Nature's Pictures*.

Later, in *Sociable Letters*, Cavendish rephrased her interest in highlighting the danger of allowing competing sensibilities to be made public. "[D]ifferent Opinions in Religion and Laws in a Commonwealth, cause Cruel Civil Wars . . . whereof the late Wars in this Country are a woful Example, all being brought to Confusion with Preaching and Pleading, on the one side Preachers and Pleaders became Souldiers, on the other side, Souldiers became Preachers and Pleaders, so that the Word and the Sword made great Troubles, and grievous Calamities in these Nations, and though there hath been much Blood Shed, many lives Lost, Men Banish'd, and Families Ruined, yet there are Divisions still."[40] One might conclude, then, that the point of book 1 of *Nature's Pictures* is to illustrate the ease with which the word leads to the sword.

Orations of Divers Sorts (1662) deploys a similar rhetorical strategy. By 1662, of course, Cavendish and her husband had returned to their estate at Welbeck Abbey, which had been partly destroyed during the English civil wars.[41] Surrounded by evidence for the ease with which the conflict of immaterial ideas escalated into material violence, she turned to another narrative frame in order to highlight conflict and its consequences. We are warned in the preface to *Orations* to expect controversy since "the Generality of the People [are] more apt to make Warr, than to keep Peace."[42] The wreckage of war is highlighted throughout the volume as it is in the catalog of calamities provided by the following oration: "In truth, there is Nothing so Miserable, Hatefull, Cruel, and Irreligious as Civil Warr, for it is an Enemy against Law, Nature, and

God, it Pulls down the Seats of Justice, Throws down the Altars of Religion, Diggs up the Urns of their Parents, Disperses the Dust and Bones of their Dead Ancestors, Spills the Blood of their Fathers, Sons, Brethren, Friends, and Country-men, and makes a Total Destruction and Dissolution" (264-65). The orations within the volume help to account for this destruction by illustrating the inevitability of disagreement on key issues.

As with *Nature's Pictures,* the point of *Orations* is that conflict is inevitable. Some orations argue for war, others for peace; some argue for mutiny, others against mutiny; some for liberty of conscience, others against liberty of conscience. To illustrate the divisive nature of controversy, Cavendish composes a series of misogynistic orations that "so Anger[s]" the women that "after the Mens Orations are ended, they Privately Assemble together, where three or four take the place of an Orator, and Speak to the rest" (sig. a4r). Thus, part 11 of *Orations* is segregated from the rest of the text and titled "Femal Orations." The first of these female orations calls on women to change their status by "unit[ing] in Prudent Counsels, to make our Selves as Free, Happy, and Famous as Men," adding "the truth is, we Live like Bats or Owls, Labour like Beasts, and Dye like Worms" (225-26). Yet no greater consensus is reached within this smaller group than was arrived at by the larger group. One orator urges women to imitate men; another argues that doing so would be unnatural. One orator complains that "our Words to Men are as Empty Sounds, our Sighs as Puffs of Wind, and our Tears as Fruitless Showres"; another retorts that men "Dig to the Centre of the Earth for Gold for us; they Dive to the Bottom of the Sea for Jewels for us; they Build to the Skies Houses for us. . . . [L]et us Love men, Praise men, and Pray for men" (226-28). Tempting as it might be to extract one of these statements and allow it to represent Cavendish's political thought, it is important to take seriously the context in which these statements appear. Her overriding concern is with the disputatious nature of the human mind. Although she was piercingly aware of women's problematic political status, she was more concerned with the inevitable conflict of opposing and often unverifiable moral, political, and religious beliefs. Taken as a whole, *Orations* is thus less a feminist statement than it is a cautionary warning about the disputatious nature of the human mind.[43]

Later, she explained her rhetorical strategy in the process of defending *Orations* from charges that she was engaging in controversy. "As for my *Orations,* I have heard, that some do Censure me for speaking too Freely, and Patronizing Vice too much, but ... it is not out of Love to Vice that I Plead for it, but only to Exercise my Fancy, for surely the Wisest, and Eloquentest Orators, have not been Ashamed to defend Vices upon such Accounts, and why may not I do the like? for my Orations for the most part are Declamations, wherein I speak *Pro* and *Con,* and Determine nothing."[44] According to this passage, we are to understand the various orations as mere exercises of fancy, exercises central to Renaissance theories of eloquence and designed more to sharpen oratorical skill than to arrive at truth.[45] But behind her defense lies a concern about the power of eloquence to move its audience. The scenes of wartime destruction that serve as a backdrop for *Orations* highlight the volume's emphasis on the destructive power of language. Like Hobbes, who attributed the civil war to the abuse of words, Cavendish also worried about the abuse of words; for both, rhetoric was "that faculty, by which we understand what will serve our turn concerning any subject to win belief in the hearer."[46] And for both, the rhetorical interest in persuasion—in "win[ning] belief"—rather than in truth posed a material threat to political stability.

CAVENDISH'S CRITIQUE OF HOBBES

For Cavendish, however, the Erastian solution of deferring to an absolute monarch was not, finally, a satisfactory response to the problem of competing definitions, perhaps because she seems to have held an even more pessimistic view of human nature than did Hobbes. Partly as a result of having watched Henrietta Maria's disastrous attempts at imposing religious change on an unwilling country, Cavendish could never bring herself to put forward any sort of conclusive reforming vision, not even an Erastian vision. She directly questions Erastianism itself in *Blazing World* (1666), where she adopts in its stead political quietism. In *Blazing World* Cavendish creates a fictional character who becomes an empress with "an absolute power to rule and govern all that World as she pleased" (13).[47] The problem, of course, is that having absolute power does not guarantee political stability. Not unlike Henrietta Maria in the 1630s, the Empress finds her subjects' religion defective, and she sets about "convert[ing] them all to her own Religion," and to that end she resolved to build Churches, and make also up a Congregation of Women, whereof she intended to be the head her self, and to instruct them in the several points of her Religion" (60). By organizing a congregation of women and building two magnificent churches, the sheer beauty of which is designed to draw converts, the Empress imitates Henrietta, whose household was organized by rules resembling those of a religious order and whose magnificent chapel at Somerset House had been built in 1636 precisely for the purpose of attracting converts. One of the Empress's churches is lined with diamonds and firestone. By the peculiar properties of firestone, which when wet flames fire, she achieves the necessary effects for sermons "of terror to the wicked" (62). The other church is lined with star-stone, the cooler light of which is more appropriate for the "Sermons of comfort" preached there (62). With these two magnificent churches, she converts the inhabitants of the Blazing World to her own religion.

Although one might argue that Erastian politics are clearly at work in the Empress's institution of her own religion, that Erastianism is visibly complicated when the Empress later confesses that

> although this World was very well and wisely order'd and governed at first, when I came to be Empress thereof; yet the nature of Women being much delighted with change and variety, after I had received an absolute Power from the Emperour, did somewhat alter the Form of Government from what I found it; but now perceiving that the world is not so quiet as it was at first, I am much troubled at it; especially there are such continual contentions and divisions . . . that I fear they'l break out into an open Rebellion, and cause a great disorder the ruine of the Government; and therefore I desire your advice and assistance, how I may order it to the best advantage.
>
> [120-21]

The Empress is advised by the duchess of Newcastle, who appears as a character in *Blazing World*, "to introduce the same form of Government again, which had been before" (121). Peace is restored when the Empress takes this advice.

In *Blazing World* Cavendish illustrates the idea that though making the sovereign the political arbiter of truth looked efficient in theory, it was hardly likely to work in practice. Her experience at the court of Henrietta Maria would certainly have reinforced such a conclusion. Yet

Blazing World also reveals Cavendish's awareness that the urge to implement change so as to bring the external world into accordance with internal ideals could not be entirely eradicated from the human spirit. Shortly after entering the Blazing World as a character and immediately after advising the Empress to suppress her instinct to impose changes on the Blazing World, the Duchess confesses her own ambition to be an empress and to have absolute authority. Her ambition reflects what Cavendish must have considered to have been a universal human instinct to bring the external world into accord with inner ideals. The solution presented to the Duchess is quite simply to turn inward, to direct one's reforming energies to the fictional worlds of the mind, which can be controlled unproblematically with an efficient simplicity unattainable in the external world. The sages of *The Blazing World,* immaterial spirits, summarize the considerable benefits of turning inward, away from the external world:

> For you can enjoy no more of a material world then a particular Creature is able to enjoy, which is but a small part, considering the compass of such a world; and you may plainly observe it by your friend the Empress here, which although she possesses a whole world, yet enjoys she but a part thereof; neither is she so much acquainted with it, that she knows all the places, Countries and Dominions she Governs. The truth is, a Sovereign Monarch has the general trouble; but the Subjects enjoy all the delights and pleasures in parts; for it is impossible, that a Kingdom, nay, a Country should be injoyed by one person at once. . . . Wherefore . . . why should you desire to be Empress of a material world, and be troubled with the cares that attend Government? when as by creating a world within your self, you may enjoy all both in whole and in parts, without controle or opposition, and may make what world you please, and alter it when you please, and enjoy as much pleasure and delight as a world can afford you?
>
> [97-98]

Both the Empress and the Duchess turn to creating imaginary worlds, an emblem for the political quietism Cavendish seems finally to have adopted, not without apparent difficulty.[48] Cavendish's compulsive writing career can similarly be understood as a redirection of energy away from correcting or reforming the external world to shaping the more governable worlds of the mind.

⌐She put this problem differently in *Philosophical Letters* (1664), which contains an extended critique of Hobbes's philosophy. There she explains that no artificial mechanism could govern subjects who do not already agree:⌐"If men do not naturally agree, Art cannot make unity amongst them, or associate them into one Politick Body and so rule them. . . . The truth is, Man rules an artificial Government, and not Government Man, just like as a Watch-maker rules his Watch, and not the Watch the Watch-maker."[49] For Cavendish, no machine, not even the monstrous artifice of Hobbes's *Leviathan,* could finally impose order on a disorderly body politic.

Here she turns Hobbes's own pessimism about the impulse to reform against Hobbes. Hobbes used the legend of Medea throughout the course of his career to warn that reform was dangerous and ultimately futile. In *Leviathan,* for example, he explained that "they that go about by disobedience, to do no more than reform the commonwealth, shall find they do thereby destroy it; like the foolish daughters of Peleus, in the fable; which desiring to renew the youth of their decrepid father, did by the counsel of Medea, cut him in pieces, and boil him, together with strange herbs, but made not of him a new man" (pt. 2, chap. 30).[50]⌐Yet, although the danger attending the impulse to reform haunted both writers, Hobbes seems to have felt comfortable putting forward a solution to the problem of maintaining political order with a confidence Cavendish resisted. Any political reform she envisioned was imposed on imaginary worlds or carefully placed within contexts that highlighted the dangers of trying to impose reform on the material world.⌐

As in Hobbes's *Leviathan,* both Newcastle's scheme to keep the populace ignorant and Davenant's utopian literary approach to the problem of maintaining public order were based on a faith in reform that Margaret Cavendish finally did not share.⌐She was as interested in the problem of maintaining public order as Hobbes or her husband or Davenant, but she was forced to find her own solution, and it departed radically from those being circulated by the exiled Royalists.⌐Her work documents her anxiety regarding the disputatious nature of the human mind, an anxiety she shared with Hobbes. Although she finally disagreed with Hobbes's mechanistic view of human nature, she absorbed his political thought, taking it to its logical extreme. In the end she was more of a Hobbesian than Hobbes. Rather than encouraging her to engage with her society, her return from exile had the opposite effect of causing her to retreat further into the worlds of her mind. Seeing that the external world could not be put in order, she chose to devote her reforming energies to textual worlds, thus retreating to the exiles of the mind. She had no other choice; as she had put it in 1653, she had no house "but what my Mind is lodg'd in."[51]

5

Rationalism versus Experimentalism

Cavendish's Satire of the Royal Society

However, although it be the Mode, yet I, for my part, shall not
follow it, but leaving to our Moderns their Experimental, or
Mode-Philosophy built upon deluding Art, I shall addict my
self to the study of Contemplative-Philosophy, and Reason
shall be my Guide.

— *Margaret Cavendish*

By the time Cavendish returned to England from her "long banishment,"
she had integrated the role of exile into the core of her identity. It had
ceased to be a geographical imposition and had become instead a voluntary interiority, a retreat from the ungovernable external world to the
more tractable worlds of the mind constructed within her texts. Perhaps
remembering Henrietta Maria's interest in the contemplative life,
Cavendish had devoted herself to it, claiming repeatedly to prefer retirement and isolation to a more public life. Yet her retirement from the
world was, due to her prolific publishing career, very public; in fact, she
explored interiority more openly and more publicly than any other writer
of her time. Writing itself had become her chief link with the world,
transforming her private experience into publicly shared experience.
Within her texts, interiority is presented as a refuge, a space in which
ideas could be pursued freely and safely. Thus, although she was no longer
banished, after 1660 she presents herself as inhabiting an exclusively textual world, one that allowed her to sustain the "strange enchantment" of
living both in the world and out of it.

We can trace this retreat in *CCXI Sociable Letters*, which, begun in exile and completed after the Restoration, has with good reason been read autobiographically.[1] The contents correspond roughly to the known details of Cavendish's life.[2] The inclusion of what appear to be actual letters from Cavendish to Eleanor Duarti and to her sisters Anne and Catherine further heightens the volume's autobiographical appearance. Furthermore, the volume is described in the preface as consisting of "the Correspondence of two ladies" who wish to "Discourse by Letters, as they would do if they were Personally together."[3] Only one-half of the correspondence appears in the volume, conveniently allowing for an autobiographical monologue that returns consistently to familiar themes: Cavendish's melancholy temperament, the instability of political institutions, the importance of avoiding controversy, and most of all, the merits of retiring from the world. That the volume is autobiographical in tone is not in question. But though guesses have been ventured as to the identity of the correspondent, there is no reason to believe that the bulk of the letters were actually mailed to or even composed for an actual correspondent.[4] Neither is there reason to assume that all the people mentioned in the letters—generally through the use of initials such as "the Lady S.P."—are actual people rather than embellishments of Cavendish's imagination.[5] Yet, however much she may have embellished and even created many of the characters and their actions, no other volume reveals her mental life more immediately than *Sociable Letters*.

The title, *Sociable Letters*, is emblematic of the irony that characterizes Cavendish's writing life: the affectionate letters document her "sociable" compulsion to write at the same time that they insist that happiness must be found inwardly, even solipsistically, in withdrawing from the world. As she makes clear early in the volume, retiring from the world is necessary: "Indeed the world is so foolishly Wicked, & basely Foolish, that they are happiest who can withdraw themselves most from it" (9). That her desired retreat from the world resulted partly from continued depression is evident in her frequent references to emotional distress. Psychologically, she could not tolerate company because her mind was "in too deep a Melancholy to be diverted" (10). Instead, she looked to the consolation of philosophy, which urged interiority, bringing philosophers "all the Delights of the Mind, and Pleasures of Thoughts." "They [philosophers] can Conquer their Unruly Passions, Unsatiable Appetites, and order their Minds according to their Fortunes; they are Happy in any Condition, having their Happiness always with them, and in them,

& not without them" (22). She insisted that her retired life was "voluntary," that she chose to live a "Home Life, free from the Intanglements, confused Clamours, and rumbling Noise of the World" (56). "None enjoyes truly himself, but those that live to themselves as I do," she claimed, paraphrasing Charles I's confession: "[W]e have learnt to own ourself by retiring into ourself" (58).[6] She would not exchange her retired life for a public life, "for I should not desire to be Mistress of that which is too Big to be Commanded, too Self-willed to be Ruled, too Factious to be Govern'd, too Turbulent to live in Peace" (62). "Happiness," she explains, is to be found "Inwardly in the Mind" (114). She had learned the hard way of the vanity of relying on external circumstances for happiness: "a Wise man carries his Happiness still Within him, and a Fool is always Seeking it Without him" (206). She complained of the cold and even of the ill health induced by her exile in Antwerp, but she concluded that her retired life was preferable to a social life: "a Retired Life is most Happy, as being most Free from Censures, Scandals, Disputes, and Effeminate Quarrels" (331). She was happiest, she makes clear, alone with her thoughts.

⌐Rather than encouraging her to re-engage with the world, her return to London after the Restoration confirmed her confidence in the wisdom of retiring from it.⌐Her husband returned to London before she did, no doubt hoping for some sort of role in the new government. He was sixty-seven years old, and it is easy in retrospect to see that his hopes were unrealistic, but he had every reason, at least in his own mind, to expect some gesture toward compensation for his considerable wartime losses. He had financed an army; his estates had been confiscated; his family had been separated; he had been banished on pain of death. Moreover, he had once held the privileged position of being the Prince of Wales's governor. With the execution of Charles I, Newcastle had felt that his experience and guidance were all the more necessary for the young Prince of Wales; correspondingly, he had synthesized his thoughts in print twice, once briefly in a letter and again at greater length in his *Advice*.[7] Surely there would be a place, even a need, for him in the new political order.

Accordingly, he had left for London in 1660 full of expectation. Margaret Cavendish had been left behind in Antwerp as a "Pawn for his debts." When she rejoined her husband some months later in London, she found that he had again been ousted from Charles's inner circle, as he had been throughout his exile. There would be no position of power to compensate for his sacrifices. Newcastle was now, aside from the forgotten Henrietta Maria, the most notorious live player on the losing side of the war. Although his estates were eventually returned to him, they were badly damaged.[8] On discovering this state of affairs, Margaret Cavendish found that her frustration with the world was complete. "Out of some passion," she writes, "I desir'd him to leave the Town, and retire into the Countrey." Her instincts were right. London was by now an unfamiliar world, governed by an ethos foreign to Caroline courtiers. The Restoration was not a return to the past. There was little to do other than to retire to Welbeck and begin the considerable project of repairing the damaged estates of Welbeck and Bolsover.[9]

As her husband oversaw repairs to the estates, she reconstructed their post-Restoration image through her writing. In dedicating the revised version of *Philosophical and Physical Opinions* (1663) to her husband, she presented their new pastoral image: "Since your Return from a long Banishment into your Native Country, retiring to a Shepheard's Life, I your Shepheardess was resolved, to imploy all my Thoughts and Industry in good Huswifery, knowing your Lordship had great Debts after your great Losses . . . yet I cannot for my Life be so good a Huswife, as to quit Writing, to follow my Sheep so Carefully, but that they will go Astray some times; the truth is, I have somewhat Err'd from good Huswifery, to write Nature's Philosophy" (sig. A2r). By depicting her life in terms of pastoral romance, she was romanticizing her husband's blasted political hopes by publicizing their new exile at Welbeck as a voluntary and attractive choice. But she was also publicizing her compulsion to write, which she would do again using similar imagery in the preface to *Sociable Letters:* "I am not a Dunce in all Imployments, for I Understand the Keeping of Sheep, and Ordering of a Grange, indifferently well, although I do not Busie my self much with it, by reason my Scribling takes away the most part of my Time" (sig. b1v). By admitting that her compulsion to write interfered with her "huswifery," she was signaling the degree to which she had begun to live in the written worlds of her texts rather than in the external world.

By portraying herself as a shepherdess so occupied with her writing that she was disregardful of her sheep, she was also highlighting her Neoplatonic rationalist stance. *Philosophical and Physical Opinions,* like her other scientific work, is a theoretical and deductive work rather than the product of experiment and observation. It appeals repeatedly though sometimes improbably to deduction through "sense and reason," implying that her claims are self-evident to those faculties. Her rationalist epistemology ran directly counter to the spirit prevailing among natural philosophers in post-Restoration London. Just as she returned to England promoting an idiosyncratic version of Cartesian rationalism, the Royal Society was in the process of receiving its charter and attempting to codify its experimental program. While she urged rationalist deduction, they focused on induction through experiment and observation. Ironically, the members of the Royal Society espoused experimentalism for the same reasons she espoused rationalism. Both Cavendish and the members of the Royal Society believed that their particular approach to natural philosophy was best at avoiding "the passions and madness" that had led to civil war.[10] Cavendish warned against making statements about the external world, fearing that claims of objective certainty might be contested in ways that subjective claims could not be. Her scientific works were the result not of experiment and observation but of her subjective thoughts, which, by definition, could not be challenged.[11] For their part, the members of the Royal Society worried that "discussions of hypotheses, like discussions of politics and religion, were ever likely to lead to disputes and wrangling, upsetting the properly quiet atmosphere of learned debate, while experiment and observation could usually be spoken of without passion and dispute."[12] Thus, both Cavendish and the members of the Royal Society worried about the controversy that might arise from dissension surrounding natural philosophy, but they proposed opposing solutions to the problem of dissent. The unusual history of Cavendish's critique of the Royal Society has been largely overlooked; in particular, we need to examine Cavendish's disagreement with the man appointed by the Royal Society to be the curator of experiments, Robert Hooke.[13]

Between 1662, when the Royal Society received its royal charter, and 1667, when Thomas Sprat's *History of the Royal Society* attempted to codify the Royal Society's mission, the Society had struggled to articulate its methodology. Although it is a mistake to conceive of the early history of the Society as an institution designed with the "central purpose" of "building up new sciences," it is true that this group shared, to varying degrees, an interest in experiment and in the usefulness of optical instruments to experimentalist methodology.[14] Moreover, to the reading public not privy to the Royal Society's internal debates or to its members' varied commitment to experimentalism, the Society made every effort to present itself as solidly experimentalist.

The Royal Society's experimental program did, of course, have critics. Steven Shapin and Simon Schaffer have examined the controversy between Robert Boyle and Thomas Hobbes during the 1660s and 1670s over the proper approach to natural philosophy: "Robert Boyle maintained that proper natural philosophical knowledge should be generated through experiment and that the foundations of such knowledge were to be constituted by experimentally produced matters of fact. Thomas Hobbes disagreed. In Hobbes's view Boyle's procedures could never yield the degree of certainty requisite in any enterprise worthy of being called philosophical."[15] Boyle's experimental program relied largely on instruments like the air pump, which he transformed into "an emblem of the Royal Society's experimental programme" (32). Together with optical instruments like the microscope and the telescope, instruments like the air pump promised "to enhance perception and to constitute new perceptual objects" (36). Although Hobbes saw that experiments could be useful, he attacked the Royal Society's reliance on the "art" of machines, making clear that "machine-minders" were not, in his view, "to be accounted philosophers." He had made clear that "the systematic doing of experiments was not to be equated with philosophy" (129). He articulated his position in "Considerations on the Reputation, Loyalty, Manners, and Religion of Thomas Hobbes": "It is laudable, I confess, to bestow money upon curious or useful delights; but that is none of the praisis of a philosopher. And yet, because the multitude cannot judge, they will pass with the unskilful, for skillful in all parts of natural philosophy. . . . So also of all other arts; not every one that brings from beyond seas a new gin, or other jaunty device, is therefore a philosopher. For if you reckon that way, not only apothecaries and gardeners, but many other sorts of workmen, will put in for, and get the prize."[16]

By publishing *Observations Upon Experimental Philosophy* in 1666, Cavendish joined this controversy over theorizing the new science. Like Hobbes, she critiqued the Royal Society's reliance on instruments, though she focused her attack not on the air pump but on the use of optical instruments. Two works in particular had been published recently celebrating the usefulness of optical instruments to experimental philosophy: the first was Henry Power's *Experimental Philosophy* (1663);[17] the second, and more famous, was Robert Hooke's lavishly illustrated and carefully annotated *Micrographia; or, some Physiological Descriptions of Minute Bodies Made by Magnifying Glasses with Observations and Inquiries Thereupon* (1665). *Micrographia* was undertaken under the auspices of the Royal Society; it and Sprat's *History* can be read "as companion volumes that addressed similar issues, problems, and audiences but with very different rhetorical strategies and resources."[18] It was to *Micrographia* that Cavendish responded.

ROBERT HOOKE'S INDUCTIVE PROJECT: *MICROGRAPHIA*

Micrographia originated in Hooke's faithful and frequent presentations of his observations made by looking through optical instruments. Presenting these observations at the Society's meetings was a responsibility assigned to him as curator of experiments. By 1664 Hooke had completed *Micrographia,* and the Royal Society licensed him to print his "microscopical book," but only after commanding him "to give notice in the dedication of that work to the Society, that though they [the members of the Royal Society] have licensed it, yet they own no theory, nor will be thought to do so: and that the several hypotheses and theories laid down by him therein, are not delivered as certainties, but as conjectures; and that he intends not at all to obtrude or expose them to the world as the opinion of the Society."[19] Hooke's preface testifies to the care with which he responded to the Royal Society's caution about laying down hypotheses. Thus, although in actuality Robert Hooke was not as committed to experiment as Boyle, "to the reading public Hooke was a thoroughgoing experimentalist."[20] As John T. Harwood has noted, "at a time when the Royal Society was a kind of gentleman's club and the New Philosophy a spectator sport, Hooke emphasized the existence of an interpretive community committed to serious questions and likely to achieve significant, highly visible results."[21]

In *Micrographia* Robert Hooke suggested that the eyepieces of telescopes and microscopes functioned as correctives to the infirm and corrupt senses through which we know the world. They offered the utopian promise of mastering the world; through them could be found "a new visible World discovered to the understanding. By this means the Heavens are open'd, and a vast number of new Stars, and new Motions, and new Productions appear in them, to which all the antient Astronomers were utterly Strangers. By this the Earth it self, which lyes so neer us, under our feet, shews quite a new thing to us, and in every little particle of its matter, we now behold almost as great a variety of Creatures, as we were able before to reckon up in the whole Universe it self" (sig. a2v). For Hooke and for his fellow experimentalists, "the Science of Nature" had for too long been an exclusive product of "the Brain and Fancy" (sig.

b1r). Through observation and experiment, the secret workings of nature could be accurately examined, and the "light, by which our actions are to be guided . . . be renewed, and all our command over things . . . be establisht" (sig. a1r).

Accordingly, the Baconian reformation in natural philosophy that Hooke proposed in the preface to *Micrographia* insistently subordinated the operations of the mind to the exact observations of the eye aided by an optical glass; it required neither "strength of Imagination, [n]or exactness of Method, [n]or depth of Contemplation . . . [so much as it required] a sincere Hand, and a faithful Eye to examine, and to record, the things themselves as they appear" (sig. a2v). Hooke's reformation will be recognized as an echo of Francis Bacon, who argued for a new science in which anyone might participate: "The course I propose for the discovery of sciences is such as leaves but little to the acuteness and strength of wits, but places all wits and understandings nearly on a level."[22] Correspondingly, *Micrographia* is a compendium of pieces of the new world that Hooke found as he gazed through the eyepieces of microscopes and telescopes. His precise drawings of fleas, ants, bookworms, the face of the moon, and other items from the natural world constituted the empiricist product of a cycle of inquiry that left little room for what Hooke understood to be the faulty operations of sense, memory, or reason. In fact, according to *Micrographia*, the cycle of observation to be used by the new experimental philosophers was mechanistic, an idea he conveyed by comparing the cycle through which an object is perceived and then inscribed onto paper to the circulation of the blood:

> So many are the links, upon which the true Philosophy depends, of which, if any one be loose, or weak, the whole chain is in danger of being dissolv'd; it is to begin with the Hands and Eyes, and to proceed on through the Memory, to be continued by the Reason; nor is it to stop there, but to come about to the Hands and Eyes again, and so, by a continual passage round from one Faculty to another, it is to be maintained in life and strength, as much as the body of man is by the circulation of the blood through several parts of the body, the Arms, the Fat, the Lungs, the Heart, and the Head.
>
> [sig. b2r]

Like many others, Hooke seems to have been influenced by William Harvey's study of the circulation of the blood: the new physiology Harvey presented seemed to suggest that man was a machine or an automaton.[23] Accordingly, Hooke portrays his new natural philosopher as an automaton-scribe whose single function is to record accurately with his "sincere Hand" what is seen through the glass with his "faithful eye." There is little room for the vagaries of the mind to interfere in this process.

Hooke's exclusive focus on the external world, his dismissal of deductive thinking, his mechanistic portrait of the scientist and of scientific activity, his zeal in putting forth the utopian promise to "command" the natural world—each of these aspects of his text troubled and even angered Cavendish. She could not have read *Micrographia* without comprehending that it contested, however unknowingly, her work and her interest in deduction. She responded swiftly. *Micrographia* was published in 1665, the same year she became duchess of Newcastle.[24] The next year Cavendish published her response to Hooke and to the Royal Society in *Observations upon Experimental Philosophy: to which is added, The Description of a New Blazing World.* Even a cursory glance at *Observations* by one of the members of the Royal Society would have revealed the volume's attack on optical instruments and more generally on the Society's experimental program and on the Society itself.

OBSERVATIONS UPON EXPERIMENTAL PHILOSOPHY

In her dedication of *Observations* (1666) to her husband, Cavendish turns one of the chief arguments used to defend experimentalism—its utilitarian promise—on its head. Her purpose in *Observations*, she explains, is to review the modern craze for optical instruments.

> In this present Treatise, I have ventured to make some observations upon Experimental Philosophy, and to examine the Opinions of some of our Modern Microscopical or Dioptrical Writers; and though your Grace is not onely a lover of Vertuosoes, but a Vertuoso your self, and have as good, and as many sorts of Optick Glasses as any one else; yet you do not busie your self much with this brittle Art, but employ most part of your time in the more noble and heroick Art of Horsemanship and Weapons, as also in the sweet and delightful Art of Poetry, and in the useful Art of Architecture ... which shews

that you do not believe much in the Informations of those
Optick glasses, at least think them not so useful as others do
that spend most of their time in Dioptrical inspections. The
truth is, My Lord, That most men in these latter times, busie
themselves more with other Worlds, then with this they live
in, which to me seems strange, unless they could find out some
Art that would carry them into those Celestial Worlds.

[sig. b1v]

By opposing her husband's preference for the "useful" arts of this world to
the experimentalists' interest in other worlds seen through optical instruments, Cavendish questions the utilitarian defense of the experimental
program made by writers like Hooke.[25] Pointing to the practical difficulty
of carrying observers to the material worlds observed through optical instruments was also a way of suggesting the imaginative power of her narrative; although no experimentalist narrative could actually transport its
reader to the worlds observed though a microscope, her narrative could
successfully transport readers to the textual worlds she created.

Her attack on the enthusiasm surrounding optical instruments
becomes more <u>intemperate</u> within the volume itself:

Art has intoxicated so many mens brains, and wholly imployed
their thoughts and bodily actions about phaenomena, or the
exterior figures of objects, as all better Arts and Studies are
laid aside; . . . But though there be numerous Books written
of the wonders of these Glasses, yet I cannot perceive any such,
at best, they are but superficial wonders, as I may call them.
But could Experimental Philosophers find out more benefi-
cial Arts then our Fore-fathers have done, either for the better increase of Vegetables and brute Animals to nourish our
bodies, or better and commodious contrivances in the Art of
Architecture to build us houses, or for the advancing of trade
and traffick . . . it would not onely be worth their labour, but
of as much praise as could be given to them: But, as Boys that
play with watry Bubbles . . . are worthy of reproof rather then
praise, for wasting their time with useless sports; so those that
addict themselves to unprofitable Arts, spend more time then
they reap benefit thereby.

[10-11]

Appearing just ten pages into her volume, this assault on the "art" of optical instruments, which was accompanied by blow-by-blow refutations of Hooke's meticulous and widely admired observations, was likely to have been read by members of the Society and, once read, passed around to others.

⌐Cavendish's objections to microscopy focused on problems of perception and epistemology. She claimed that magnification could distort an image, a claim that held some truth since cracked or imperfect lenses could literally distort an object.²⁶ Hooke was keenly aware of this problem, and in his preface to *Micrographia* he included an extensive explanation of the glasses he had selected for use in his observations, complaining in the process that the glasses were so imperfect that "there may be perhaps ten wrought before one be made tolerably good, and most of those ten perhaps every one differing in goodness one from another, which is an Argument, that the way hitherto used is, at least, very uncertain."²⁷ Cavendish pushed this claim to its extreme, writing that "the more the figure by Art is magnified, the more it appears mis-shapen from the natural" (9). She provides a brief catalog of mistaken impressions obtained by looking through a microscope: a louse appears, under a microscope, to look like a lobster (8); a knife that appears blunt under a microscope is, in fact, still able to cut (9).

More problematic was what could *not* be seen through the microscope: if, she explains, an artist were to draw the portrait of a beautiful lady by peering at her through a microscope, the artist would be unable to represent the lady's beauty accurately (10). Because microscopy went "no further then the exterior Parts of the Object presented," it presented only an external view of a given object, and this should not be mistaken for the object's essence (8).

She viewed Hooke's claim that optical instruments could improve on the otherwise erroneous "process of humane Reason," as fallacious: "[W]e have no power at all over natural causes and effects" (6). A fool would not be able "to order his understanding by [optical] Art, if Nature has made it defective" (7), she adds. In fact, no art can "inform us of the Truth of the Infinite parts of Nature" (5). To claim as much is to claim that "man [is] a degree above Nature" (6). Finally, she argues that the "Experimental and Mechanick Philosophy cannot be above the Speculative part, by reason most Experiments have their rise from the Speculative, so that the Artist or Mechanick is but a servant to the Student" (7). No glass, no matter how sophisticated, could eliminate all the defects of a viewer or that viewer's subjectivity.

In addition to raising questions about Hooke's assumptions regarding epistemology and perception, Cavendish objected to his mechanistic view of the world, which he presented unproblematically with what one biographer describes as a "constant state of irrepressible aesthetic enjoyment."[28] In *Micrographia* Hooke claimed that nature worked "Mechanically" (171); it was capable of the "most stupendious Mechanisms and contrivances" (154). Seeds, for example, were "little automatons or Engines" (154). The legs of spiders were "long Leavers" (199). The "structure of Vegetables [was] altogether mechanical," he explained, comparing the intake of water through plant pores to the intake of water of the Thames by the waterworks at London Bridge.[29] He tried to identify the mechanisms at work and at times seemed to reduce sensibility itself to a mechanism. For example, in describing the beard of a wild oat, he noted that "if you take one of these Grains, and wet the Beard in Water, you will presently see the small bended top to turn and move round, as if it were sensible" (147). Viewed under a microscope, the mechanism of the beard's sensibility became visible: the microscope revealed "a kind of Spongie substance, which, for the most part, was very conspicuous neer the knee, as in the cleft K K, when the Beard was dry; upon the discovery of which, I began to think, that it was upon the swelling of this porous pith upon the access of moisture or water that the Beard, being made longer in the midst, was streightned, and by the shrinking or subsiding of the parts of that Spongie substance together, when the water or moisture was exhal'd or dried, the pith or middle parts growing shorter, the whole became twisted" (148-49). The wreathing and unwreathing of the oat beard, which Hooke first compared to sensibility, was thus reduced to a mechanism. Citing this example, Cavendish responded that "if Animate Motion was produced this way, it would, in my opinion, be but a weak and irregular motion. Neither can I conceive how these, or any other parts, could be set a moving, if Nature her self were not self-moving, but only moved" (22). To her mind, Hooke was replacing a world governed organically by the force of nature with a mechanistic universe.[30]

Unlike the experimentalists, who devoted themselves to "other worlds" without discovering an "Art that would carry them into those Celestial Worlds," Cavendish presents herself as being in possession of such an art (sig. b1v). Against Hooke's inductive experimentalism, Cavendish juxtaposes rationalism, or what she calls "an Arguing of the mind," as an alternative approach to knowing the world. In the preface to *Observations,* Cavendish compares rationalism directly with experimentalism: "Discourse shall sooner find out Natures Corporeal figurative Motions, than Art [the deluding art of optical glasses] shall inform the Senses; By Discourse, I do not mean Speech, but an Arguing of the mind, or a Rational Inquiry into the Causes of Natural effects; for Discourse is as much as Reasoning with our selves" (sig. e2v-f1r). Through the use of narrative, she carries readers into the worlds of her mind. For example, she opens *Observations* with an "Argumental Discourse" that locates the volume's source not in the external world but in the "rational inquiry" that occurred in her mind. She proceeds to take her readers through the internal "argument" that fueled *Observations*. "When I was setting forth this Book of *Experimental Observations*, a Dispute chanced to arise between the rational Parts of my Mind concerning some chief Points and Principles in Natural Philosophy; for, some New Thoughts endeavouring to oppose and call in question the Truth of my former Conceptions, caused a war in my mind, which in time grew to that height, that they were hardly able to compose the differences between themselves, but were in a manner necessitated to refer them to the Arbitration of the impartial Reader" (sig. h1r).[31] The controversy within her mind becomes heated, until finally "Some Rational thoughts, which were not concerned in this dispute, perceiving that they became much heated, and fearing they would at last cause a Faction or Civil War amongst all the rational parts, which would breed that which is called a Trouble of the Mind, endeavoured to make a Peace between them" (sig. q1v-q2r). The argument is referred to the "judicious and impartial" reader, who is to decide which theory makes more sense. Cavendish closes the "Argumental Discourse" by warning the reader not to let "Self-love or Envy corrupt you, but let Regular Sense and Reason be your onely Rule, that you may be accounted just Judges, and your Equity and Justice be Remembred by all that honour and love it" (sig. q2r). Read as a response to the confidence with which the Royal Society was espousing its experimental program, the detailed replay of Cavendish's internal argument foregrounds her interest in deduction rather than in induction.

Cavendish's attack on Hooke was unmistakable. *Observations* printed large sections of *Micrographia*'s arguments, italicizing them so that they might be recognized more readily as quotes. She rejected both Hooke's experimental program and his mechanistic view of the world; she also argued that his exclusive attention to what could be seen prevented him from comprehending the vastness and variety of nature: "The truth is, there's not any thing that has and doth still delude most mens understandings more, then that they do not consider enough the variety of Natures actions, and do not imploy their reason so much in the search of natures actions, as they do their senses; preferring Art and Experiments before Reason, which makes them stick so close to some particular opinions, and particular sorts of Motions or Parts, as if there were no more Motions, Parts, or Creatures in Nature, then what they see and find out by their Artificial Experiments" (86).[32] She added that there was more to the world than what could be seen. Like C.S. Lewis, three hundred years later, she objected to the Baconian focus on conquering nature rather than reconciling oneself to it.[33] She reviewed and contested Hooke's observations of needles, knives, flint, stings of bees, flies, moss, the beard of a wild oat plant, seeds, snails, charcoal, and salt, repeating her assertion that men should "employ their time in more profitable studies, then in useless Experiments" (103).

BACKGROUND: CAVENDISH'S NATURAL PHILOSOPHY

In addition to disagreeing with the Royal Society's experimental philosophy, Cavendish was also, no doubt, annoyed at the Society's apparent disregard for her published theory of natural philosophy, which had reached its fullest and clearest articulation in *Philosophical and Physical Opinions* (1663). In 1664 she added *Philosophical Letters,* which presented thoughtful critiques of Hobbes, Descartes, Henry More, and Jan Baptista Van Helmont. It is worth discussing her natural philosophy so as to identify her place among the theorists of the new science. In *Philosophical Letters,* she positioned herself between the Paracelsian mysticism modernized by Van Helmont, much of which she dismissed as "Chymaeras and Fancies," and the atomistic mechanistic systems articulated by Hobbes and Descartes and taken up by many members of the Royal Society. In this she was not alone; the transition from Helmontian to atomist was "a not uncommon intellectual pattern in the seventeenth century." Paracelsian thought had experienced a resurgence in England in the 1640s.[34] Cavendish's friend Walter Charleton had early on embraced Paracelsian thought only to drop it for his own version of atomism.[35] Cavendish could have absorbed Paracelsian ideas from a number of sources: her physician, Theodore Mayerne, was a Paracelsian; Charleton, also a physician, had studied and translated Van Helmont; Cavendish, too, read and responded in print to Van Helmont.[36] As early as 1655, she had praised John Gerarde's *Herball* (1597), which included chemical remedies.[37]

Although she rejected the more arcane and mystical elements of Paracelsian thought, she embraced its organic view of nature, in which the human world is not above nature but within it. Paracelsus had criticized as "foolish and vain" that philosophy "which leads us to assign all happiness and eternity to our element alone, that is, the earth. And that is a fool's maxim which boasts that we are the noblest creatures. There are many worlds: and we are not the only beings in our own world." In the course of refuting Hobbes's claim that the human mind excelled the minds of all other creatures, Cavendish echoed Paracelsus by suggesting that other creatures also used reason, though admittedly they used it differently than man did. "By reason [creatures reason] not after the same manner or way as Man, Man denies, they can do it at all; which is very hard; for what man knows, whether Fish do not Know more of the nature of Water, and ebbing and flowing, and the saltness of the Sea? or whether Birds do not know more of the nature and degrees of Air, or the cause of Tempests?"[38]

Similarly, in discussing Henry More's *Antidote Against Atheism,* she attributed the claim that man is above all other creatures to human arrogance. In the process she articulated an early concern for humanity's potentially destructive influence on the environment:

> If we observe well, we shall find that the Elemental Creatures are as excellent as man, and as able to be a friend or foe to Man, as Man to them, and so the rest of all Creatures; so that I cannot perceive more abilities in Man then in the rest of natural Creatures; for though he can build a stately House, yet he cannot make a Honey-comb; and though he can plant a Slip, yet he cannot make a Tree; though he can make a Sword, or Knife, yet he cannot make the Mettal. And as Man makes use of other Creatures, so other Creatures make use of Man, as far as he is good for any thing: But Man is not so useful to his neighbour or fellow-creatures, as his neighbour or fellow-creatures to him, being not so profitable for use, as apt to make spoil.[39]

Humanity's potential to "make spoil" of the surrounding environment was particularly evident in the destruction of the forests and parks surrounding the Newcastle estates.

Like the Paracelsian J.B. Van Helmont, Cavendish posited a vitalist view of nature. In her natural philosophy, there was only one substance: matter, or what she refers to as "only Matter." All matter could be divided into two categories: inanimate matter and animate matter. The latter category could be further divided into sensitive animate matter and rational animate matter.[40] As one might expect, inanimate matter was grosser than sensitive animate matter, which, in turn, was not as fine as rational animate matter. These three degrees of matter were intermixed so that all matter was infused by sense and reason: "As the Sensitive or Vital Animate part of Only matter liveth in the Unanimate part of Only matter, so the Rational or Radical part of Animate matter liveth in the Sensitive part of Animate matter, so that all degrees of Only and Infinite matter are Intermixed." Soul, thoughts, ideas—all were part of rational *matter*. She campaigned to present a view of nature governed organically by "reason"; the "glue or cement" that held the universe together was, she argued, "sense and reason." These served as "the Architect or Creator of all figures of Natural matter."[41]

In presenting these arguments, she differed from mechanists, who leaned toward positing a universe that, like a machine, consisted of inert matter.[42] In her materialist monism, she also differed from dualists who posited a clean division between material and spiritual substances. She directly criticized Descartes, for example, who claimed

> [t]hat the Mind . . . is a substance really distinct from the body, and may be actually separated from it and subsist without it: If he mean the natural mind and soul of Man, not the supernatural or divine, I am far from his opinion; for though the mind moveth onely in its own parts, and not upon, or with the parts of inanimate matter, yet it cannot be separated from these parts of matter, and subsist by its self, as being a part of one and the same matter the inanimate is of, (for there is but one onely matter, and one kind of matter, although of several degrees,) onely it is the self-moving part; but yet this cannot impower it, to quit the same natural body, whose part it is.[43]

Her view of the material world more nearly resembles certain strands of modern-day cognitive scientists than that of most of her contemporaries.

In Cavendish's vitalist universe, then, all of nature was infused with reason: "There is not any Creature or part of nature without this Life and Soul; and that not onely Animals, but also Vegetables, Minerals and Elements, and what more is in Nature, are endued with this Life and Soul, Sense and Reason." She argued that reason might be seen at work in drugs, vegetables, and minerals: "Neither can I perceive that man is a Monopoler of all Reason, or Animals of all Sense, but that Sense and Reason are in other Creatures as well as in Man and Animals; for example, Drugs, as Vegetables and Minerals, although they cannot slice, pound or infuse, as man can, yet they can work upon man more subtilly, wisely, and as sensibly either by purging, vomitting, spitting, or any other way, as man by mincing, pounding and infusing them, and Vegetables will as wisely nourish Men, as Men can nourish Vegetables."[44]

Finally, unlike experimentalists like Robert Boyle and Robert Hooke, who "consistently displayed themselves as a godly community" whose work might efficaciously "convince men there is a God," Cavendish placed theology outside of the boundaries of natural philosophy. She conceded with Henry More that all men believed in some sort of God, but she stipulated quite clearly that the province of natural philosophy was confined exclusively to the material world and could in no way admit theological speculation: "Neither can Theology and Natural Philosophy Agree, for Philosophy is Built all upon Human Sense, Reason, and Observation, whereas Theology is onely Built upon an Implicit Faith, which is an Undoubted Belief of that, which the Nature of the Creature cannot possibly Comprehend or Conceive, whilst it is in this World." Natural philosophy could be explored through logical deduction in a way that theology could not. By positing a supernatural or divine realm about which nothing could be known, she eliminated from her natural philosophy the possibility of potentially controversial discussions about the nature of God. Like Hobbes, she was concerned about the political implications of the experimentalists' interest in allying natural philosophy with theology: the civil wars had shown the destructive power of individual theological speculation, and she thus dismissed all such discussion by positing the knowable world as a materialist monism: "Nature is material, and not any thing in Nature, what belongs to her, is immaterial; but whatsoever is Immaterial, is Supernatural, Therefore Motions, Forms, Thoughts, Ideas, Conceptions, Sympathies, Antipathies, Accidents, Qualities, as also Natural Life, and Soul, are all Material."[45]

Having established the basic principles of her natural philosophy before 1666, *Observations Upon Experimental Philosophy* was the first part of Cavendish's public campaign to correct what she saw as the experimentalists' mistaken approach to natural philosophy. By publicly critiquing Robert Hooke's experimental program, she joined the controversy over experimental practice taking place during the 1660s between Robert Boyle and Thomas Hobbes. As a theorist of the new science, Cavendish finally differed, however, both from Hobbes and from the experimentalists. While she shared Hobbes's view that the experimental program was fundamentally mistaken, she differed from him and from many experimentalists by contesting their mechanism. In particular, she worried that Hobbes, like the experimentalists, threatened to replace an organism with a machine: matter, she insisted, was not inert; it was self-moving.

BLAZING WORLD

Observations was only the first half of Cavendish's attack on experimentalism. To *Observations* she appended a fictional illustration of its rationalist precepts, *The Description of a New Blazing World.*[46] *Blazing World* is Cavendish's most extended examination of her interest in retreating to the worlds of her texts, and by extension, into the worlds of the mind. Readers tend to read *Observations* and *Blazing World* separately, but the two are in fact companion pieces; although the former takes the form of scientific discourse and the latter of romantic fantasy, both are philosophical texts aimed at contesting the Royal Society's experimental program by specifically targeting Hooke's celebration of microscopes and telescopes. Both volumes value rationalist narrative over inductive observation. In including a work of fiction within a volume on natural philosophy, Cavendish was not acting without precedent; Thomas Stanley's *History of Philosophy* included a translation of Aristophanes' *The Frogs,* through which Stanley hoped to illustrate Aristophanes' critique of Euripides' philosophy of mind. But appending a work of fiction to *Observations* was also part of a larger strategy aimed at highlighting the inner life of the mind and its vagaries, which the experimentalists seemed to overlook. Read as a companion to *Observations, Blazing World* embodies Cavendish's complex response to the Royal Society's experimental philosophy.

The defenders of the new science frequently used geographical tropes because they proved particularly useful in foregrounding the errors of Aristotle and other ancients and thus in outlining the progress already made and yet to be made by modern science. The relatively recent remapping of the world caused by the Copernican revolution, by Columbus's discovery of a new world, and by increased travel, had proved beyond doubt that ancient cosmographers had partial or erroneous knowledge. By analogy, there were other things too that the ancients had missed and that the moderns might usefully discover. As Richard Foster Jones demonstrated long ago, the image of Hercules' Pillars became an emblem for the ancients' closing off of new worlds to the moderns through the tyrannical sway they held over modern minds. The pillars were alleged to have been inscribed with the phrase "Ne plus ultra," commanding travelers to go no farther. Francis Bacon asked why "a few received authors [should] stand up like Hercules' Columns, beyond which there should be no sailing or discovering." As Joseph Glanvill remarked in *The Vanity of Dogmatizing* (1661), had learning stopped with the ancients, "Hercules his Pillars had still been the worlds *Non ultra.*"[47] His use of geographical metaphors reveals his utilitarian hope for the new science: "There is an *America* of secrets, and an unknown *Peru* of Nature" still to be discovered by the experimental philosophy.[48] The title of his 1668 volume would be *Plus Ultra.* Henry Power prefaced his *Experimental Philosophy* with the promise that the microscope, that "Modern Engine," could reveal the "eminent signatures of Divine Providence" and even actual atoms, thereby contesting the claims that nature "must have a non-ultra of her subdivisions."[49] The experimentalists directed their energies to what they considered to be matters of fact; these were "discovered rather than invented."[50]

It is significant, then, that in the prefatory poem Newcastle contributed to *Blazing World,* he uses a geographical trope similar to those deployed by defenders of the new science. But whereas the moderns used geographical tropes to emphasize the discovery of new worlds, he focuses attention on his wife's invention of new worlds:

> Our Elder World, with all their Skill and Arts,
> Could but divide the World into three Parts:
> Columbus, then for Navigation fam'd,
> Found a new World, America 'tis nam'd;
> Now this new World was found, it was not made,
> Onely discovered, lying in Times shade.
> Then what are You, having no Chaos found
> To make a World, or any such least ground?
> But your creating Fancy, thought it fit

To make your World of Nothing, but pure Wit.
Your *Blazing-world,* beyond the Stars mounts higher,
Enlightens all with a Coelestial Fier.
[sig. 'A1r']⁵¹

Margaret Cavendish's *Blazing World* is a new world like Columbus's new
world, but whereas Columbus's was found, Cavendish's world is made.
Newcastle's focus on the created worlds in Cavendish's text highlights her
interest in a different sort of space from the cosmic space being mapped,
measured, and *discovered* by the experimental philosophers; she is interested, as Newcastle makes clear, in worlds that the mind *creates.*

⌐In *Blazing World* Cavendish defines her role as author in opposition to the image of the experimentalist gazing into his microscope; instead of peering through a glass in order to serve as a Hooke-like scribe
through whom an observed fraction of the external world appears re-
produced and magnified on paper, Cavendish looks inward, freely exer-
cising her subjective use of perspective over the worlds within her head.⁵²
The inventive, wildly improbable, and self-referential narrative that results calls into question Hooke's objective certainty by displaying the
unpredictability of the self and its inevitable interposition in the process
of perception. Like René Descartes or Thomas Hobbes, who more me-
thodically but no less certainly trusted the workings of the mind to arrive at the truth, Cavendish looks inward to find what truth can be found.
Unlike Descartes or Hobbes, however, she finds no need for convincing
proof; the narrative aims at delight and surprise rather than proof. By
inscribing her own subjective eccentricity onto her narrative, she highlights the problem she sees as inherent in Hooke's plan: if, Cavendish
seems to point out, an observer can be as eccentric as she reveals herself
to be, how are we to rely on such an observer's "eye" for empirical objec-
tivity? In *Blazing World,* as in *Observations,* Cavendish focuses on the
subjectivity in which our inquiry into the world is, according to her, inevitably trapped.

Cavendish first defines herself in opposition to Hooke's experimentalist in the narrative frame constructed in the preface to *Blazing World.*
There she claims that her ambition in the external world has caused her
to turn to the imaginary worlds of her mind:

I am . . . as Ambitious as ever any of my Sex was, is, or can be;
which makes, that though I cannot be Henry the Fifth, or

Charles the Second, yet I endeavour to be Margaret the First. And although I have neither power, time nor occasion to conquer the world as Alexander and Caesar did; yet rather than not to be Mistress of one, since Fortune and the Fates would give me none, I have made a World of my own: for which no body, I hope, will blame me, since it is in every ones power to do the like.

[sig. b2r]

Critics have tended to read Cavendish's extravagant expression of her desire for fame literally; as a consequence, they tend to explain her interest in fame as psychological evidence for her character rather than as a philosophical positioning of the "self" that allows for an exploration of the problem of subjectivity.[53] Yet her announcement of ambition serves at least two philosophical purposes. First, by claiming the Blazing World as an exclusive product of her brain and fancy, Cavendish locates it within the subjective realm of her imagination, thereby guarding herself from making Hooke-like claims of objective certainty regarding the external world. Second, and perhaps more importantly, by calling attention to her own ambition, she calls into question Hooke's portrayal of a series of interchangeable, passive, and ambitionless experimentalists. By parading her own allegedly boundless will and ego, Cavendish questions the degree to which the subjective interference of the self can be eliminated, thus problematizing the premise on which Hooke's objective certainty was based.

Blazing World begins as a story of an unnamed young woman who, somewhat improbably, accidently enters the Blazing World, so overwhelming its emperor with her beauty that he reveres her as a divinity, marries her, and gives her absolute authority over the Blazing World, after which he disappears from the narrative. As the newly crowned empress familiarizes herself with her new world and experiments with her absolute authority over it, she explores two competing modes of inquiry. The first mode—experimentalism—is presented by a collective group of experimental philosophers, astronomers, and various other natural philosophers, most of whom actively practice a Hooke-like induction; the second mode—rationalism—is presented by a second main character, the duchess of Newcastle herself, who appears as a character within her own narrative. In order to distinguish the character from the author, the character will be referred to hereafter simply as "the Duchess."

The Empress is naturally curious about the world she suddenly finds under her command, and observing that each sort of creature follows a profession "most proper for the nature of [its] Species," she encourages the pursuit of the arts and sciences by erecting schools and founding several societies (15). In the subsequent satire of the Royal Society—in which giants present themselves as architects and parrot-men as orators—the Empress's newfound experimentalism is tested and falters. In particular, her exchanges with her experimental philosophers, whose enthusiasm for optical instruments appears boundless, problematize the value of optical instruments and of the "eye" as the exclusive bases for knowing the world. When, for instance, she asks the experimental philosophers to use their telescopes in order to resolve a dispute troubling her astronomers regarding the true nature of thunder and lightning, the "Telescopes caused more differences and divisions amongst them, then ever they had before," each observer arguing for his own interpretation of what is seen through the telescope (26). The Empress eventually becomes impatient with their quarrels and commands them to break their telescopes, explaining that "if . . . glasses were true informers, they would rectifie . . . irregular sense and reason; But . . . Nature has made your sense and reason more regular then Art has your Glasses; for they are meer deluders, and will never lead you to the knowledg of Truth" (27-28). The Empress's argument here, like Cavendish's parallel argument in *Observations,* that glasses distort images and that sense and reason are sufficient for understanding the world, directly contradicts Hooke's claim that eyepieces of microscopes could function as correctives to otherwise deficient senses. The Hooke-like experimental philosophers are so visibly crushed by the Empress's command to break all telescopes that she eventually relents and allows them to keep the telescopes "upon the condition, that their disputes and quarrels should remain within their Schools, and cause no factions or disturbances in State, or Government" (28). Their enthusiasm for optical glasses remains undiminished and, hoping to make amends for her displeasure with the telescope, they present her their microscopes.

The Empress observes through a microscope a fly, charcoal, a nettle, a flea, and a louse, each of which are illustrated and discussed in Hooke's *Micrographia.* The flea and the louse appear "so terrible to her sight, that they had almost put her into a swoon," and when she recovers, she inquires, as her author similarly inquires in *Observations,* into the utilitarian value of such observations: "The Empress, after the view of those strangely-shaped Creatures, pitied much those that are molested with them, especially poor Beggars, which although they have nothing to live on themselves, are yet necessitated to maintain and feed of their own flesh and blood, a company of such terrible Creatures called Lice. ... [A]fter the Empress had seen the shapes of these monstrous Creatures, she desir'd to know whether their Microscopes could hinder their biting, or at least shew some means how to avoid them?" (31-32). The general fruitlessness of the experiments also disappoints the author, Cavendish, whose intrusive narrative reveals her impatience with optical instruments and includes a direct barb at Hooke's lengthy and detailed observations in *Micrographia:* "To relate all their optick observations through the several sorts of their Glasses, would be a tedious work, and tire even the most patient Reader, wherefore I'le pass them by" (32-33). But Cavendish's real criticism lies neither in the experimentalists' tediousness nor in their lack of utility; her concern lies in their unwillingness to acknowledge the inevitable interference of their own subjectivity.

Were Cavendish writing, as she seems to claim in the preface, simply to compensate for her frustrated ambition at being a subject rather than a monarch, she might now conclude her tale, deriving compensatory satisfaction from the Empress's absolute command over the Blazing World's considerable imaginary wonders.[54] But Cavendish's attention in the preface to her own political disappointments and to her personal status as subject is a rhetorical device meant to advance her philosophical interest in questions of epistemology and perception. Having provided a satire of Robert Hooke and his experimental philosophy in the first half of the narrative, she explores the problem of rationalism in the course of the second half of the narrative. In attempting to impose its vision on the world, rationalism, too, could lead to the kind of unchecked reforming zeal that Cavendish associated with experimental practice.

Equipped with absolute authority and her own religious dogmatisim, the Empress sets in motion a program of religious reform (discussed in part in chapter 4). She builds two spectacular churches, which gain converts, and she begins conversations with the immaterial spirits of the Blazing World about the possibility of writing a Jewish cabala, a millenarian project that sought to revive esoteric lost evidence convincing enough to convert Jews to Christianity, which was necessary if the hoped-for millennium was to be reached.[55] This was exactly the sort of reforming project that Cavendish worried about. Somewhat reluctantly, the immaterial spirits agree to help the Empress, but because they are immaterial spirits and cannot write, they suggest she find a scribe to take their dictation. The Empress considers various ancient authorities—Aristotle, Pythagoras, Plato, Epicurus—but the spirits suggest that each of these ancients is "so wedded to their own opinions, that they would never have the patience to be Scribes" (89). She considers moderns—Galileo, Gassendi, Descartes, Van Helmont, Hobbes, Henry More—all of whom, so the spirits tell her, are "so self-conceited, that they would scorn to be Scribes to a Woman" (89). The spirits recommend instead the duchess of Newcastle, and the Empress agrees to import her into the Blazing World as her scribe.

Once the Duchess enters the narrative as a character, she quickly puts a stop to the Empress's utopian and millenarian vision. She advises against writing any sort of cabala, and when the Empress persists, the Duchess suggests that she write "a Poetical or Romancical Cabbala, wherein you can use Metaphors, Allegories, Similitudes, &c. and interpret them as you please" (92-93). The Duchess also advises that the Empress

> dissolve all their societies; for 'tis better to be without their intelligences, then to have an unquiet and disorderly Government. The truth is, said she [the Duchess], wheresoever is Learning, there is most commonly also Controversie and Quarrelling; for there be always some that will know more, and be wiser than others; some think their arguments come nearer to truth, and are more rational than others; some are so wedded to their own opinions, that they'l never yield to Reason; and others, though they find their Opinions not firmly grounded upon Reason, yet for fear of receiving some disgrace by altering them, will nevertheless maintain them against all sense and reason, which must needs breed factions in their Schools, which at last break out into open Wars, and draw sometimes an utter ruin upon a State or Government.
>
> [122-23]

Cavendish's argument for abolishing learned societies echoes the argument her husband advanced in his *Advice,* that political stability required keeping the people in ignorance. For Cavendish, the experimentalists' attempt at mapping and measuring material space posed a threat to political stability for the simple reason that reason could not be relied on, disputes were therefore inevitable, and conflict would result.

The dangers of trying to govern or command the external world are highlighted further when the Duchess herself succumbs to envy and ambition. Dazzled as she is by the Blazing World's wonders, her initial enthusiasm dims as she begins to feel the effects of her own "extreme ambition" and falls into a melancholy out of envy for the Empress's power (93). When the Empress asks the Duchess to identify the cause of her melancholy, the Duchess confesses, "I would fain be as you are, that is, an Empress of a World, and I shall never be at quiet until I be one" (94). Like Robert Hooke and his fellow experimentalists, who hoped that by discovering the secret workings of nature a "command over things" might be reestablished, the Duchess also yearns, at least initially, for command over the external world.

The Empress promises to do everything in her power to help the Duchess, and she turns once again to her immaterial spirits for advice, asking them whether other worlds exist to be commanded, and if so, whether the Duchess might become the empress of one of them. The spirits in turn ask why the Duchess wishes to command a "gross material World," which can only be known in parts, when she can create a world "within" herself, which she can know and govern absolutely (97). They advise her to turn to the worlds of her mind, which she can enjoy "without controle or opposition" (98). After trying to create imaginary worlds according to a variety of philosophical systems including those of Thales, Pythagoras, Plato, Epicurus, Aristotle, Descartes, and Hobbes, she happily and industriously applies herself to creating a world entirely of her own invention. Unlike Hooke, who would banish the products of "the Brain and Fancy," keeping his eye servilely fixed on fragments of the external physical world, and unlike the Empress, who struggled to impose her ideals on an unyielding external world, the Duchess turns inward to the speculative and subjective pleasures of the mind. In this she takes "more delight and glory, then ever Alexander or Cesar did in conquering this terrestrial world" (sig. I1r).[56]

Just as Cavendish claims in the preface to create the fictional Blazing World because fortune provided her with no external world over which to be mistress, the Duchess rejects the material world for the worlds "within" her mind. By reenacting her author's decision to look inward, the character's behavior begins what Catherine Gallagher has called "a process of infinite regression . . . Presumably, the character['s] . . . world will, like the blazing world, also contain a Margaret Cavendish who wishes to be Empress of a world and decides instead to create a microcosm, etc. ad infinitum."[57] But Cavendish's narrative is more than a giddy musing on infinity. It reenacts a series of magnifications of the self; Cavendish responds to Hooke, finally, by providing a micrographia of the mind. To his "small pictures" of magnified bits and pieces of the external physical world, Cavendish provides "small pictures" of the ongoing, unpredictable discourse of the mind. Whereas Hooke in *Micrographia* uses his lens to observe items from the physical world, Cavendish in *Blazing World* uses her narrative to preserve what she can of the subjective and often erratic musings of the self. These two volumes form an interesting, important, and early antinomy in the historical debate over empiricism and rationalism.

Reading *Blazing World* and *Observations* primarily as philosophical texts and, in particular, as responses both to Robert Hooke's *Micrographia* and to the Royal Society helps to explain Cavendish's unsystematic procedure and her willful eccentricity in these works. In *Blazing World* she encapsulated her philosophy more clearly and more economically than she did anywhere else. Steeped in a skepticism positing that "we are in Utter Darkness," Cavendish had, like Descartes, fallen back on the only thing about which she could be certain—the nature of her thinking life.[58] The experimentalists of the Royal Society threatened to dismiss that life through their tyrannical focus on the visible world. Ever fearful of confrontation, she reacted in the best way she knew how, by presenting two written narratives, one scientific, the other a fantasy, both of them urging interiority.

FOREGROUND: CAVENDISH'S VISIT TO THE ROYAL SOCIETY

Observations upon Experimental Philosophy and *Blazing World* appeared as a single volume in 1666. It must have come as something of a surprise to members of the Royal Society when the following year Cavendish made known her desire to attend one of its meetings. At its meeting on 23 May 1667, the minutes record that

> Lord Berkeley mentioned, that the duchess of Newcastle had expressed a great desire to come to the society, and to see some of their experiments; but that she desired to be invited. This was seconded by the earl of Carlisle and Dr. Charleton, who

pressing, that it might be put to the vote accordingly, whether the duchess of Newcastle should at her desire be invited to be present at the meeting on the Thursday following; it was carried in the affirmative.

The ceremonies and the subjects for her entertainment were referred to the council.[59]

Although the minutes suggest that the Society readily dispatched the invitation, Samuel Pepys describes the decision as being arrived at only "after much debate pro and con, it seems many being against it, and we do believe the town will be full of ballets of it."[60]

The nature of the debate can be guessed at from the list of entertainments decided upon for the duchess's visit. "1. Those of colours. 2. The mixing of cold liquors, which upon their infusion grow hot. 3. The swimming of bodies in the midst of water. 4. The dissolving of meat in the oil of vitriol. 5. The weighing of air in a receiver, by means of the rarefying engine. 6. The marbles exactly flattened. 7. Some magnetical experiments, and in particular that of terrella driving away the steel-dust at its poles. 8. A good microscope." Through these entertainments, the Royal Society staged a presentation of its experimental program. Both the weighing of air and the experiment of cohesion (demonstrated through the use of two perfectly smoothened marbles) were experiments that employed the use of the air pump. As Shapin and Schaffer have demonstrated, they were vital for Robert Boyle's experimental program. Just as Robert Hooke had used the microscope as an icon for the Royal Society, so too had Robert Boyle used the air pump to create an iconography for the Royal Society's experimental program.[61]

It is, however, the last item, carefully qualified as a "good" microscope, that could not have been arrived at without some debate. Cavendish had made it abundantly clear that she considered microscopy a "brittle Art." She had also announced in print what many people knew, that her household contained "as good, and as many sorts of Optick Glasses as any one else [had]."[62] The members of the Royal Society may have concluded that her desire to attend a meeting suggested a change of heart, but if they had glanced at either *Observations* or *Blazing World,* they must have wondered what their critic intended by asking to attend a meeting.[63] The two men charged with "provid[ing]" and "tak[ing] care of" the proposed list of entertainments were none other than Robert Boyle and Robert Hooke.[64]

Cavendish arrived at the meeting late, and with what John Evelyn described as "greate pomp," she took her seat at the president's right hand, and watched as the entertainments were presented.[65] The only record of what she said comes from Samuel Pepys, who reported disappointment at not "hear[ing] her say anything that was worth hearing, but that she was full of admiration, all admiration." He continues, "After they had shown her many experiments, and she cried still she was 'full of admiration,' she departed, being led out and in by several Lords that were there."[66]

The members had raised, however obliquely, the issue of optical instruments before their avowed critic, but she did not use her visit to advance her arguments against experimental philosophy. In fact, she seems to have feigned uncritical admiration for the Society. Yet John Evelyn seems to have been aware of the irony of the meeting. He commemorated the visit in a ballad, which, like the significance of Cavendish's visit to the Royal Society, has gone largely unnoticed. Perhaps remembering the moment in *Blazing World* when its empress becomes alarmed by viewing things through a microscope, he attributes to Cavendish a similar distress as she, too, was asked by experimental philosophers to view things through a microscope:

> But oh a stranger thing, this Dame
> A Glasse they shew'd with an hard name
>   I cannot fix upon't
> That made a Louse to looke as big
> As any Sow that's great with pig
>   Some Swore an Eliphant.[67]

Evelyn was aware of Cavendish's published criticism of the experimental program; other members were undoubtedly also aware, despite Cavendish's claim to be full of admiration, that they were entertaining a critic. Although Pepys was disappointed not to hear anything other than that she was full of admiration, other members may well have been relieved by her silence.

In many ways Cavendish's apparently admiring silence during this visit was emblematic of her life: unable to negotiate public conversations, let alone debates, outside the small circle of her family, she channeled her energies into her writing, where she explored her ideas boldly and freely. We might, however, conclude something of the true nature of her reaction to the Society's "entertainments" from the fact that the following year, she reissued *Observations* and *Blazing World.* Her debate with the Royal Society was, characteristically, entirely confined to textual space.⌋

Conclusion

The Exiles of the Mind

Margaret Cavendish spent her last years revising and republishing her work with characteristic energy. *Orations* reappeared in revised form in 1668, as did *Poems, or, Several Fancies in Verse, Grounds of Natural Philosophy,* and a Latin version of her biography of her husband translated by the faithful Walter Charleton.[1] To these she added a new volume, *Plays, Never Before Printed,* which was probably composed earlier. In 1671 she added revisions of *Nature's Pictures* and *The World's Olio.* She had written compulsively throughout her mature life, "convers[ing] with few" and engaging with the world on her own terms—exclusively through her texts.[2] When she died on 15 December 1673 at the age of fifty, she was the author of twenty-three volumes, slightly less than half of which were revisions of earlier work. Her public interest in acknowledging the flux and fluidity of conscious experience—in what William James would later refer to as the "blooming buzzing Confusion" of the mind—marks her as a modern thinker, even as her interest in exploring the world through correspondences and analogies places her habits of mind in an order that was being overthrown as archaic even in her day.[3]

When we consider, however, that her primary interest lay not in the nature of the physical universe but rather in the nature of the human mind, her interest in correspondences and analogies seems both more relevant and strikingly modern. She defined herself against those who were coming to view the universe, in increasing numbers, no longer as an organism but as a clockwork mechanism. For her, mechanism threatened the utterly human, and consequently less predictable, worlds of the mind. She insisted on the varied experience and richness of the inner life, by focusing attention squarely on "the powerful inchoate feelings and affinities and fears which dispute with us the control of our lives."[4]

Perhaps because she appreciated the richness and variety of the inner life, she warned against trying to impose its ideals on the external world. It was of the utmost importance, she argued, to reconcile oneself to the external world rather than to try bringing it into conformity with one's ideals or mastering it through solving its mysteries. Like the Caroline masques she imitated, she focused attention on the regulation of the mind.

She was a profoundly pessimistic thinker, and she did not view the monumental intellectual revolution she witnessed simply as consisting of a chain of improvements that constituted what many referred to as human progress. She was presciently aware, as her more optimistic contemporaries were not, of the darker aspects of that revolution. Although she did not live long enough to see it performed, she would have appreciated Thomas Shadwell's *The Virtuoso*, which was dedicated to Newcastle, Shadwell's faithful patron. When, for example, the scatter-brained virtuoso, Nicholas Gimcrack, presents as his utopian project a stentorophonic tube that promises to carry the king's voice throughout the country, he describes it with the kind of zeal she had warned against: "I have thought of this to do the king's service. For when I have perfected it, there needs but one parson to preach to the whole country. The king may then take all the church lands into his own hands and serve all England with his chaplains in ordinary."[5] Cavendish had campaigned against utopian projects for most of her life. The flux of life was, for her, much more complex than the idea of progress suggested—and much more tragic.

That her husband appreciated her character is suggested by the magnificent monument he had erected in her honor in Westminster Abbey and the careful arrangements he made for her burial on 7 January 1674. On the monument he had inscribed a narrative of retirement and loss that will sound familiar to her readers: "Here lyes the Loyall Duke of Newcastle and his Dutches his second wife, by whome he had noe issue her name was Margarett Lucas, yongest sister to the Lord Lucas of Colchester, a noble familie for all the Brothers were Valiant, and all the Sisters virtuous. This Dutches was a wise wittie & Learned Lady, which her many Bookes do well testifie: she was a most Virtuous & a Loueing & carefull wife & was with her Lord all the time of his banishment & miseries & when he came home never parted from him in his solitary retirements."[6] It is a pleasant irony that the writer who renounced caring "into what part of the Earth I shall be thrown," found a memorial that perfectly encapsulated the iconic myth of the exiled cavalier she constructed throughout her work.

Newcastle also arranged for the publication in 1676 of *Letters and Poems in Honour of the Incomparable Princess, Margaret, Dutchess of Newcastle*. She had made clear, however, that her true monument would be the body of texts she bequeathed to the world. Repeatedly, she addresses a future audience. "Who knows," she told the universities of Oxford and Cambridge, "but after my honourable burial, I may have a glorious resurrection in following ages, since time brings strange and unusual things to passe." She had committed her remarkable life to paper, not just in *A True Relation* but throughout her many volumes, justifying her pursuit of fame by reminding her readers that "there is little difference between man and beast, but what ambition and glory makes." In this determination to inscribe herself onto paper, she entered the debate over words and things prominently embodied by the Royal Society's adopting as their motto on 17 September 1662, "Nullius in Verba."[8] The history of their efforts at making words stand for things is well known. Although Cavendish did not entirely disagree with their stand, she understood that words also create things, including the elusive texture of the self. It was through words, not things, that she sustained the "strange enchantment" of both engaging with and retiring from the world. In this, she joined the early philosophers of mind in pioneering a voyage into one of the realms that most concerns the modern era: the exiles of the mind.

Appendix A

Problems in the Dating of Margaret Lucas's Birth

Margaret Lucas's year of birth is variously given as 1617, 1623, or 1624. The *Dictionary of National Biography* indicates 1624 as her year of birth, but most modern biographers—Grant, Mendelson, and Jones—have agreed on 1623.[1] Supporting the claim that Lucas was born in 1623 is Anthony Wood's claim that she was fifty when she died on 15 December 1673.[2]

Richard Goulding suggests 1617, on the basis that Joseph Lemuel Chester "quotes from her funeral certificate the statement that she was in her fifty-seventh year when she died."[3] If she were born in 1617, however, she would have been twenty-six when she joined Henrietta Maria's court in 1643, which is a little older than usual for a maid of honor. Although it is by no means impossible that she was born in 1617, this date is called into question by Cavendish's own claim that she was an infant when her father died in 1625.[4]

In *Poems and Fancies,* Cavendish provided an allegory of her life that may contain a clue to her year of birth. She compared herself to a ship:

> A Ship of youth in the Worlds Sea was sent,
> Balanc'd with Self-conceit, and Pride it went.
> And large Sailes of Ambition set thereon,
> Hung to a tall Mast of good Opinion.
> . . . .
> But when that she had past nineteen Degrees,
> The Land of Happinesse she no longer sees:
> For then Rebellious Clouds foule black did grow,
> And Showers of Blood into those Seas did throw.[5]

If by these lines she means that at the age of nineteen ("nineteen De-grees") the "Rebellious Clouds" of war appeared, she identifies her year of birth as 1623. She wrote nothing to contradict such a conclusion, and, lacking further evidence, we might conclude that Chester's note is thus an error and that Margaret Lucas was born in 1623.

Appendix B

The Letters of Margaret Lucas
Addressed to William Cavendish

The following undated letters were written by Margaret Lucas to William Cavendish during their courtship, which took place between 10 April 1645, when Newcastle arrived in Paris, and 20 December 1645, the date of a letter from Margaret Lucas's mother, Elizabeth Lucas, congratulating the couple on their marriage. (A modernized transcript of Elizabeth Lucas's letter appears in chapter 3, in the section titled "World and Mind in Conflict.") During this time Lucas attended Henrietta Maria as a maid of honor in exile in France. The first characteristic one notices about Lucas's youthful letters is their sprawling handwriting. Even in mature life, her handwriting remained, by her own acknowledgment, poor. It may be of interest to note in passing that Elizabeth Lucas had substantially neater handwriting than her daughter. In *Nature's Pictures* (1656), the mature Margaret Cavendish attributed her poor handwriting to the race to commit her thoughts to paper:

> [T]he brain being quicker in creating than the hand in writing, or the memory in retaining, many fancies are lost, by the reason they ofttimes out-run the pen, where I, to keep speed in the Race, write so fast as I stay not so long as to write my letters plain, insomuch as some have taken my hand-writing for some strange character, & being accustomed so to do: I cannot now write very plain, when I strive to write my best, indeed my ordinary hand-writing is so bad as few can read it, so as to write it fair for the Press.
>
> [384]

The letters reveal Lucas's acute sense of herself as an exile—from court culture, from England, and more generally from the world. In

Newcastle she found a source of solace, not least because of his own ambivalent status as an illustrious member of a passing order. She summarizes her attraction to him in letter 13: "my lord, I have not had much expereanse of the world, yet I have found it such as I could willinly part with it, but sence I knew you, I fear I shall love it to well, becaus you are in it, and yet me thinkes, you are not in it, becaus you are not off it; so I am both in it and out off it, a strang in chantment." The language of Platonic love seems to have provided her with welcome relief from the turmoil and pettiness of court life by opening up the worlds of the mind as a refuge.

Lucas wrote in some haste and at odd hours, sometimes by candlelight; her letters read like an abbreviated epistolary novel. In them the drama of the couple's courtship can be seen to unfold. We observe Lucas responding to Newcastle's queries about court gossip regarding the illegitimacy of her oldest brother (1), to his professions of passion for her (14), to his bawdy love poems (17), to her receipt of his portrait and a love token (6, 9), to the queen's displeasure at learning of the courtship (1, 19, 20), to Lucas's own melancholy, which apparently affected her health (8), and finally to the preparations for marriage at the chapel of Sir Richard Browne (17). Lucas was still at court when Marie-Louise de Gonsague-Nevers married Vladislav VII of Poland on 8 November 1645; she and Newcastle must therefore have married after that date, sometime during late November or early December (see letter 8).

The original letters are in the British Library, MS Additional 70499 ff. 259-97. They have been printed faithfully in Richard W. Goulding, *Letters Written by Charles Lamb's "Princely Woman, the Thrice Noble Margaret Newcastle" to her Husband* (London, 1909). Margaret Lucas's spelling, like that of her husband, is idiosyncratic. Furthermore, she provided no punctuation and no capitalization. For the most part, I have relied on Richard Goulding's transcription, retaining his punctuation marks and his glosses while also adding my own, and departing from his edition only where I found discrepancies between his text and the manuscript. Unlike Goulding, however, I have distinguished between the letters *u* and *v*, despite the fact that Lucas makes no distinction. These minimal changes make the text more readable. The order of the letters is the same as the order in which they appear in the manuscript collection.

1

my lord,

ther is but on acsident which is death to mak me onhapy
ether to my frindes or fame or your affeetion, tho the last I
prefer equall to the firest, but I fear others foresee we shall
be unfortunat, tho we see it not our seleves [ourselves], or
elles ther would not be such paynes taking to unty the knot
of our affeetion. I must confes as you have had good frindes
to counsell you, I have had the like to counsell me and tell
me they heer of your profesions of afeetion to me; which
they bed me tak hed of, for you had ashured your selfe to
many and was constant to non. I answred that my lord
newcastll was to wis and to honest to ingag himself to many,
and I hard the qeene should tak it ell that I ded not mak her
aquainted befor I had resolved. I asked of what; they sayed
of my resolution to you. I asked if I should aquant the
qeene with every conplement that was bestod on me, with
many other idell descouerses, which would be to long to
wright, but pray doe not think I am inquisitive after such
frivolus talk, for I avoyd company to avoyd ther descours;
for the king and qeenes favour, my lord, I think you will
never be in danger of loosing it, for I never hard that any
body perfeetly had it; for my lord jermyne,[1] I think you
know your self to well to seek so loe, tho I will not say but
pollisee somtimes makes ues [use] of inferiours, but it is the
glorie of the inferiours to neglect when they get the
advantag of ther superiours; they they [sic] that tould you
of my mother has beter inteligenc then I, and shur, my lord,
I threw not my self away when I gave my self to you, for I
never ded any act worthy of prays [praise] before, but tis
the natur of those that cannot be happy to dessir non elles
should be so, as I shall be in haveing you, and will be so, in
spit of all malles [in spite of all malice], in being, my lord,
you most humbell sarvant
Margreat Lucas
pray lay the falt of my wrighting to my pen.

2

me lord,
I deed not dessir to delever up the intrest I had in you out
of any in constansee in me, but out of a considdarashoin of
you; me lord, me lord widdrington[2] in his advies [advice]
has don as a nobell and a true affectshoinit frind would doe,
yet I find I am infinnightly obleged to you whos afeetshoins
are above so powerfull aparswashon; my lord, if I doe not
send to you, pray exques [excuse] me, for if I doe, thay well
say I parsue you for your affectshoin, for though I love you
extremely well, yet I never feard my modesty so smalle as it
would give me leve to court any man; if you ples to ask the
queen, I think it would be well understod. I thank you for
the fear you have of my ruin, who cannot be happy in
nothing more then being, my lord, your most umbell
sarvant
Margreat Lucas

3

my lord,
pardon me if I have wright [writ, written] any thing that is
not agreable, but if I be carfull in things that may arise to
the scandall of my repetaion [reputation] is for fear of a
refleckion, becaus I am yours, for though it is imposabll to
keep out of the rech of a slandering toung from an enves
parson [envious person], yet it tis in my power to hender
them from the advantag of a good ground to beld [build]
ther descoures on, for know, me lord, saintiarmanes [St.
Germain] is a place of much sencour [censure, gossip] and
thinks I send to often; me lord, I am sory you should think
your love so much transends mine, but suer it tis as
uncomble [uncomely] to see a woman to kaind as to see a
man to necklegant, but, me lord, I know you are a man of
so much honour that I may safly rule my actions by your
directions, and beleve my tim best spent when you ples to
command, me lord, your most humbell sarvaunt
Margreat Lucas

4

my lord,
I think you have a plot against my healt in sending so early
for I was forst to reed your leter be a candell light, for ther
was not day enouf, but I had rather reed your leter then
slepe, and it doth me more good; my lord, I hop you are not
angare for my advise of st jermenes. I gave it semply for the
best; as for mr porter[3] he was a stranger to me, for before I
cam in to france I ded never see hem, or at lest knew hem
not to be mr porter, or my lord of newcastlls frind, and, my
lord, it is a custtom I obsarve that I never speek to any man
before they addres them selves to me, nor to look so much
in ther face as to invit ther descours, and I hop I never was
unsevell [uncivil] to any parson of what degree so ever, but
to morrow the qeene comes to pares [Paris], they say, and
then I hope to iusttifie my selfe to be, my lord, the most
humbell sarvant to you and your sarvants
Margreat Lucas

5

my lord,
ther is non could be more sory to part with any thing thay
love so well as I doe you, but it was my affeetion to you, not
to my self, as made that dissir to leve me. I consider non so
much as to be desplesd or deslik any thing in you for any
considdarion of what others can say, for that you think to
be best shall ples [please] me most; my lord I have hard
thay that have many sutes to prosequt [prosecute] of ther
one [own] selddom prefers any other, or, if they doe, so
slitly as not to be regarded, wherfor I beleaf my lord jermyn
has to many implymentst [employments] of the queens for
to desspash yours; it was say [said] to me you had declared
your marreg to my lord jermyn. I ansurred it was mor then
I could doe, but heer is so many idell descores as it would
werre [weary] me to tell them, and you to heer them. I wish
my self beter not only for my advantag but that I may be

worth your acseptance, which I shall indever to be the mor
becaus I am, my lord, your most humbl sarvant
Margreat Lucas
if you cannot reed this leter, blam me not, for it was so early
I was half a slep.

6

my lord,
your verses are more like you then your peckter, though it
resembelles you very much, but heer art has not bene so
good a courtiar as it eues [used] to be; my lord, the only
blesing I wish for heer is I may desarve your afectshion
which is onvalabell [invaluable]. I have sent this hear in
obedance to your commands, which I shall allways be redy
to exsequit [execute] with that obsarvances as becomes, my
lord, your most umbell sarvant
Margraet Lucas

7

my lord,
pray beleve I am not factious, espashally with you, for your
commands shall be my law, but supos me now in a very
mallancolly humer, and that most off my contempaltions
[contemplations] are fext [fixed] on nothing but
dessolutions [dissolutions], for I look apon this world as on
a deths head for mortefication, for I see all things subiet to
allteration and chaing, and our hopes as if they had takin
opum [opium]; therfore I will despis all things of this
world, I will not say all things in it, and love nothing but
you that is above it, but I should be lost to thos thoughts if I
ded not meet som off you [yours] to restor me to my self
againe; my lord, I hear the qeen comes to parres [Paris] this
next week to the solemetes [solemnities] of prences marys⁴
marrag, and I am in a dessput wither I should com with
her, if I can get leve to stay; my reson is becaus I think it will
stop the scors of ther descors [course of their discourse] of

us when they see I doe not com, but I shall not doe any
thing without your apprebation, as be comes your most
humbl sarvant
Margreat Lucas
My lord lett your ere lemet [ear limit] your poetry.

8

my lord,
as grace drawes the sole to life, so natuer, the pencell of god,
has drawen your wit to the birth, as may be seene by your
verses, though the subget is to mene for your mues [though
the subject is too mean for your muse]; the medeum and
species of my sight and understaning are flated to all things
in respeck of what comes from you, and more unighted and
contracted that [than] is represented from your lordship. I
should be sory your afeetshion should be as brokin as the
case of your pickter; it can be no ell oment of my part. I
know not what it may be of yours. I hope it is not raven like
to give woring [warning] of deth, but I wish life only to be
still, my lord, your hon. umbell sarvant
Margraet Lucas

9

my lord,
I thank you for the toaken of love you sent me, for I must
confes I want it, wer it but to returne it on your self againe,
for tho I give you all the love I have, yet it tis to lettell for
your meret, or could I wish for mor love then ever was or
shall be, yet my wish could not be so scopus [copious], but
you would be stell as farre beyound it as your worth is
above other mens; my lord, I am sory you should bedd me
keepe the ferses [verses] you sent, for it lookes as tho you
thought I had flung thos awey you sent before; shurly I
would keep them wer it with deficulty, and not to part with
your muses so easely, and beleve me I will part with nothing

that you shall command me to keep, nor with the nam of
being, my lord, your most humbell sarvant
Margreat Lucas
my lord the qeen coms not tell friday, if then.

10

my lord,
I am a lettell a shamed of my last letter, more then of the
others, not that my affeetion can be to larg, but I fear I
discover it to much in that leter, for wemen most love
silently, but I hop you will pardon the [letter] still, becaus
the intension was good; my lord, I can beleve nothing but
what is in honour of you, and I besech you to beleve that I
have ever truth of my sid, tho naked; therfor I never sayed
any such thing as you menshioned in your leter of your
peckter, nor never so much as shewed it to any cretur
[creature] befor yesterday that I gave it to mend, but I find
such enemenys [enemies] that what soever can be for my
disadvantag tho it have but a resemblance of truth shall be
declard. I hop my innocens will gard me, but suer, my lord,
you have many frindes, tho I have many enemenys, or eles
this is a counselling age, but if I shall preiudgice you in the
affaires of the world, or in your iudgment of your bad
choyce, consider and leve me, for I shall desir to life no
longer then to see you hapy, which am so much, my lord,
your most humble sarvant
Margreat Lucas
it is not ushall [usual] to give the queen gloves or any thing
eles, but, my lord, if you ples, I will give them her.

11

my lord,
I am sory you have metamorphosis [metamorphosed] my
leter and made that masculen that was efemenat; my
ambition is to be thought a modest woman and to leve the
title of a gallante man to you, for natuer would seme as

defective to give a woman the courage of a man as to give a man the weknes of a woman, but shurly, my lord, I shall be content to be any thing you would have me to be, so I am yours; my lord, I am sory you have such a defluction in your eies. I fear your wrighting may draw downe the rhum [rheum], so, much tho I rejoyce at nothing mor then your leters, but in sted of ioy they would bring me sadnes if I reseved then [them] at such a disadvantag as to hurt them, and let me intreat you to lase [lose] no mor [more (time)] at the leters of her who is so much, my lord, your humbell sarvant
Margreat Lu[c]as

12

my lord,
I may very well tak all your faltes to me, and yet be excusable for what is yours though not for my one [own], and tis no mercie to signe a pardon wher ther has bene no offence. I must confes my discression dede never aper [appear] so much as by my affeetion to love a parson of so much woreth as your self, and yet, me lord, I must tell you I am not esly [easily] drawen to be in love, for I ded never see any man but your self that I could have marred; my lord, if my desert dede not hendere me mor then the vissitts I reseve in my chamber, I may be [by] the favour of mr. stuarte be one of the queene of spayne [Spain's] maydes without deshonour to her parson. I never knew the vice of envy, but I must have a large proporsion of grace to arme me against it, if I had a rivall in your affeetion, espeshially a nemeies [an enemy's] daughter, but wer I suer you should hat [hate] me as I hop you love me, yet I well be, my lord, your most humbell sarvant
Margreat Lucas
the queen takes noe notes [notice] of any thing to me.

13

my lord,
I wounder not at my love, but at yours, becaus the obiet
[object] of mine is good. I wish the obiet of yours wer so,
yet me thinkes, you should love nothing that wer ell,
therfore if I have any part of good tis your love makes me
so, but loved I nothing elles but you, I love all that is good,
and loving nothing above you I have loves recompens; my
lord, I have not had much expereanse of the world, yet I
have found it such as I could willinly part with it, but sence
I knew you, I fear I shall love it to well, becaus you are in it,
and yet me thinkes, you are not in it, becaus you are not off
it; so I am both in it and out off it, a strang in chantment
[strange enchantment], but pray love so as you may love me
long, for I shall ever be, my lord, your most humbl sarvant
Margreat Lucas
my lord, they say the qeen comes to morrow.

14

my lord,
it may be the triall, but it tis not true love that absence or
tim can demenesh, and I shall as sone forget all good as
forget you; me lord, you are a parson I may very
confeedently one [own] unles morell [moral] meret be a
scandall, but, me lord, ther is a cusstumare law that must be
sineed [signed] before I may lawfully call you husban; if you
are so passhonit as you say, and as I dar not but belefe, yet it
may be feared it cannot last long, for no extrem is
parmenttary [permanent], but how so ever unworthy I am
in my self, I am estemabell [esteemable] as on thas [one
that] is, me lord, your most faithfull and umbell sarvant
Margreat Lucas

15

my lord,
wer I much sicker then I was, your kaind car [care] would

cuer me. I am a feard it wer an ambeshion to desir much of
your love, knowing my self of lettell dessart and yet, me
thinks, it should be no sinne when the disir is good; my
lord, I sent a leter by my mayd; I should be sory if you
thought any line can come from you could be any others
wayes then plesing to me, for that is only troublesom which
is foolesh or emperttenent, with which you will never be
taxed, nor your iudgment, unles now in choosing me, but
being as your choyes makes it good, and so I shall valu
[value] my self, which elles I should not, and esteming my
self the more for being my lord, your most umbell sarvant
Margreat Lucas

16

My lord,
I have reseved your leter which semes to satisfi mee aginest
the noies [noise] of a cort, but when I rede your lordsp
justificashon under your one [own] hand, I consider tis all
the sattisfackshon can be given from a parson of honnor,
but now, having so great a in gongshon [an injunction] as is
laid upon mee in the nam of a brother, which has so great a
powr [power], together with your lordps excues that having
som ocashones of my one this week that will drae [draw]
me to pares [Paris], of which I belefe your lordps may hear
of, my lord, your humbell sarvant
M.L.

17

my lord,
ther is nothing will pleas me more then to be wher you are,
and I begen to admire parres [Paris] be caus you are in it;
my lord, the reson I had to consele [conceal] our affeetions
was becaus I thought it would be agreabl to your dissir, but
for my part I would not car [care] if the trumppet of fame
blue it throw out all the world, if the world wer ten times
biger then it tis, for it would be an advantag to me and my
iudgment, and tho I am gelty of falts I may be a shamed to

one [own], yet sence they are knowin in heven I car not
what can be knowin on earth, and I dout not but heven
doth a prove and will geve a blesing to my affeetions to you,
but seting a sid all my falts I shall never leve to have that
vertue as to be, my lord your most humbl sarvant
Margreat Lucas

18

my lord,
I should be sory if your busnes be not a corden to your
dissir, and pray, me lord, consider well wither marring me
will not bring a troubl to your self, for, beleve me, I love you
to well to wesh you unhapy, and I had rather lose all
hapines my selfe then you should be unforteenat, but if you
be resoveled, what day soever you ples to send for me, I will
com; my lord, I know not what counsell to give conserning
the quine [queen], but I fear she will tak it ell if she be not
mad aquanted with our intenshoins, and if you ples to right
a leter to her and send it to me I will delever it that day you
send for me. I think it no pollese [policy] to desples the
quine, for though she will doe us no good, she may doe us
harme. I have sent my mayd about som busnes, and she and
my lady broune[5] shall agre a bout the other things you spak
of. I understand the parswashon [persuasion] of som
againest your marreg, suer thay would not perswad you but
for your good; but if you think you have don unadvisedly in
promesis [promising] your self to me, send me word, and I
will resing [resign] up all the intrist I have in you, though
unwillingly; but what would I not doe for any thing that
may condues [conduce] to your content, for heerafter, if
you should repent, how unfortunat a woman shoud I be. I
have bene very ell this three days, but health can not be so
plesing to me as knowing my self to be, my lord, your most
umbell sarvant
Margreat Lucas
pray me lord, doe not messtrust me, for telling of any thing
that you have commanded my silance in; for though I am a

woman, I can keep counsell, but I hav [have] not power ofer the emmaganacions [imaginations] of others; pray consider I have enemyes.

19

my lord,
it can be in no bodyes powr to ues [use] me ell if you ues me well. I have not ben with the qeen as yet be [by] reson I am not well, but I heer she would have me acknowledg my self in a falt and not she to be in any, but it will be hard for me to accuse my self and to mak my self guilty of a falt when I am innocent, but if it be the duty of a sarvant to obaye all the commandes of [a] mestres, tho it be against my self, I will doe it, if it be but to bring my self in to ues [use] of obedience against I am a wife; for the hindirance of our marrag, I hop it is not in ther power, I am sure they can not hinder me from loving, for I must be and will be and am, my lord, your admiring, loving, honouring humbell and obedient sarvant
Margreat Lucas

20

my lord,
my health will be according as I imagin your affeetion, for I shall never be sicke so long as you love me; my lord, I hop the qeene and I am frindes; she sayeth she will seme so at lest, but I finde, if it had bene in her power, she would a crost [have crossed] us. I hard not of the leter, but she sayed to me she had it in wrightin that I should pray you not to mak her acquainted with our desines; my lord, sence our affeetions is poubleshed, it will not be for our honours to delay our marreg; the qeene dos intend to com on mondday; if not, I will send you word. I will wayt on her furst to paris, and then I am at your sarves [service] to be commanded as, my lord, your most humbell sarvant
Margreat Lucas

21

my lord,

I dessir nothing so much as the continueuanc of your affeetion, for I think my self recher [richer] in haveing that then if I wer a monarch of all the world; my lord, I hop the qeene and I shall be very good frindes againe, and may be the beter for the deffarances we have had; it was reported heer that you would be with us before we could be with you, and be ashured I will bring non to our wedding but thos you ples. I find to sattesfy the opinon we are not marred allredy, we must be marred by on [one] of the prestes heer, which I think cousens[6] to be the fettes [fittest]; we shall not com tell mondday, if then, but ther is no tim can allter my affeetion, I know not what it can doe your[s], for I am parfeetly, my lord, your most humbell sarvant Marg. Lucas

Notes

1. INTRODUCTION

1. Cavendish, *The Life of... William Cavendishe* (1667), sig. b1r.

2. See Appendix A. Thomas Lucas died 25 September 1625. See Morant, *Essex*, 124; and Mendelson, *The Mental World of Stuart Women*, 14.

3. Cavendish, *A True Relation of my Birth, Breeding, and Life*, in *Nature's Pictures* (1656), 370-71; all subsequent citations are to this edition. In some copies of this edition "vertues" has been emended by hand as "virtuous."

4. Cavendish, *A True Relation*, 372; see Gardiner, *The Great Civil War*, 1:12; Morant, *Essex*, 124; Ryves, *Mercurius Rusticus*, 1-4.

5. Public Record Office, *Calendar of State Papers, Domestic*, 1649-50, 39. (Hereafter, I will refer to this collection as *Cal. S.P. Dom.* followed by the reign and the date.) There was some discussion about whether Newcastle should receive such harsh treatment. In November the House of Lords had to be convinced by the House of Commons to include him with the six others excepted from the pardon. See the entry for 21 Nov. 1648 in *Journals of the House of Lords* (London, 1767/1770-), 10:598. See also Grant, *Margaret the First*, 103.

6. See the entry for 10 Dec. 1651 in the Public Record Office, *Calendar of the Proceedings of the Committee for Compounding 1643-1660* (London, 1891), 1733-34. The grounds of the committee's refusal were that the earl of Newcastle had been excepted from the pardon and that Margaret Cavendish had married him after "he became a delinquent, so that at the time of marriage he had no estate" (1734). She describes her meeting with the committee as follows: "[F]or my brother, the Lord Lucas did claim in my behalf, such a part of my Lords Estate, as wives had allowed them, but they told him, that by reason I was married since my Lord was made a Delinquent, I could have nothing, nor should have any thing, he being the greatest Traitor to the State, which was to be the most loyall Subject, to his King and Countrey: but I whisperingly spoke to my brother to conduct me out of that ungentlemanly place, so without speaking to them one word good or bad, I returned to my Lodgings, & as that Committee was the first, so was it the last, I ever was at as a Petitioner." Cavendish, *A True Relation*, 379-80.

7. Osborne, *Letters to Temple*, 79.

8. Pepys, 18 March 1668, *Diary*, 9:123; J. Evelyn, 30 May 1667, *Diary*, 3:482-83; Makin, *Essay*, 10; Mary Evelyn to Ralph Bohun, ca. 1667, in M. Evelyn, "Letters," 4:9.

9. Pepys, 26 April 1667, *Diary,* 8:186; Pepys, 1 May 1667, *Diary,* 8:196; Pepys, 10 May 1667, *Diary,* 8:209.

10. For an interesting discussion of types of biography, see James L. Clifford's chapter entitled "Forms—Types of Biography," in his *Puzzles to Portraits,* 83-98. The term "silhouette biography" is Marchette Chute's (83).

11. Cross-dressing had been a fad in the 1630s with Henrietta Maria's fashions; in the 1660s the fad was revived in part as a reminiscence of a lost order. See Backscheider, "The Cavalier Woman."

12. J. Evelyn, "Ballad," f. 131; Charles Lyttelton to Christopher Hatton, 7 Aug. 1665, in Thompson, *Correspondence of the Family of Hatton,* 1:47.

13. Mary Evelyn to Ralph Bohun, ca. 1667, in M. Evelyn, "Letters," 4:9.

14. Leon Edel, *Literary Biography* (Garden City, N.Y.: Doubleday, 1959), 88.

15. Douglas Grant suggests that Cavendish knew Katherine Philips. He identifies Cavendish as the Lady M. Cavendish in Katherine Philips's "To My Lady M. Cavendish, choosing the name of Policrite," noting that the choice of the name "Policrite" (critic of many things) reflects Margaret Cavendish's sense of herself as a satirist. The Lady M. Cavendish addressed by Philips is, however, Mary Butler, daughter of the duke of Ormonde; Mary Butler married William, Lord Cavendish (later the first duke of Devonshire) on 27 October 1662. There is no conclusive evidence that Margaret Cavendish actually met Katherine Philips, though they would certainly have known of each other. I am indebted to Elizabeth Hageman for help with this matter.

16. Cavendish, *A True Relation,* 386; Cavendish, *Philosophical and Physical Opinions* (1655), sig. B3v.

17. Cavendish, *Philosophical and Physical Opinions* (1663), 88, 86; Cavendish, *Nature's Pictures* (1656), sig. C3v.

18. Cavendish, *Observations* (1666), sig. h1r.

19. For a detailed discussion of the making of the modern self, see Taylor, *Sources of the Self,* 111-99.

2. A STRANGE ENCHANTMENT

1. Gerolamo Agostini, Venetian Secretary in England, to the Doge and Senate, *Calendar of State Papers and Manuscripts, Relating to English Affairs, Existing in the Archives and Collections of Venice* (1642-1643), 279-80. See also the entries in *Journals of the House of Commons* for 23 May 1643 in 3:98 and for 21 June 1643 in 3:139. A full-scale biography of Henrietta Maria, one that takes into account her religious and political interests, is needed. Bone, *Henrietta Maria,* provides a useful point of departure. See also Oman, *Henrietta Maria.* Harbage's *Cavalier Drama* has been criticized for its monolithic treatment of court culture as "cavalier," but it provides one of the fullest explorations available of Henrietta's theatrical activities. More recently, Veevers's groundbreaking *Images of Love and Religion* supplied the first full-scale examination of the interdependence of the queen's religious, aesthetic, and social interests. A new edition of Henrietta Maria's letters is also needed, although the standard edition edited by Green has in-

formed most biographies of the queen because of its useful notes.

2. H.A. Doubleday and Howard de Walden, eds., *The Complete Peerage,* 13 vols. (London: St. Catherine Press, 1936), 9:523. For the approximate date of their marriage, see Appendix B. A letter from Margaret's mother, Elizabeth Lucas née Leighton, dated 20 December 1645, thanks Newcastle for having honored her by his letters and "my Daughter much more by marrage." This letter is revealing in two ways. First, we get a suggestion of Elizabeth Lucas's dim view of marriage through her remark that by marrying Margaret Lucas, Newcastle "made her extremely happie: for oftentimes these [marriage and happiness] come not together, but by yourselfe she hath attained to both." Second, the letter is interesting in that Elizabeth Lucas's handwriting is so much neater than her daughter's. The manuscript of the letter is in the British Library, MS Add 70499, f. 299. It is printed accurately in Goulding, *Letters from the Originals,* 2. See also the modernized transcription in chapter 3.

3. Pope Urban VIII hoped that by becoming "the Esther of her oppressed people" Henrietta might bring Catholics in England relief. Green, *Letters of Henrietta Maria,* 7.

4. Platonic love doctrine could, of course, serve as a veil for fleshly lovers. That Cavendish was aware of this, at least later in life, is evident in her satirical description of the cult of Platonic love at court: "Praying is not usual for a Courtier, yet those Ladies [at Court] that are Beautiful are made Saints there, and the men are their Devouts, which offer them Vows, Prayers, Praises, and sometimes Thanksgiving, and many times they are Penitents; but when the Ladies Beauties decay, the men become Apostates. Thus you may see many of our Sex are made Saints, though they be Sinners, but they are Sainted for their Beauty, not for their Piety, for their outward Form, not for their inward Grace: Indeed they are worldly Saints, and the Court is their Heaven and Nature their Goddess." *Sociable Letters,* 15-16. Throughout her life, however, she seems to have appreciated Platonic love doctrine's attention to the mind.

5. Cavendish, *A True Relation,* 372. Oman reports that "pastoral plays were performed [that summer] for the queen's amusement in college gardens." *Henrietta Maria,* 151.

6. Rich, "Autobiography," 4; Butler, *Theatre and Crisis,* 103.

7. Butler, *Theatre and Crisis,* 106; Gregorio Panzani conveyed the queen's habit of blending religious interests with pleasure when he sent instructions regarding the selection of a suitable agent for the queen's household to Cardinal Barberini. The instructions were based on his conversation with the queen's confessor, Father Philip. According to Father Philip, the agent should be "about 35 years of age, youth and old age being neither of them capable of that desirable mixture of gravity and spirit requisite in a public minister; that he ought to be noble, rich, handsome, and affable in conversation; a good economist, observing strict order in his family; grave and reserved, yet complaisant, especially to the ladies of the court, and still here very guarded, the king and queen being strictly virtuous, and professed enemies to immodesty and gallantry." *Memoirs,* 188.

Recent work by Martin Butler, Kevin Sharpe, and Malcolm Smuts has foregrounded the diversity of religious and political positions embraced by members of the court elite. My intention is not to suggest that court culture was uniform but that Henrietta's religious and aesthetic sensibility, which visibly shaped court culture in the 1630s, would have continued to exert influence within her household in the 1640s and especially in exile in France. See Butler, *Theatre and Crisis;* Sharpe, *Criticism and Compliment;* and Smuts, *Court Culture.*

8. Sharpe, *The Personal Rule,* 538.

9. Ibid., 188-90.

10. *Cal. S.P. Dom.—Charles I,* 1625-1626, 273. In this volume see also pages 179, 193, 485, 580 (additional references to Henrietta's theatrical activity can be found in *Cal. S.P. Dom.—Charles I* 1629-1631, 509, 512, and 516; *Cal. S.P. Dom.— Charles I* 1631-1633, 484); John Davys to Henry, earl of Huntingdon, 21 July 1625, Historical Manuscripts Commission, *The Manuscripts of the Late Reginald Rawdon Hastings,* 2 (1930): 68; Amerigo Salvetti (or, more correctly, Alessandro Antelminelli) to the grand duke at Florence, 6 March 1626, Historical Manuscripts Commission, *Manuscripts of Henry Duncan Skrine, Esq.,* 11, Part 1 (1887): 47.

11. Adams, *Sir Henry Herbert,* 56. The queen's appearance at the masque performed at the Middle Temple has been discussed by Martin Butler, who argues that the pro-Spanish faction at court "manipulated" Henrietta, "realizing her potential as a lever by which 'opposition' pressure could be brought against Charles" and the Caroline stage "engaged in the debate of these [political] issues" (*Theatre and Crisis,* 322-23). More recently, Erica Veevers has argued that although politics informed the Caroline stage, Henrietta's involvement must first be understood within the terms of conservative feminism and of her religion. See Butler, "Entertaining the Palatine Prince"; Veevers, *Images of Love,* 5-8; Smuts, "Puritan Followers."

12. John Peacock, "The French Element in Inigo Jones's Masque Designs," in Lindley, *The Court Masque,* 154; Sensabaugh, "Platonic Love and the Puritan Rebellion"; see also Sensabaugh's "Love Ethics in Platonic Court Drama." Sensabaugh presents a problematically uncritical review of Puritan opposition to Henrietta's Platonic love doctrines. See Erica Veevers's response to Sensabaugh in *Images of Love,* 56-65.

13. See *The New Catholic Encyclopedia* entry for "Humanism, Devout." See also Bremond, *Religious Thought in France,* 1:55-100; Veevers, *Images of Love,* 75-109; and Peacock, "The French Element," 156.

14. Sales, *A Devoute Life,* 279:351, 350. For Henrietta's devotion to *The Imitation of Christ,* see Oman, *Henrietta Maria,* 332.

15. Veevers, *Images of Love,* 75. See also J. Evelyn, *Diary,* 3:45. William Prynne attacked Cosin's book for its "popishness" in *Censure of Mr Cozens.*

16. A second book at the Folger Shakespeare Library, a sermon by Lancelot Andrewes, also carries Henry Cavendish's signature and the date of 1676, which suggests that he may have signed a number of the books he inherited with his father's title. See Andrewes, *The Copie of the Sermon Preached VI April 1604,* Folger Shakespeare Library, Washington, D.C.

17. The literature on the précieuse cult is extensive and varied. In addition to Veevers's work, see Vincent, *Hôtel de Rambouillet and the Précieuses;* Fletcher,

"Précieuses at the Court of Charles I"; Laidler, "A History of Pastoral Drama in England"; Tieje, "The Expressed Aim of the Long Prose Fiction"; Lynch, *The Social Mode of Restoration Comedy;* Lynch, "Conventions of Platonic Drama"; Gagen, "Love and Honor in Dryden's Heroic Plays"; Harbage, *Cavalier Drama;* Upham, *The French Influence in English Literature;* Fletcher, *The Religion of Beauty in Woman;* Dalziel, "Richardson and Romance"; de Mourgues, *Metaphysical Baroque and Précieux Poetry;* and Dammers, "Female Characterization."

18. Lynch, *The Social Mode of Restoration Comedy,* 80; Vincent, *Hôtel de Rambouillet and the Précieuses,* 40.

19. Lynch, *The Social Mode of Restoration Comedy,* 52; Veevers, *Images of Love,* 16.

20. See Orgel and Strong, *Inigo Jones;* Howell, *Letters,* 317-18. Howell's letters seem to provide the point of departure for most discussions of Platonism and the précieuse tradition in England in the 1630s.

21. Cavendish, *The Lady Contemplation,* in *Playes* (1662), 226; Cavendish, *The Presence,* in *Plays, Never Before Printed* (1668), 7; Newcastle's *Advice to Charles II* can be found in Slaughter, *Newcastle's Advice to Charles II,* 60. The letter was written in late 1658 or early 1659 and presented to Charles in the spring of 1659 (xi). See also Rogow, *Thomas Hobbes,* 118.

22. John Peacock has traced Henrietta's influence on Inigo Jones, describing her as a "chief collaborator" along with the king after 1630. "The French Element," 158. Veevers, *Images of Love,* 89.

23. Veevers, *Images of Love,* 136-37; Orgel and Strong, *Inigo Jones,* 2:599, 2:601.

24. Smuts, *Court Culture,* 228. Veevers, *Images of Love,* 142. See also Bone, *Henrietta Maria,* 101; Cyprien de Gamache, *Memoirs of the Mission in England of the Capuchin Friars from the year 1630 to 1669,* in Thomas Birch, *Court and Times of Charles the First* (London, 1848), 2:311-14.

25. Cratander, the royal slave in William Cartwright's play of that name, refers to the queen Atossa's beauty, "where honour is transmitted in a true / Mysterious Gage of an Immaculate minde." Cartwright, *The Royall Slave.* (Oxford, 1639), sig. E4r. By linking beauty with intellectual purity or power, the Platonic drama of the 1630s included women in the world of the mind.

26. Peter William Thomas, *Sir John Berkenhead,* 101. Recent critics, among them Kevin Sharpe, Martin Butler, and Malcom Smuts, have argued successfully that the traditional image of a monolithic Stuart court culture does not sufficiently take into account the "factional rivalries, jockeyings for place and favour, the differing political and religious views, the attempted palace coups and heated Council debates which lay behind the illusory uniformity of Whitehall." Sharpe, *Criticism and Compliment,* 10. This is undoubtedly true, and it may be more accurate to speak of court cultures than court culture. Nevertheless, those who positioned themselves against the court found it convenient to depict a unified court culture when they attacked it. Despite the considerable differences between Henrietta and Charles, for example, opponents of the court, such as Prynne, worried that the royal couple was too unified and that Henrietta exerted undue control over the king's affairs. That Prynne continued to attack the queen and

her imagined hold on court culture is evident in his *Popish Royall Favourite.* There he blames the king's leniency toward Catholics in large part on the fact that Catholics had "Queen Mary her selfe in the Kings own bed and bosome for their most powerfull Mediatrix, of whom they might really affirme in reference to his Majesty, what some of their popish Doctors have most blasphemously written of the Virgin Mary in relation to God and Christ, That all things are subject to the command of Mary, even God himself" (56).

27. Harbage, *Cavalier Drama,* 94. That Lucas may actually have read *The Shepheard's Paradise* seems likely; it is quite possible that a manuscript copy accompanied the queen into exile in France.

28. The Royalist newsbook *Mercurius Aulicus* reported that John Pym promised members of both Houses that "if their Lordships would have patience but a little while, they should see them get so good a pawne into their hands, that they might make their own conditions" (see *Mercurius Aulicus,* 17 Jan. 1643, 29).

29. Bone, *Henrietta Maria,* 157.

30. Green, *Letters,* 167. All references are to this edition; subsequent references will be provided in the text.

31. "A Short History of the Troubles in England," in *Memoirs for the History of Anne of Austria,* 1:220. This volume does not identify its translator; it is dedicated to Sarah, duchess of Marlborough.

32. Cavendish, *Life of . . . William Cavendishe* (1667), 23.

33. In one pamphlet Henrietta is reported to be using "all the labours, and endeavours can possible bee, conceived to raise what armes Shee can." See *Strange and Terrible Newes,* sig. A3v. She is accused in *A Mappe of Mischiefe* of "endeavour[ing] to overthow [the] Common-wealth"; *Mercurius Aulicus,* 27 Feb. 1643.

34. Cavendish, *A True Relation,* 373; Gardiner dates the disturbance that involved the Lucas property as occurring on 22 August 1642. See Gardiner, *The Great Civil War,* 1:12. See also Morant, *Essex,* 124.

35. Ryves, *Mercurius Rusticus,* 1-4.

36. Ibid., 4. See note 37.

37. See Madan, *Oxford Books,* 2:497, 2:430-33. The first issue of *Mercurius Rusticus* carrying the story of the plundering of the Lucas home at Colchester is dated 20 May 1643. In March 1646 Bruno Ryves published a collected edition of the issues of *Mercurius Rusticus.* It is in the 1646 collected edition that the engraved title page with scenes of parliamentary atrocities appears.

38. Fanshawe, "Memoirs," f. 13.

39. Cavendish, *A True Relation,* 374.

40. See Oman, *Henrietta Maria,* 161; Cavendish, *A True Relation,* 372.

41. In *Poems and Fancies* Cavendish writes that she "underst[ood] no other Language; not French, although I was in France five yeares" (sig. A6r); Bone, *Henrietta Maria,* 186.

42. Trease, *Portrait of a Cavalier,* 145.

43. The manuscripts of Margaret Lucas's letters to William Cavendish are in the British Library, MS Add 70499, ff. 259-97. They have also been printed faithfully in Goulding, *Letters from the Originals,* 5-18. For the letters quoted, see Appendix B, letters 7 and 1. See also Morant, *Essex,* 124.

44. See Appendix B, letters 10, 1.

45. Ibid., letters 8, 13.

46. Ibid., letter 12; Cavendish, *A True Relation,* 374-75.

47. As Peter William Thomas has shown, John Berkenhead's newsbook, *Mercurius Aulicus,* for example, employed the literature of the court to present Royalist commanders as "brave, noble, and sensitive men conquering by generic right." That Berkenhead's code name was "Cratander" after the heroic slave in William Cartwright's *The Royall Slave* suggests the degree to which court life was interpreted in terms of literature. See Thomas, *Sir John Berkenhead,* 102.

Similarly, as Lois Potter has demonstrated, "the habit of seeing events in literary terms was common to both sides in the civil wars, as was the attempt to 'place' those events by assigning them to the correct genre." See Potter, *Secret Rites and Secret Writing,* 73.

48. Cavendish, *Playes,* sig. A3r.

49. Cavendish, *Sociable Letters,* 295; William Cavendish to Edward Nicholas, 15 Feb. 1657, *Cal. S.P. Dom. (1656-1657),* 279.

50. Ezell, "'To Be Your Daughter in Your Pen,'" 294. Ezell argues convincingly that playwriting had a significant domestic social function within the Newcastle household, one in which "like Donne and other coterie poets, but unlike the duchess, the Cavendish sisters retained control of their readership" (294). It is true that unlike her step-daughters, Margaret Cavendish published her plays, but her sense of purpose in writing them may not have differed from that of the Cavendish sisters as much as Ezell suggests. See also *"The Concealed Fansyes: A Play by Lady Jane Cavendish and Lady Elizabeth Brackley"*; excerpts of their other work can be found in *Kissing the Rod,* ed. Germaine Greer et al. (New York: Farrar Straus Giroux/The Noonday Press, 1988): 109-18.

51. Cavendish, *Love's Adventures* and *The Lady Contemplation* appear in *Playes,* 1662. Jacqueline Pearson has noted that Cavendish's "silent women challenge assumptions about women's duties, [and] society's insistence that a woman must be prepared to sacrifice her inner life to the demands of her family." This is undoubtedly true, but Cavendish's psychological investigation does not stop with this certainty. Rather, she goes on to explore competing truths about the relation between mind and world, using her plays as a sort of laboratory for her psychological investigations. See Pearson, *The Prostituted Muse,* 129.

52. For discussions of Royalist female characters in plays of the early 1660s, see Backscheider's excellent "Cavalier Woman"; and N.H. Keeble's "Obedient Subjects? The Loyal Self in Some Later Seventeenth-Century Royalist Women's Memoirs," in Maclean, *Culture and Society in the Stuart Restoration,* 201-18.

53. The reference to the king's failure to provide pay occurs on page 9.

54. James Fitzmaurice, "Margaret Cavendish on Her Own Writing: Evidence from Revision and Handmade Correction," *Papers of the Bibliographical Society of America* 85 (Sept. 1991): 302.

55. Harbage, *Cavalier Drama,* 37; Cavendish, *Plays, Never Before Printed* (1668), sig. A1v.

56. In an effort to explain the contradictions inherent in Cavendish's plays, Linda Payne claims, justly but without developing the idea fully, that "the pres-

ence of unresolved conflicts can be a powerful force on the page rather than the stage." Linda R. Payne, "Dramatic Dreamscape: Women's Dreams and Utopian Vision in the Works of Margaret Cavendish, Duchess of Newcastle," in Schofield and Macheski, *Curtain Calls,* 31. Drawing on the work of Roger Chartier, Marta Straznicky argues correctly that Cavendish appreciated the fact that her plays were meant to be read rather than performed: "Cavendish uses the resources of print to create an intimate, private relation between text and reader, and this is where closet drama *is* palpably different from published stage drama." "Reading the Stage," 378. Cavendish's interest in the proper relation between text and reader is, as this chapter attempts to demonstrate, complex. For an overview of the context of Cavendish's writing, see Randall, *Winter Fruit,* 313-36.

57. Cavendish, *Love's Adventures,* in *Playes* (1662), 35, 28.

58. Cavendish, *Youth's Glory and Death's Banquet,* in *Playes* 166, 171.

59. For an interesting discussion of the relationship between marriage and authorship in *Youth's Glory and Death's Banquet,* see Rosenthal, *Playwrights and Plagiarists,* 77-81. My interest in the dialectics between Cavendish's active and contemplative cavaliers offers an alternate, though not entirely contradictory, interpretation to Rosenthal's argument that Cavendish presents "marriage as irreconcilable with authorship" (77). Referring to Lady Sanspareille's death, Linda R. Payne asks, "Was it just too inconceivable that this remarkable woman could continue to bloom in a public role?" This question seems to overlook the complexity of the ambivalence expressed throughout Cavendish's work regarding the active and contemplative lives. Payne, "Dramatic Dreamscape," 29.

60. The Princess in the play is angry at her maid of honor's marriage just as Henrietta was displeased with Lucas's marriage. John Evelyn writes that Newcastle "had obligation to my Wives mother, for his marriage, there, That is his Dutchesse had, who was Sister to my L: Lucas, & maide of honor then to Q: Mother; married in our Chapel at Paris." J. Evelyn, 24 April 1667, *Diary,* 3:480-81; Goulding, *Letters from the Originals,* 16; Grant, *Margaret the First,* 17. See also Appendix B, letters 1, 19, 20.

61. *Horace: Satires, Epistles and Ars Poetica,* ed. H. Rushton Fairclough (Cambridge: Harvard Univ. Press/Loeb Library, 1978), 451.

3. CAVENDISH'S REVIEW OF THE NEW ATOMISM

1. Lucretius, *On the Nature of the Universe,* trans. R.E. Latham (London: Penguin, 1951), 60.

2. See chapter 2, note 41.

3. Elizabeth Lucas to William Cavendish, marquess of Newcastle, 20 Dec. 1645, MS Add 70499, f. 299, British Library. See also Goulding, *Letters from the Originals,* 2. I have modernized the spelling in this letter.

4. Cavendish, *A True Relation,* 374.

5. Ibid., 377. This is actually page 376, but it is misnumbered as page 377.

6. Gardiner, *The Great Civil War,* 4:149. See also Whitelock, *Memorials of the English Affairs,* 2:362.

7. J. Evelyn, 8 July 1656, *Diary,* 3:177. See also Morant, *Essex,* 72; and Gardiner, *The Great Civil War,* 4:203.

8. Gardiner, *The Great Civil War,* 4:198.

9. *The Loyall Sacrifice,* 87-88; Historical Manuscripts Commission, *The Manuscripts of the Duke of Beaufort,* Twelfth Report, appendix, pt. 9 (1891): 28; Thomas Fairfax to Edward, earl of Manchester, Speaker of the House of Peers, 29 Aug. 1648, in Rushworth, *Historical Collections,* 7:1243.

10. Theodore Mayerne to the marquis of Newcastle, 24 May 1648, "Letters to William Cavendish," f. 14r., 14v. Mayerne's letter, most of which is directed at providing recommendations for Newcastle's health, furnishes evidence for a reconsideration of Newcastle's character as an untroubled dilettante.

11. Mayerne to Newcastle, 24 May 1648, f. 19v-20r; Mayerne to Newcastle, 22 May 1649, f. 25r.

12. Cavendish, *A True Relation,* 375-76.

13. Ibid., 377, 372. One example of Royalist interest in the Book of Job can be found in Anne Fanshawe's description of her surprise at finding herself at Oxford suddenly as "poor as Job." Fanshawe, "Memoirs," f. 13. The most illustrious example of interest in the Book of Job, of course, comes from a more ambiguous Royalist, Thomas Hobbes, whose *Leviathan* refers directly to Job.

14. Kargon, *Atomism in England,* 68; Gelbart, "The Intellectual Development of Walter Charleton," 156. See also Clucas, "The Atomism of the Cavendish Circle."

15. Petty, *Discourse,* epistle dedicatory, sig. A8v-A9v. The Cavendish salon is discussed in the following works: Kargon, *Atomism in England,* 63-76; Meyer, *The Scientific Lady in England,* 1-15; H. Jones, *The Epicurean Tradition,* 196. More recently, Stephen Clucas has reexamined Kargon's "narrative for the development of the atomistic hypothesis," arguing that Gassendi may not be as central a figure in the modernization of atomism that took place in the midcentury as has been thought. Although Clucas is right to point to the ease with which ideas were disseminated, he focuses exclusively on the physical properties of atoms and thus does not sufficiently take into account the metaphorical uses Cavendish made of atomism. See Clucas, "The Atomism of the Cavendish Circle." See also his article "Poetic Atomism in Seventeenth-Century England."

16. Aubrey, *Letters Written by Eminent Persons,* 2.2:626.

17. In 1664 John Rolleston paid out £39.14s in book purchases for Cavendish. See Trease, *Portrait of a Cavalier,* 188. See also Grant, *Margaret the First,* 200. That she was also allowed to lavish money on her books is evident by their magnificent engravings. Walter Charleton noted in a letter to Margaret Cavendish that she "bestow[ed] also great summs of Money in Printing" her books. Walter Charleton to Margaret Cavendish, 7 May 1667, in *Collection of Letters and Poems,* 108.

18. Cavendish, *The World's Olio* (1655), 47. The pagination of this volume is faulty; the printed page 47 is actually page 49, probably because the unnumbered two-page "Epistle" constituting pages 47-48 was added at the last moment. I refer to the actual (and unnumbered) page 47. Cavendish repeated these claims about her education in *Philosophical and Physical Opinions* (1655), when

she claimed to have had "by relation, the long and much experience of my Lord, who hath lived to see and be in many changes of fortunes, and to converse with many men of sundry nations, ages, qualities, tempers, capacities, abilities, wits, humors, fashions and customes" (sig. A4r).

19. For another application of the analogy between words and worlds, see *Youth's Glory and Death's Banquet.* There Lady Sanspareile compares the creation of nature with the creation of words out of letters, computation out of numerals, and music out of notes: "For well may Nature, if many by Art can make infinite varietye, by change of few principles, as for example in musick, from 8 Notes, by change, infinite Tunes, are, or can be made; from the figure of 1 to 9 what Multiplication? From 24 letters, how far can the mind dictate it self in, numerous words, and different languages? Thus Nature the tutress to man, and onely man, have taught him to imitate her" (138). Joshua Sylvester's translation of Du Bartas's *The Divine Weeks* contains a similar play on words and worlds:

> Or, as of twice-twelve Letters, thus transpos'd,
> This world of Words is variously composed;
> And, of these Words, in divers order sow'n,
> This sacred Volume that you read, is grow'n.
> [I, ii, 272-81]

See Grosart, *Complete Works of Joshua Sylvester.* Cavendish mentions Sylvester admiringly in "An Epistle to the Reader, for my Book of Philosophy" in *Philosophical and Physical Opinions* (1655), sig. a2r.

20. Cavendish, *Philosophical and Physical Opinions* (1655), sig. A1v.

21. Miriam Reik calls attention to A.R. Hall's observation that the postal organizations of the early seventeenth century served to spread scientific news: "Problems could be exposed for general consideration: and criticism could be provoked and collated. In the mid–seventeenth century a number of men occupied a prominent position, less on account of their own intellectual capacities, than because of their indefatigability as correspondents." See A.R. Hall, *The Scientific Revolution,* 191. Jean Jacquot notes that men like Charles Cavendish "contributed to the advancement of learning mainly by providing an appreciative audience, by asking intelligent questions or formulating valuable objections, and by helping the circulation and exchange of scientific information." See Jacquot, "Sir Charles Cavendish," 13. See also Reik, *Golden Lands,* 206.

22. Reik, *Golden Lands,* 208 n. 62.

23. The letter is reprinted in Hervey, "Hobbes and Descartes," 87.

24. Clarendon, *Life of Edward Earl of Clarendon,* 2:250. Similarly, in *The History of the Rebellion,* Clarendon refers to Charles Cavendish as having "the noblest and largest mind, though the least and most inconvenient body that lived" (3:374).

25. Cavendish, *Poems and Fancies,* sig. A7r. See also chapter 1, note 6.

26. In the "Epistle to Time" prefaced to *Philosophicall Fancies,* Cavendish wrote that the volume was "in three weeks begun, and finisht all" (sig. A3r). In another preface "To the Reader" in the same volume, she apologizes for the volume's "false Stitches," explaining that "it was huddl'd up in such hast, (out of a desire to have it joyned to my *Booke* of Poems) as I took not so much time, as

to consider throughly; For I writ it in less then three weekes; and yet for all my hast, it came a weeke too short of the Presse. Besides my desire (to have those Works Printed in *England,* which I wrote in *England,* before I leave England) perswaded me to send it to the Presse, without a further inlargement" (10-11). On the last page of *Poems and Fancies* she advertises her hastily concluded work, writing "Reader, I have a little *Tract* of *Philosophicall Fancies* in *Prose,* which will not be long before it appear in the world" (214). *The World's Olio,* which was not published until 1655, was actually begun in 1650 (see *Philosophicall Fancies,* 90).

27. In the preface to *The World's Olio* (1655) she acknowledges having begun the volume five years earlier: "This Book, most of it was written five years since, and was lockt up in a Trunk as if it had been buried in a Grave, but, when I came out of England, I gave it a Resurrection" (sig. A3v).

28. Notable exceptions are Robert Kargon's *Atomism in England* and Meyer's *The Scientific Lady in England.*

29. Woolf, "The Duchess of Newcastle," 74.

30. J. Evelyn, 12 May 1656, *Diary,* 3:173; Charles Trawick Harrison traces the influence of the ancient atomists in English literature: "Except, then, for the quaint work of [Nicholas] Hill, the apparently unremarked sympathies of Bacon, and the sensitive criticism of Sir Thomas Browne, the ancient Atomists produced little effect on English thought of the first half of the seventeenth century. The generation of Hobbes and Boyle, and of the establishment of the Royal Society, is another matter." Harrison, "The Ancient Atomists," 20. More recently, Howard Jones has argued, "It is fair to say, then, that during the sixteenth and early seventeenth centuries, Epicurus was known to the general English public almost exclusively in his medieval role as the champion of sensual living, and we look in vain for evidence of any comprehensive and coherent grasp of the Epicurean philosophy as a whole." See H. Jones, *The Epicurean Tradition,* 187.

31. Charleton, *The Darknes of Atheism,* 40-43.

32. For Cavendish's materialist monism, see chapter 5. The term "sea-change" is Jones's. He notes that in the process of purging Epicurean doctrine of offending elements, Gassendi changed it "from a purely materialist and mechanistic system in which divine power is expressly denied a creative or operational role" to "one in which the immaterial is preserved as an essential element and God placed at the very centre." H. Jones, *The Epicurean Tradition,* 180. Gassendi's Epicurean works are as follows: *De vita et moribus Epicuri libri octo; Animadversiones in decimum librum Diogenis Laertii;* and *Philosophiae Epicuri syntagma.* On Gassendi's Christianized atomism see Margaret J. Osler, "Fortune, Fate, and Divination: Gassendi's Voluntarist Theology and the Baptism of Epicureanism," in Osler, *Atoms, Pneuma, and Tranquillity,* 155-74.

33. Charleton, *Physiologia Epicuro-Gassendo-Charltoniana,* 126; René Descartes, *Principles of Philosophy,* in *The Philosophical Writings of Descartes,* 1:240. Robert Kargon summarizes the three types of atoms in Descartes's system: "a fine dust which gets between the interstices of larger corpuscles and permits no void, larger but still subtile round particles (*matière subtile* or aether) and, finally, relatively larger particles composing gross matter." Kargon, *Atomism in England,* 64. All natural phenomena, for Descartes, could be explained in terms

of matter and motion. That motion was bestowed upon atoms by God.

34. Howard Jones emphasizes that Hutchinson's translation is the first English translation and dates it to the late 1640s or early 1650s, using as evidence her claim that she "turned it into English in a roome where my children practiced the severall quallities they were taught with their Tutors." H. Jones, *The Epicurean Tradition,* 258 n. 34. Hutchinson was married in 1638 and had children soon afterward. See also the following articles: Wiess, "Dating Mrs. Hutchinson's Translation of Lucretius"; Munro, "Mrs. Lucie Hutchinson's Translation of Lucretius," 121-39.

One of the interesting moments in Hutchinson's lengthy apology for having translated Lucretius is that she claims to have translated him "only out of youthful curiosity to understand things I heard so much discourse of at second hand." *Memoirs,* 400. Her claim substantiates Stephen Clucas's argument that interest in atomism in England was not entirely dormant until Gassendi's atomism was reintroduced in the 1650s. See Clucas, "The Atomism of the Cavendish Circle," 247. Nevertheless, Cavendish's exploration of atomism remains the boldest early exposition to appear in English.

35. Hutchinson, *Memoirs,* 2:401; J. Evelyn, *On the First Book of T. Lucretius,* sig. A8v. Two recent attempts to discuss Milton's use of atomism in his description of Chaos include Norton, "'The Rising World,'" 91-110; and J. Rogers, *The Matter of Revolution,* 103-43. Both accounts are suggestive, but neither is entirely satisfactory. Milton's Christianized version of Chaos was consistent with those of other Renaissance writers. See, for example, Du Bartas, *Divine Weeks* (London, 1608), 8. Cf. Milton, *Paradise Lost,* bk. 2, ll. 896-903.

36. For a fuller discussion of Boyle's and Newton's cultural work of Christianizing atomism, see Jacob, *The Cultural Meaning of the Scientific Revolution.*

37. Cavendish, *Poems and Fancies,* 163 (this page number refers to the actual page 163, which appears as 'sig. Aa2r' before the pagination begins again between page 160 and an incorrectly numbered page 141).

38. Nicolson, *Voyages to the Moon,* 66; Richard Waller, *The Life of Dr. Robert Hooke,* in Gunther, *Early Science in Oxford,* 6:9.

39. Sarasohn, "Science Turned Upside Down," 293; Cavendish, *Observations Upon Experimental Philosophy* (1668), sig. h3v.

40. Cavendish, *The World's Olio* (1655), 1.

41. Ibid., 46.

42. Walter Charleton to Margaret Cavendish, 7 May 1667, *Collection of Letters and Poems,* 111.

43. See Grant, *Margaret the First,* 196; Kargon, *Atomism in England,* 75.

44. That this proverb captured her imagination is evident in the fact that she repeats it in *Observations upon Experimental Philosophy* (1668), 68.

45. John Dryden articulated a similar thought twenty-five years later in the dedication of *Aureng-Zebe:* "As I am a man, I must be changeable: and sometimes the gravest of us all are so, even upon ridiculous accidents. Our minds are perpetually wrought on by the temperament of our bodies." Dryden, *Aureng-Zebe* (London, 1676, sig. a1r-v).

46. Cavendish, *The World's Olio* (1653), 116. Cf. Godwin, *The Man in the*

Moone: "That there should be Antipodes was once thought as great a Paradox as now that the Moon should bee habitable. But the knowledge of this may seeme more properly reserv'd for this our discovering age: In which our Galilaeusses, can by advantage of their spectacles gaze the Sunne into spots, & descry mountaines in the Moon" (sig. A4r-A4v).

47. Cavendish, *The World's Olio,* 139.

48. See chapter 5, the section titled "Robert Hooke's Inductive Project: *Micrographia.*"

49. See "A Condemning Treatise of Atomes" in *Philosophical and Physical Opinions* (1655), sig. A3v. See also Sarasohn, "Science Turned Upside Down," 297; Clucas, "The Atomism of the Cavendish Circle," 260.

4. "No House But My Mind"

1. Cavendish, "A Condemning Treatise of Atomes," in *Philosophical and Physical Opinions* (1655), sig. a3v.

2. Cavendish, *Philosophical and Physical Opinions* (1663), sig. C2r. Cavendish's rejection of "the Dancing and Wandering and Dusty motion of Atoms" sounds similar to Hutchinson's rejection of the "casual, irrational dance of atoms." But whereas Hutchinson objected to the Epicurean emphasis on chance rather than divine plan as the explanation for all things, Cavendish's objections to atomism proceeded from what she saw as the democratic political implications of atomism, which, by threatening hierarchy, led to an anarchic political system. See Hutchinson, *Memoirs,* 2:401.

John Rogers in *The Matter of Revolution* argues that Cavendish's "physical vision functions most powerfully as a utopia of female rule" (202). In order to read her natural philosophy as an embodiment of what he calls a "liberatory" discourse, he argues that her natural philosophy "simply never descends from the airy realm of scientific theory to the mundane world of political philosophy" (204). Such a claim is called into question, however, by Cavendish's repeated recourse to analogies between the physical world and the political world.

3. Cavendish, *Philosophical and Physical Opinions* (1663), sig. C2r-C2v.

4. For discussions of Hobbes's frontispiece, see K. Brown, "The Artist of the *Leviathan* Title-Page"; K. Brown, "Thomas Hobbes and the Title-Page of *Leviathan*"; and Rogow, *Thomas Hobbes,* 155-60. Similarities between Oliver Cromwell's face and the face of the sovereign on Hobbes's frontispiece led some to conclude that *Leviathan* supported Cromwell's bid for power. For a refutation of this claim, see Goldsmith, "Hobbes's Ambiguous Politics."

5. Jacob and Raylor, "Opera and Obedience," esp. 216. Both Davenant's *Gondibert* and Newcastle's *Advice* to Charles II are heavily indebted to Hobbes; both focus squarely on the problem of maintaining public order.

6. Rogow writes that "Hobbes's influence on the duchess is unknown, but there can be no doubt of his influence on Newcastle." Arnold Rogow and Thomas P. Slaughter argue that Newcastle's *Advice* is heavily indebted to Hobbes. See Rogow, *Thomas Hobbes,* 118; Slaughter, *Newcastle's Advice to Charles II,* xiii. See

also Anzilotti, *An English Prince;* Conal Condren, "Casuistry to Newcastle: 'The Prince' in the World of the Book," in Phillipson and Skinner, *Political Discourse.*

7. Hobbes, *Leviathan,* in *Works,* 3:113. Chapter numbers for citations to *Leviathan* are provided in the text.

8. Hobbes, *Works,* 3:41.

9. For Quentin Skinner, Hobbes was motivated to create a science of politics in large part because of his concern over the tradition of disputation and the pliability of human judgment it exposed. For Skinner's excellent account of Hobbes's complex response to Renaissance theories of eloquence, see his *Reason and Rhetoric,* 267-84.

10. Skinner, "Hobbes and His Disciples," 163. See also Malcolm, *The Correspondence of Thomas Hobbes,* 1:xxxiii.

11. Hobbes's recent biographer, Arnold Rogow, gives the difference in age between Newcastle and Thomas Hobbes as four years. Geoffrey Trease has, however, convincingly suggested that Newcastle's christening date—16 December 1593—is evidence that he was born not in 1592 as had traditionally been thought but in 1593. Hobbes was born 5 April 1588, making their difference in age closer to five years. See Trease, *Portrait of a Cavalier,* 18. See also Rogow, *Thomas Hobbes,* 110. For Newcastle's date of baptism see also E.B. Fryde, D.E. Greenway, S. Porter, and I. Roy, eds., *Handbook of British Chronology* (London: Offices of the Royal Historical Society, 1986), 472.

12. Hobbes to William Cavendish, 26 Jan. 1634, in Malcolm, *The Correspondence of Thomas Hobbes,* 1:19.

13. Rogow cites Newcastle's cool treatment by the court of Charles I as one reason for Hobbes's decision to remain in the Devonshire household in 1636. Newcastle had hoped to become governor to the Prince of Wales, but his appointment was not announced until March 1638. Rogow adds that the Devonshire household may have become more attractive as some of Hobbes's domestic duties were replaced with "less menial, more respectable chores" and as the third earl "turn[ed] his attention to the creation of a remarkable library." *Thomas Hobbes,* 112. A brief review of the acquaintance between Hobbes and Newcastle can also be found in Malcolm, *The Correspondence of Thomas Hobbes,* 2:812-15.

14. Hobbes, "Autobiography," 26.

15. Hobbes, "The Optiques." In the dedication to Newcastle, Hobbes wrote, "that which I have writt of it, is grounded especially upon that which about 16 yeares since I affirmed to your Lordship at Welbeck, that light is a fancy in the minde, caused by motion in the braine" (f. 3r). This identifies the year of their discussion of light and optics as 1630.

16. Hobbes published *Humane Nature: or The Fundamental Elements of Policie* in English in 1650. Cavendish's reading of Hobbes is particularly evident in *Philosophical Letters* (1664), where she provides frequent citations to both *Leviathan* (1651) and to *Elements of Philosophy. The First Section, Concerning Body* (1656), which was the English translation of Hobbes's *De Corpore.* See Cavendish, *Philosophical Letters,* 1-97.

17. Thomas Hobbes to Margaret Cavendish, 9 Feb. 1662, in *Collection of Letters and Poems,* 67-8; Malcolm, *The Correspondence of Thomas Hobbes,* 2:524.

18. Hobbes's influence on Davenant's theory of the imagination is well known. See Jacob and Raylor, "Opera and Obedience"; Thorpe, *The Aesthetic Theory of Thomas Hobbes;* Dowlin, *Sir William Davenant's Gondibert.*

19. The *Preface* is reprinted in Gladish's edition of *Gondibert.* See Davenant, *Gondibert,* 3. See also Sharpe, *Criticism and Compliment,* 103.

20. Condren, "Casuistry to Newcastle," 164-86. I would neither want to insist that Newcastle's *Advice* is purely Hobbesian nor that Margaret Cavendish was unfamiliar on some level with the political thought of Machiavelli; rather, I explore Cavendish's fear of the printed word as a fear she shared with Hobbes.

21. Slaughter, *Newcastle's Advice to Charles II,* 20. The argument that a surplus of learned men was a threat to government had been in the air throughout the seventeenth century. Noting that admissions to the two universities tripled between 1560 and 1590, David Riggs observes that "by the last decade of the sixteenth century, however, the demand for new Bachelors of Arts had long since been satisfied, and the surplus graduates, many of whom congregated in London, made up a small but highly visible group of discontented intellectuals.... Men in positions of authority recognized that such persons constituted a threat to the commonwealth." *Ben Jonson: A Life,* 55-56.

22. Aubrey, *Brief Lives,* 154; Hobbes, "Autobiography," 24.

23. Cavendish, *Nature's Pictures* (1656), sig. C3v; Cavendish, *Philosophical and Physical Opinions* (1655), sig. B2v.

24. Hobbes, "Autobiography," 24; see also Aubrey, *Brief Lives,* 156; Alan Ryan, "Hobbes's Political Philosophy," in Sorell, *The Cambridge Companion to Hobbes,* 209.

25. As cited in Hibbert, *Cavaliers and Roundheads,* 293.

26. Cavendish, *The World's Olio* (1655), 163. Her concern for the problem of subjectivity in natural philosophy becomes particularly evident in her response to the experimental philosophy of Robert Hooke. See chapter 5.

27. In addition to naming two of his books *Leviathan* and *Behemoth,* both beasts mentioned in Job, Hobbes chose to inscribe the title page of *Leviathan* with a quotation from Job that constitutes a significant part of God's response to Job: "Non est potestas super terram quae comparetur ei." That response emphasizes the inadequacy of trying to explain cosmic order in human terms. See Job 41.

28. Mintz, *The Hunting of Leviathan,* 28. Mintz's note on the use of the term "Erastian" is worth repeating. Mintz uses the term "as it was commonly applied to Hobbes in the seventeenth century, and not as it was originally intended by Erastus" (28 n. 3).

29. Cavendish, *Philosophical and Physical Opinions* (1655), sig. B2r; Cavendish, *The World's Olio* (1655), 39.

30. Cavendish, *Life of . . . William Cavendishe* (1667), 162.

31. Ibid., 14.

32. William Cavendish, *A Letter of Instructions,* f. 111v; Condren, "Casuistry to Newcastle, 168.

33. Cavendish, *Sociable Letters,* 356-57.

34. Cavendish was particularly nervous about gazettes. In *The Life of . . .*

William Cavendishe, she records her husband's concern that "it is a great Error in a State to have all Affairs put into Gazettes (for it over-heats the people's brains, and makes them neglect their private Affairs, by over-busying themselves with State-business)" (173). In *Sociable Letters,* she warned that the gazettes contained "more Falshoods than Truth" (340). William Cavendish attacked newspapers in his *Advice to Charles II* (presented to Charles probably around 1659). There, he advised that "there is an other Error that doth over heate your people Extreamly And doth your Majestie much hurte, which is that Every man now Is become a state man, & itt is merly the weekly Corants, Both att home & a broad, therefore they should bee forbid Eyther Domesticke or forayne news, as also such fellowes As Captin Rosingame, that made £500 a yeare with writing Newes to severall persons, this did as much hurte as the other if not more, for in a letter hee might bee bolder Then they Durste bee in printe this too, not only to bee For-biden absolutly butt to bee punisht, severly if they offend in this, kinde, this will so Coole the nation & quiett state speritts, as your Majestie & your subiects will finde greate Ease in itt,—so all our discourse will be of Hunting & Hawkeing, Boling, Cocking, & such things, & bee Ever ready To serve your Majestie." Slaughter, *Newcastle's Advice to Charles II,* 56. Slaughter argues that Newcastle's *Advice* was influenced by Hobbes's *Leviathan* (xiii); for arguments that the *Advice* is essentially Machiavellian, see Anzilotti, *An English Prince,* 59-75; Condren, "Casuistry to Newcastle," 164-86.

35. In *The Life of . . . William Cavendishe* (1667), Cavendish dates her extended reading as occurring after the Restoration: "After I was returned with your Lordship into my Native Country, and led a retired Country life, I applied my self to the reading of Philosophical Authors, of purpose to learn those names and words of Art that are used in Schools" (sig. a2r).

36. Cavendish, *Philosophical Letters* (1664), sig. a1r.

37. Cavendish, *The Life of . . . William Cavendishe,* 167.

38. Cavendish, *Orations of Divers Sorts* (1662), 63. In some copies of this volume, the imprint date has been altered in ink to 1663.

39. Cavendish, *Sociable Letters* (1664), 54.

40. Ibid., 84-5. The method of book 1 seems to be reflected in the volume's frontispiece engraving by Abraham van Diepenbeeck. There, the Newcastle family is portrayed sitting at a long rectangular table. Either because of the animation of the storytelling or because of the excessive fire in the fireplace, a steward is in the process of opening a window, a suggestion that the environment has become overheated. Whether the engraving is a joke played by the artist on his eccentric patron or whether he was instructed as to the method of book 1, there is an interesting match between the engraving and book 1's narrative frame. Both represent troubled atomistic systems.

41. For interesting discussions of the estates, see Goulding, *Bolsover Castle;* Turberville, *A History of Welbeck Abbey;* Girouard, *Robert Smythson & the Elizabethan Country House.* Cavendish describes the ruined estates in *The Life of . . . William Cavendishe* (1667), 90-107.

42. Cavendish, *Orations* (1662), sig. a3v.

43. Scholars have been troubled by Cavendish's problematic feminism. Hilda

Smith in *Reason's Disciples* notes the "interpretive problems" posed by the fact that Cavendish's feminism is "at once the most radical and far-reaching and the most contradictory . . . She appears to have understood, better than any of her sisters, the multifaceted nature of women's oppression . . . [yet] she could also be as critical of her sisters as the staunchest misogynist" (75-76). Others, notably Catherine Gallagher, Rachel Trubowitz, and Sandra Sherman, try to account for Cavendish's problematic feminism by suggesting that it collided in various ways with her Filmerian ideology. The evidence suggests, however, that Cavendish's primary interest was in the disputatious nature of the human mind and that she viewed her own lucid feminist observations as potentially disruptive to the stability of the body politic, despite or perhaps even because of their accuracy. In addition to Smith, see Gallagher, "Embracing the Absolute"; Trubowitz, "The Reenchantment of Utopia"; Sherman, "Trembling Texts."

44. Cavendish, *Sociable Letters,* sig. c1v-c2r.

45. For Hobbes's comparable response to Renaissance theories of eloquence, see Skinner, *Reason and Rhetoric,* 267-84.

46. Hobbes, *The Art of Rhetoric* (1637), in *Works,* 6:424.

47. Cavendish, *Observations upon Experimental Philosophy: to which is added, the Description of a New Blazing World* (1666). *The Description of a New Blazing World,* hereafter referred to simply as *Blazing World,* first appeared in 1666, both separately (as *the Description of a New World, Called the Blazing-World*) and bound together with *Observations.*

48. For a more extensive discussion of *Blazing World,* see chapter five.

49. Cavendish, *Philosophical Letters,* 47-48.

50. Hobbes, *Works,* 3:326-27.

51. Cavendish, *Poems and Fancies,* sig. A7r.

5. RATIONALISM VERSUS EXPERIMENTALISM

1. Douglas Grant, for example, argues that the "naturalness" of the epistolary form "allowed [Cavendish] to give a clearer and fairer impression of her own character than in any of her other works." *Margaret the First,* 168. Similarly, James Fitzmaurice reads much of this volume autobiographically, locating its focus on the theme of marriage. See Fitzmaurice, *Margaret Cavendish,* xiii.

2. Cavendish's *Sociable Letters* discusses exile (196) and life in Antwerp, including riots (359), national "Pastimes" of Antwerp (405), and trouble Cavendish had with her maids (249, 311). The letters also discuss the Restoration (169, 343) and the frustration of trying to recover and repair estates (449). Letters are included in which she first envisions writing *Orations* (367) and *Philosophical Letters* (452). The letters are not ordered chronologically, and they seem to be written from two different places: one group is written from a city, probably Antwerp, where neighbors are so close that a garden door "Belongs to our Garden, but Opens into" the neighbor's garden (249); the other group of letters is written from a more isolated country estate, probably Welbeck, where she is free from "the several Noises that are made in Populous Cities" (449).

3. Cavendish, *Sociable Letters,* sig. c2r-c2v.

4. Grant advances Elizabeth Chaplain, later Elizabeth Topp, as a candidate for the correspondent. Many of the letters note the physical distance between correspondents, however, which would seem to eliminate Elizabeth Topp, who was part of Cavendish's household. Grant also argues that the letters "were actually addressed to someone and were not simply self-communings." This seems unlikely, given the monologic tone of the letters. *Margaret the First,* 167.

5. James Fitzmaurice has argued that since the initials frequently correspond, sometimes in transposed form, to her name, to her maiden name, to her husband's name or, as in the example cited above, to names of her characters such as the Lady Sanspareille, that some "of the characters were actual people more or less carefully hidden behind initials and anagrams." *Margaret Cavendish,* xii. This seems too broad a claim, one that ignores both Cavendish's social isolation and her interest in speculative activity.

Read as fiction, *Sociable Letters* can be seen as a precursor to the epistolary novel. B.G. MacCarthy places *Sociable Letters* firmly in the tradition of the epistolary novel, citing the observation of the nineteenth-century critic J.J. Juserand that "many collections of imaginary letters had, as we have seen, been published before, but never had the use to which they could be put been better foreseen by any predecessor of Richardson." *The Female Pen,* 245.

6. Charles I to the Prince of Wales, 29 Nov. 1648, in Petrie, *Letters, Speeches and Proclamations,* 240; Sharpe, *The Personal Rule,* 190.

7. William Cavendish, "A Letter of Instructions"; for the *Advice,* see chapter 4, note 6.

8. Cavendish, *The Life of . . . William Cavendishe* (1667), 86. Cavendish describes the effect on her husband of seeing the ruined estates: "And although his Patience and Wisdom is such, that I never perceived him sad or discontented for his own Losses and Misfortunes, yet when he beheld the ruines of that Park, I observed him troubled, though he did little express it, onely saying, he had been in hopes it would not have been so much defaced as he found it, there being not one Timber-tree in it left for shelter" (92).

9. Ibid., 88. Cavendish describes the ruin in detail. Part of her description includes the following summary: "His two Houses Welbeck and Bolsover he found much out of repair, and this later half pull'd down, no furniture or any necessary Goods were left in them but some few Hangings and Pictures, which had been saved by the care and industry of his Eldest Daughter the Lady Cheiny" (91). See also chapter 4, note 41.

10. Sprat, *History,* 53.

11. Cavendish differed from her husband, who seems to have despaired of arriving at any conclusions at all when the subject was natural philosophy. In *Philosophical and Physical Opinions* (1663), he interjects the following claim: "This is my Opinion, which I think can as hardly be Disproved as Proved, since any Opinion may be Right or Wrong, for any thing that any body knows, for certainly there is none can make a Mathematical Demonstration of Natural Philosophy" (464). Newcastle's addendum does not appear in the 1655 edition of *Philosophical and Physical Opinions.* It suggests that he was hostile to the new

science's and to the Royal Society's interest in method. Although Cavendish shared her husband's skepticism toward the Royal Society, she called for a heightened awareness of the variety of internal realities, not for an abandonment of the enterprise of natural philosophy.

12. Hall, *Promoting Experimental Learning*, 11. Thomas Sprat suggested that a remedy to the nation's "Civil differences" could be found in "assembl[ing] in some calm, and indifferent things, especially Experiments." *History*, 426.

13. Hooke was appointed on 5 November 1662. See 'Espinasse, *Robert Hooke*, 1; Shapin and Schaffer, *Leviathan and the Air-Pump*, 235. The chief articles on Cavendish's encounters with the Royal Society are Mintz, "The Duchess of Newcastle's Visit to the Royal Society"; Meyer, *The Scientific Lady in England*, 1-15; Nicolson, *Pepys's Diary and the New Science*, 103-75; Kargon, *Atomism in England*, 63-76; Sarasohn, "Science Turned Upside Down."

14. Skinner, "Thomas Hobbes," esp. 233-34. See also the following books by Michael Hunter: *Science and Society; The Royal Society and its Fellows; Establishing the New Science; Science and the Shape of Orthodoxy.*

15. Shapin and Schaffer, *Leviathan and the Air-Pump*, 22, 32, 36, 129.

16. Hobbes, "Considerations on the Reputation, Loyalty, Manners, and Religion of Thomas Hobbes," in *Works*, 4:436-37.

17. The date on Henry Power's *Experimental Philosophy* is 1664, but the volume actually appeared in 1663.

18. John T. Harwood, "Rhetoric and Graphics in *Micrographia*," in Hunter and Schaffer, *Robert Hooke*, 147. See also Mulligan, "Robert Hooke and Certain Knowledge."

19. Gunther, *The Life and Work of Robert Hooke*, vol. 6 of *Early Science in Oxford*, 219. Nicolson, *Science and Imagination*, 163.

20. M. Hall, *Promoting Experimental Learning*, 52. For Hooke's empiricism see also Mulligan, "Robert Hooke and Certain Knowledge"; John Henry, "Robert Hooke, The Incongruous Mechanist," in Hunter and Schaffer, *Robert Hooke*, 149-80; C. Wilson, "Visual Surface and Visual Symbol"; Macintosh, "Perception and Imagination."

21. Harwood, "Rhetoric and Graphics," 142.

22. Bacon, *Works*, 4:54-55.

23. Jonathan Sawday discusses Charleton's and Digby's deployment of the machine metaphor in "The Mint at Segovia."

24. William Cavendish was created duke of Newcastle on 16 March 1665. See Trease, *Portrait of a Cavalier*, 193; Doubleday and de Walden, *The Complete Peerage*, 9:524. Charles II had written to his aging governor: "I have received yours by your son, and am resolved to grant your request. Send me therefore word what title you desire to have, or whether you will choose to keepe your old and leave the rest to me. I do not tell you I will despatch it tomorrow; you must leave the time to me, to accommodate it to some other ends of myne; but the differing it shall not be long, nor with any circumstance that shall trouble you. I am glad you enjoy your health for I love you very well." Charles II to William Cavendish, 7 June 1664, Historical Manuscripts Commission, *Manuscripts of His Grace the Duke of Portland*, 2 (1893): 145.

25. Shapin and Schaffer make a claim that suggests that Cavendish was right to question the Royal Society's utilitarian claims: "From the best modern historical research it now appears that none of the utilitarian promissory notes [of the Royal Society] could be, or were, cashed in the seventeenth century." *Leviathan and the Air-Pump*, 340 n. 11.

26. Gerald Dennis Meyer notes that Cavendish "was not alone in her belief that 'Concave and Convex glasses, and the like . . . represent the figure of an Object . . . very deformed and misshaped: also a Glass that is flaw'd, crack'd, or broke . . . will present numerous pictures of one Object.' Bad glass meant bad reflection and refraction, as Robert Hooke, curator of the Royal Society, well knew." *The Scientific Lady in England*, 4.

27. Hooke's concern regarding the problem of obtaining good microscopes and telescopes is worth quoting in full: "The Glasses I used were of our English make, but though very good of the kind, yet far short of what might be expected, could we once find a way of making Glasses Elliptical, or of some more true shape; for though both Microscopes, and Telescopes, as they now are, will magnifie an Object about a thousand thousand times bigger then it appears to the naked eye; yet the Apertures of the Object-glasses are so very small, that very few Rays are admitted, and even of those few there are so many false, that the Object appears dark and indistinct: And indeed these inconveniences are such, as seem inseparable from Spherical Glasses, even when most exactly made; but the way we have hitherto made use of for that purpose is so imperfect, that there may be perhaps ten wrought before one be made tolerably good, and most of those ten perhaps every one differing in goodness one from another, which is an Argument, that the way hitherto used is, at least, very uncertain. So that these Glasses have a double defect; the one, that very few of them are exactly true wrought; the other, that even of those that are best among them, none will admit a sufficient number of Rayes to magnifie the Object beyond a determinate bigness." *Micrographia*, sig. d2v. He proceeds to describe the corrections he devised in order to compensate for the glasses' defects, chiefly through lighting.

28. 'Espinasse, *Robert Hooke*, 57.

29. Hooke, *Micrographia*, 161-62; 'Espinasse, *Robert Hooke*, 57.

30. Carolyn Merchant in *The Death of Nature* attributes to the scientific revolution the transformed view of the universe from organism to mechanism. Although Robert Hooke's contribution to this transformation is not in doubt, the consistency of his mechanism has been called into question recently by John Henry, who finds in Hooke's mechanism evidence of congruity, incongruity, and other "active principles." Henry's argument is persuasive, but it does not alter the fact that Cavendish would have perceived Hooke as a mechanist. See Henry's "Robert Hooke, The Incongruous Mechanist."

31. In the revised 1668 version of this passage, she refers to her work properly as *Observations Upon Experimental Philosophy*, thereby highlighting its status as a critique of the experimental philosophy rather than as an exercise in experimental philosophy.

32. This is actually page 90. The pages in the volume are misnumbered.

33. Lewis, *The Abolition of Man*, 63-87.

34. Cavendish, *Philosophical Letters,* 238; Gelbart, "The Intellectual Development of Walter Charleton," 150; M. Hunter, *Science and Society,* 22.

35. M. Hunter, *Science and Society,* 28-29; Gelbart, "The Intellectual Development of Walter Charleton," 150; Rolleston, "Walter Charleton"; Walter Page, "The Reaction to Aristotle in Seventeenth-Century Biological Thought," in Underwood, *Science Medicine and History,* 1:489-509. Useful studies of Charleton's interest in mechanism include Kargon, "The Acceptance of Epicurean Atomism in England"; and Sawday, "The Mint at Segovia." Charleton's translation of Van Helmont, *A ternary of paradoxes: the magnetick cure of wounds* (1650), for example, "contained information about the sympathetic cure of wounds communicated by Sir Kenelm Digby." Rolleston, "Walter Charleton," 405.

36. Both Cavendish and her husband claim that she learned physical terms, which some readers used as evidence that she plagiarized her work, from her physicians. In his interesting "Epistle" prefaced to the 1655 edition of *The Philosophical and Physical Opinions,* Newcastle writes that "the great Mystery of these Physical terms, I am almost ashamed to tell you; not that we have been ever sickly, but by Melancholy often supposed our selves to have such diseases as we had not, and learned Physitians were too wise to put us out of that humour, and so these tearms cost us much more then they are Worth, and I hope there is no body so malicious, as to envie our bargain, neither truly do I repent my bargain, since Physitians are the most rational men I have convert with all, and my worthy and very good friends, and truly this Lady never convert with any Physitian of any disease, but what she thought she had her self, neither hath she convert with many of that profession" (sig. A2r-A2v). Cavendish herself echoed this claim within the same volume, confessing "it is true I have convert with Physitians more then any other learned profession, yet not so much as to increase my understanding, although more then was advantagious for my health" (sig. B4r).

37. Cavendish, *The Philosophical and Physical Opinions* (1655), sig. B4r.

38. Waite, *Writings of Paracelsus the Great,* 2:269; Cavendish, *Philosophical Letters,* 40.

39. Cavendish, *Philosophical Letters,* 147.

40. Cavendish, *Philosophical and Physical Opinions* (1663), 2.

41. Cavendish, *Philosophical and Physical Opinions* (1663), 4; Cavendish, *Philosophical Letters,* 167, 168.

42. Hooke suggested that eventually the imagination and the soul could be discovered to be mechanically driven faculties: "Nor do I imagine that the skips from the one to another will be found very great, if beginning from fluidity, or body without any form, we descend gradually, till we arrive at the highest form of a brute Animal's Soul, making the steps or foundations of our Enquiry, Fluidity, Orbiculation, Fixation, Angulization, or Crystallization Germination or Ebullition, Vegetation, Plantanimation, Animation, Sensation, Imagination." *Micrographia,* 127. Cavendish objected to the mechanized view of the world Hooke presented.

43. Cavendish, *Philosophical Letters,* 111. Cf. Damasio, *Descartes' Error,* 247-52. Damasio also contests Descartes's dualism and its modern variants, arguing first that Descartes wrongly "persuaded biologists to adopt, to this day, clock-

work mechanics as a model for life processes," and secondly, that the *cogito* "illustrates precisely the opposite of what I [Damasio] believe to be true about the origins of mind and about the relation between mind and body. . . . We are, and then we think, and we think only inasmuch as we are, since thinking is indeed caused by the structures and operations of being" (248).

44. Cavendish, *Philosophical Letters,* sig. b2v, 43.

45. For Boyle's religious interests, see Shapin and Schaffer, *Leviathan and the Air-Pump,* 318-19. Cavendish, *Philosophical and Physical Opinions* (1663), sig. b2v; Cavendish, *Philosophical Letters,* 12.

46. The volumes were first published both together as one volume and separately as individual volumes in 1666. Each of these volumes was republished in 1668.

47. R. Jones, *Ancients and Moderns,* 244-48; Bacon, *Works,* 3:321 (see also 3:221 and 3:223); Glanvill, *The Vanity of Dogmatizing,* 140. Glanvill's attitude toward the new science was inconsistent, urging both a pessimistic skepticism and an "awestruck admiration for the advances of seventeenth-century science." See Stephen Medcalf's useful introduction to his edition of *The Vanity of Dogmatizing: The Three 'Versions' by Joseph Glanvill* (Hove, England: Harvester Press, 1970), xvii.

48. Glanvill, *The Vanity of Dogmatizing,* 178. See also R. Jones, *Ancients and Moderns,* 143. For an interesting discussion of the religious concerns triggered by the new science, see Jacob, *The Cultural Meaning of the Scientific Revolution.*

49. Power, *Experimental Philosophy,* sig. b2r, a3v, b1v.

50. Shapin and Schaffer, *Leviathan and the Air-Pump,* 65.

51. The pagination begins over again with a new title page for *Blazing World* on what would otherwise be page 393 of *Observations.*

52. Sylvia Bowerbank argues that *Blazing World* is "Cavendish's response to her failure as a natural philosopher [which included] retreat[ing] into fantasy." "The Spider's Delight," 402. This reading entirely overlooks Cavendish's satire of the Royal Society in *Blazing World* and echoes standard complaints regarding Cavendish's regrettable lack of education. Catherine Gallagher places *Blazing World* within the political context of Restoration London, but disregards its scientific context. See her "Embracing the Absolute." More recently, *Blazing World* has been read, problematically, as a precursor to the utopian tradition in literature. In an interesting article, Rachel Trubowitz argues that Cavendish "reclaimed" utopia "for the royalist side as an instrument by which the magic of monarchy, custom, and tradition, which the Puritans had tried to eradicate through utopian visions of rationalized politics, culture, and religion, could be reinstated." "The Reenchantment of Utopia," 236. As I argue in chapter 4, however, Cavendish critiques Erastianism in *Blazing World.* Kate Lilley also places *Blazing World* within the genre of utopian literature in her introduction to her edition of *Blazing World and Other Writings* (New York: Penguin, 1994), xxiii. Khanna argues in "The Subject of Utopia" that *Blazing World* affords "multiple figurations of female power" (30), and figures "a multiple subjectivity and connections between self-assertion and sharing" (33). Yet, though there are utopian moments in *Blazing World,* Khanna overlooks the fact that the text yields no utopian readings with-

out immediately problematizing them. Sandra Sherman, like Catherine Gallagher, argues that *Blazing World* reflects a particular moment in political history: "Cavendish, writing during the decline of the Commonwealth and into the Restoration, reflects in her preoccupation with authorship a nostalgia for absolutism, tempered unconsciously by a revision in the idea of absolute monarchy." "Trembling Texts," 186. That Cavendish is interested in the philosophical problems of subjectivity is clear; that she presents any sort of utopian vision, other than to argue problematically for solipsistic retreat to the worlds of the mind, is much less clear.

53. Jean Gagen usefully contextualizes Cavendish's interest in fame by placing it in the tradition of "Renaissance humanism out of which it arose." "Honor and Fame," 520. Missing from Gagen's intelligent account of Cavendish's immersion in Renaissance humanism is Cavendish's interest in the new science. James Fitzmaurice argues cogently that Cavendish "intended to be understood as a harmless eccentric so that she could protect herself from criticism." "Fancy and the Family," 202.

54. Dolores Paloma, in "Margaret Cavendish," argues that *Blazing World* allows Cavendish to imagine "women fighting battles and leading armies, ruling nations, and engaging in architecture, navigation, mining, and physical exercise," heroic masculine professions from which women were generally prohibited from engaging (56). Although this is true, it does not fully account for the strangeness or self-referentiality of *Blazing World*. Linda Payne argues briefly in "Dramatic Dreamscape" that *Blazing World* exposes Cavendish's "view of dreams and creativity," but she does not develop this idea fully (26).

55. Francis Mercury Van Helmont discussed cabalist scholarship with Henry More and Anne Finch, viscountess Conway, at length in the 1670s. See Coudert, "A Cambridge Platonist's Kabbalist Nightmare"; Nicolson, *Conway Letters*, 309-77 (page references are to the original edition).

56. This passage appears in the "Epilogue to the Reader" that immediately follows the text of *Blazing World*.

57. Gallagher, "Embracing the Absolute," 31-32. Gallagher's interesting article overlooks the fact that *Blazing World* is a satire of the Royal Society and of experimentalism.

58. Cavendish, *The World's Olio* (1655), 177.

59. Birch, *The History of the Royal Society,* 2:176.

60. Pepys, 30 May 1667, *Diary,* 8:243.

61. Birch, *The History of the Royal Society,* 2:177. For a thorough and lucid discussion of Boyle's use of the air pump, see Shapin and Schaffer, *Leviathan and the Air-Pump,* 44-45, 49-55, 226-81.

62. Cavendish, *Observations* (1666), sig. b1r.

63. Marjorie Nicolson suggests that the "microscopical observations were, as always, shown by Robert Hooke, probably with the assistance of some of the beautiful enlargements in the *Micrographia,* which had recently appeared." *Pepys's Diary and the New Science,* 110. Hooke undoubtedly presented the microscopical observations, but it seems unlikely that he would have trotted out *Micrographia* before its greatest critic.

64. Birch, *The History of the Royal Society,* 2:177.

65. J. Evelyn, 30 May 1667, *Diary,* 3:483; Newsletter, 30 May 1667, Historical Manuscripts Commission, *Manuscripts of S.H. Le Fleming* (1890): 49.

66. Pepys, 30 May 1667, *Diary,* 8:243. Pepys's record of the meeting is the fullest extant record of Cavendish's visit: "Anon comes the Duchesse, with her women attending her; among others, that Ferrabosco of whom so much talk is, that her lady would bid her show her face and kill the gallants. She is endeed black and hath good black little eyes, but otherwise but a very ordinary woman I do think; but they say sings well. The Duchesse hath been a good comely woman; but her dress to antic and her deportment so unordinary, that I do not like her at all, nor did I hear her say anything that was worth hearing, but that she was full of admiration, all admiration. Several fine experiments were shown her of Colours, Loadstones, Microscope, and of liquors: among others, of one that did while she was there turn a piece of roasted mutton into pure blood—which was very rare—here was Mr. Moore of Cambrige, whom I had not seen before, and I was glad to see him—as also a very pretty black boy that run up and down the room, somebody's child in Arundell-house. After they had shown her many experiments, and she cried still she was 'full of admiration,' she departed, being led out and in by several Lords that were there; among others, Lord George Barkely and the Earl of Carlisel and a very pretty young man, the Duke of Somersett" (8:243).

67. J. Evelyn, "Ballad," f. 131-32.

6. CONCLUSION

1. She was motivated to have the biography translated because, as she explained in *The Philosophical and Physical Opinions* (1655), Latin was "a general language through all Europe." Had she been fluent in Latin, she would have written all her work in Latin rather than in "my native Language, which goeth no further then the kingdom of England" (sig. a2r).

2. For the argument that Cavendish may have composed her plays much earlier than their dates of publication suggest, see "A Defamiliarized World: War and Exile," in chapter 2. Cavendish, *The Life of . . . William Cavendishe* (1667), sig. b1r.

3. William James, *Psychology: Briefer Course,* in *William James: Writings 1878-1899* (New York: Library of America, 1984), 24.

4. Taylor, *Sources of the Self,* 111.

5. Thomas Shadwell, *The Virtuoso,* ed. Marjorie Hope Nicolson and David Stuart Rodes (Lincoln: Univ. of Nebraska Press, 1966), V.ii. 58-62.

6. Goulding, *Margaret (Lucas) Duchess of Newcastle,* 25; Grant, *Margaret the First,* 239.

7. Cavendish, *The Philosophical and Physical Opinions* (1655), sig. B3r.

8. M. Hunter, *Establishing the New Science,* 17.

Appendix A

1. Grant, *Margaret the First,* 32; Mendelson, *The Mental World of Stuart Women,* 12; Jones, *A Glorious Fame,* 7. Francis Bickley claims that Cavendish was born "about 1624." *The Cavendish Family,* 104. Similarly, A.S. Turberville identifies the year of her birth as "1623 or 1624." *A History of Welbeck Abbey,* 118.

2. Wood, *Athenae Oxonienses,* 2:1114.

3. Goulding, *Margaret (Lucas), Duchess of Newcastle,* 4. See also Chester, *Registers of the Collegiate Church,* 182.

4. Cavendish, *A True Relation,* 369.

5. Cavendish, *Poems and Fancies* (1653), 155-56

Appendix B

1. Henry Jermyn, later earl of Saint Albans, secretary to Henrietta Maria.

2. William Widdrington, first Baron Widdrington of Blankney, loyal companion of Newcastle. He fought under Newcastle during the civil war and followed him to Hamburg and Paris. He followed Charles into Scotland in 1650 and into England in 1651, dying there in August after being wounded in battle. He is mentioned throughout *The Life of . . . William Cavendishe.*

3. Endymion Porter, groom of the bedchamber to Charles I.

4. Marie-Louise de Gonsague-Nevers married Vladislav VII of Poland on 8 November 1645. Henrietta Maria and her maids of honor attended the ceremony.

5. Elizabeth Browne, wife of Sir Richard Browne, English resident at the court of France, at whose chapel the marriage of the marquess of Newcastle and Margaret Lucas was celebrated. When Lady Browne died, her son-in-law, John Evelyn, wrote that she was "universally lamented, having been so obliging on all occasions to those who continually frequented her house in Paris, which was not only an hospital, but an asylum to all our persecuted and afflicted countrymen" (John Evelyn, 22 Sept. 1652, *Diary,* 2:63). That Lady Browne inspired the portrait of Mademoiselle Civility in Cavendish's *The Presence* seems evident from John Evelyn's claim that Newcastle "had obligation to my Wives mother, for his marriage" (Evelyn, 24 April 1667, *Diary,* 3:480-81).

6. John Cosin, later bishop of Durham, who served in Paris as chaplain to the Royalist exiles who belonged to the church of England.

Selected Bibliography

Manuscript Sources

Cavendish, William, Earl of Newcastle. "The Lord Newcastle to his Pupil Prince Charles, being a Letter of Instructions for his Studies, Conduct, & Behaviour." Harley 6988, ff. 111-14. British Library, London.

Evelyn, John. "Ballad." SP 29/450, ff. 131-32. Public Record Office, London.

Fanshawe, Anne. "Memoirs." MS Add 41161. British Library, London.

Hobbes, Thomas. "A Minute or first Draught of the Optiques in Two Parts." Harley 3360, ff. 1-372. British Library, London.

Lucas, Margaret. "Letters of Margaret Lucas to William Cavendish, Marquess of Newcastle." MS Add 70499, ff. 259-97. British Library, London.

Mayerne, Theodore. "Letters to William Cavendish." In *A Boke, Wherein is Contained Rare Minerall Receipts Collected at Paris from those who hath had great experiece* [sic] *of them*. Portland Manuscripts Pw V 90, ff. 14-28. University of Nottingham Library, University Park.

Primary Sources

Adams, Joseph Quincy, ed. *The Dramatic Records of Sir Henry Herbert, Master of the Revels, 1623-1673*. New Haven, Conn.: Yale Univ. Press, 1917.

Aubrey, John. *Aubrey's Brief Lives*. Ed. Oliver Lawson Dick. London: Secker and Warburg, 1949. Reprint, Ann Arbor: Univ. of Michigan Press, 1957.

———. *Letters Written by Eminent Persons in the Seventeenth and Eighteenth Centuries*. 2 vols. London, 1813.

Bacon, Francis. *The Works of Francis Bacon*. Ed. James Spedding, Robert Leslie Ellis, and Douglas Heath. 14 vols. New York, 1862-74.

Berington, Joseph, ed. *The Memoirs of Gregorio Panzani; Giving an Account of His Agency in England*. London, 1793.

Birch, Thomas. *The History of the Royal Society of London*. 4 vols. London, 1756.

Carlell, Lodowicke. *The Deserving Favorite*. London, 1629.

———. *The Passionate Lovers, a Tragi-Comedy*. London, 1655.

C[arter], M[atthew]. *A Most True and Exact Relation of That as Honourable as Unfortunate Expedition of Kent, Essex, and Colchester*. London, 1650.

Cavendish, Jane, and Lady Elizabeth Brackley. *The Concealed Fansyes*. PMLA 46 (Sept. 1931): 802-38.

Cavendish, Margaret. *CCXI Sociable Letters*. London, 1664.

———. *The Description of a New World, Called the Blazing-World*. London, 1666.

———. *The Description of a New World, Called the Blazing-World*. London, 1668.

———. *De Vita et Rebus Gestis Nobilissimi Illustrissimique Principis, Guilielmi Ducis Novo-Castrensis*. Trans. Walter Charleton. London, 1668.

———. *Grounds of Natural Philosophy: Divided into Thirteen Parts: with an Appendix Containing Five Parts*. London, 1668.

———. *The Life of the Thrice Noble, High, and Puissant Prince, William Cavendishe, Duke, Marquess, and Earl of Newcastle*. London, 1675.

———. *The Life of the Thrice Noble High and Puissant Prince William Cavendishe, Duke, Marquess, and Earl of Newcastle*. London, 1667.

———. *Nature's Pictures Drawn by Fancies Pencil to the Life*. London, 1656.

———. *Nature's Pictures Drawn by Fancies Pencil to the Life*. London, 1671.

———. *Observations Upon Experimental Philosophy: to which is added, the Description of a New Blazing World*. London, 1666.

———. *Observations Upon Experimental Philosophy: to which is added, the Description of a New Blazing World*. London, 1668.

———. *Orations of Divers Sorts, Accommodated to Divers Places*. London, 1662.

———. *Orations of Divers Sorts, Accommodated to Divers Places*. London, 1668.

———. *The Philosophical and Physical Opinions*. London, 1655.

———. *Philosophical and Physical Opinions*. London, 1663.

———. *Philosophical Letters, or, Modest Reflections upon some Opinions in Natural Philosophy: Maintained by Several Famous and Learned Authors of this Age, Expressed by way of Letters*. London, 1664.

———. *Philosophicall Fancies*. London, 1653.

———. *Playes*. London, 1662.

———. *Plays, Never Before Printed*. London, 1668.

———. *Poems and Fancies*. London, 1653.

———. *Poems and Phancies*. London, 1664.

———. *Poems, or, Several Fancies in Verse: with the Animal Parliament in Prose*. London, 1668.

———. *The World's Olio*. London, 1655.

———. *The World's Olio*. London, 1671.

Charleton, Walter. *The Darknes of Atheism Dispelled by the Light of Nature*. London, 1652.

———. *Epicurus's Morals*. London, 1670.

———. *The Immortality of the Human Soul, Demonstrated by the Light of Nature*. London, 1657.

———. *Physiologia Epicuro-Gassendo-Charltoniana: or, a Fabrick of Science Natural, upon the Hypothesis of Atoms Founded by Epicurus*. London, 1654.

A Collection of Letters and Poems: Written by several Persons of Honour and Learning, Upon divers Important Subjects, to the Late Duke and Dutchess of Newcastle. London, 1678.

Cosin, John. *A Collection of Private Devotions: in the Practise of the Ancient Church, Called the Houres of Prayer*. London, 1627.

Creech, Thomas. *Lucretius His Six Books on Epicurean Philosophy: and Manilius His Five Books*. London, 1700.

Davenant, William. *Sir William Davenant's Gondibert.* Ed. David F. Gladish. Oxford: Clarendon Press, 1971.

Davenant, William, and Inigo Jones. *Salmacida Spolia, a Masque.* London, 1640.

Descartes, René. *The Philosophical Writings of Descartes.* Ed. and trans. John Cottingham, Robert Stoothoff, and Dugald Murdoch. 2 vols. Cambridge: Cambridge Univ. Press, 1985.

Digby, Sir Kenelm. *Private Memoirs of Sir Kenelm Digby.* London, 1827.

Evelyn, John. *The Diary of John Evelyn.* 6 vols. Ed. Esmond Samuel de Beer. Oxford: Clarendon Press, 1955.

———. *An Essay on the First Book of T. Lucretius Carus De Rerum Natura. Interpreted and Made English Verse.* London, 1656.

Evelyn, Mary. "Letters." In *The Diary and Correspondence of John Evelyn,* ed. William Bray. 4 vols. London, 1862-1863.

Fontenelle, Bernard Le Bovier de. *A Discovery of New Worlds. From the French. Made English by Mrs. A. Behn,* London, 1688.

———. *New Dialogues of the Dead.* Trans. J.D., London, 1683.

Gassendi, Pierre. *Animadversiones in decimum librum Diogenis Laertii.* Lyon, 1649.

———. *De vita et moribus Epicuri libri octo.* Lyon, 1647.

———. *Philosophiae Epicuri syntagma.* Lyon, 1649.

Glanvill, Joseph. *The Vanity of Dogmatizing: Or Confidence in Opinions. Manifested in a Discourse of the Shortness and Uncertainty of Our Knowledge, And its Causes; With some Reflexions on Peripateticism; And an Apology for Philosophy.* London, 1661.

Godwin, Francis. *The Man in the Moone: or a Discourse of a Voyage Thither by Domingo Gonsales, the Speedy Messenger.* London, 1638.

Green, Mary Anne Everett. *Letters of Queen Henrietta Maria, Including Her Private Correspondence with Charles the First.* London, 1857.

Grosart, Alexander B. *The Complete Works of Joshua Sylvester.* 2 vols. Edinburgh: Edinburgh Univ. Press, 1880.

Hobbes, Thomas. "The Autobiography of Thomas Hobbes." Trans. Benjamin Farrington. *Rationalist Annual* (1958): 22-31.

———. *The English Works of Thomas Hobbes.* Ed. William Molesworth. 11 vols. Aalen, Germany: Scientia, 1962.

Hooke, Robert. *Micrographia; or, Some Physiological Descriptions of Minute Bodies Made by Magnifying Glasses with Observations and Inquiries Thereupon.* London, 1665. Facsimile reprint, New York: Dover, 1961.

Howell, James. *Epistolae Ho-Elianae: The Familiar Letters of James Howell.* Ed. Joseph Jacobs. London, 1890.

Hutchinson, Lucy. *Memoirs of the Life of Colonel Hutchinson Governor of Nottingham by His Widow Lucy.* Ed. C.H. Firth. 2 vols. London, 1885.

Hyde, Edward. *The Life of Edward, Earl of Clarendon . . . Written by Himself.* 2 vols. Oxford: Oxford Univ. Press, 1857.

Letters and Poems in Honour of the Incomparable Princess, Margaret, Duchess of Newcastle. London, 1676.

The Loyall Sacrifice. London, 1648.

Makin, Bathsua. *An Essay to Revive the Antient Education of Gentlewomen.* London, 1673.

Malcolm, Noel, ed. *The Correspondence of Thomas Hobbes.* 2 vols. Oxford: Clarendon Press, 1994.

A Mappe of Mischiefe, or a Dialogue Between V. and E., Concerning the Going of Qu. M. into V. [London?], 1641.

Memoirs for the History of Anne of Austria, Wife to Lewis XIII of France . . . translated from the Original French of Madame de Motteville. 5 vols. London, 1726.

Montagu, Walter. *The Accomplish'd Woman. Written Originally in French, Since Made English.* London, 1656.

―――. *The Shepheard's Paradise.* London, 1629 [1659].

Morant, Philip. *The History and Antiquities of the County of Essex.* London, 1768.

Motteville, Francoise (Bertaut) de. *Mémoires De Madame De Motteville sur Anne D'Autriche Et Sa Cour.* Ed. M.F. Riaux. Paris, 1869.

―――. *Memoirs for the History of Anne of Austria . . . trans. from the Original French.* 5 vols. London, 1726.

Munro, H.A.J. "Mrs. Lucie Hutchinson's Translation of Lucretius." *Journal of Classical and Sacred Philology* 4 (March 1858): 121-39.

Osborne, Dorothy. *Letters to Sir William Temple.* Ed. Kenneth Parker. London: Penguin, 1987.

Panzani, Gregorio. *The Memoirs of Gregorio Panzani.* Ed. Joseph Berington. London, 1793.

Pepys, Samuel. *The Diary of Samuel Pepys.* 11 vols. Ed. Robert Latham and William Matthews. Berkeley: Univ. of California Press, 1976.

Petty, William. *The Discourse Made Before the Royal Society . . . Concerning the Use of Duplicate Proportion in Sundry Important Particulars together with a New Hypothesis of Springy or Elastique Motion.* London, 1674.

Power, Henry. *Experimental Philosophy, in Three Books: Containing New Experiments, Microscopical, Mercurial, Magnetical.* 1664. Reprint, Sources of Science, No. 21. New York: Johnson Reprint, 1966.

Prynne, William. *A Briefe Survay and Censure of Mr. Cozens His Couzening Devotions.* London, 1628.

―――. *The Popish Royall Favourite: Or, a Full Discovery of His Majesties Extraordinary Favours to, and Protections of Notorious Papists.* London, 1643.

Rich, Mary Countess of Warwick. "Autobiography of Mary Countess of Warwick." In *Early English Poetry, Ballads, and Popular Literature of the Middle Ages,* vol. 22, ed. T.C. Croker, 1-50. London: Percy Society, 1848.

Ryves, Bruno. *Mercurius Rusticus: Or, the countries Complaint.* [Oxford], 1646.

Sales, Francois de. *Delicious Entertainments of the Soule.* Trans. by a Dame of our Ladies of Comfort of the Order of S. Bennet in Cambray. Douay, 1632.

―――. *An Introduction to a Devoute Life* (1613). In *English Recusant Literature,* vol. 279. ed. D.M. Rogers, trans. John Yakesley. London: Scolar Press, 1976.

Sprat, Thomas. *History of the Royal Society.* London, 1667. Facsimile reprint, ed. Jackson I. Cope and Harold Whitmore Jones, St. Louis: Washington Univ. Studies, 1959.

Stanley, Thomas. *The History of Philosophy.* 3 vols. London, 1655-1662.

Strange and Terrible Newes from the Queen of Holland. [London?], 1642.

Thompson, Edward Maunde, ed. *Correspondence of the Family of Hatton.* 2 vols. London, 1878.

Waite, Arthur Edward, ed. *The Hermetic and Alchemical Writings of Aureolus Philippus Theophrastus Bombast, of Hohenheim, Called Paracelsus the Great.* 2 vols. London, 1894. Reprint, New York: University Books, 1967.

Wilkins, John. *The Discovery of a World in the Moone, or, A Discourse Tending to Prove, That 'tis Probable There May Be another Habitable World in That Planet.* London, 1638.

Wood, Athony. *Athenae Oxonienses: an Exact History of all the Writers and Bishops Who Have Had Their Education in the Most Antient and Famous University of Oxford.* London, 1721.

SECONDARY SOURCES

Altick, Richard D. *Lives and Letters: A History of Literary Biography in England and America.* New York: Knopf, 1965.

Anzilotti, Gloria Italiano. *An English Prince: Newcastle's Machiavellian Political Guide to Charles II.* Pisa: Giardini, 1988.

Asch, Ronald G., and Adolf M. Birke, eds. *Princes, Patronage, and the Nobility: The Court at the Beginning of the Modern Age.* Oxford: Oxford Univ. Press, 1991.

Backscheider, Paula R. "The Cavalier Woman." *Studies in Eighteenth-Century Culture* 24 (1995): 3-27.

Baldwin, Anna, and Sarah Hutton, eds. *Platonism and the English Imagination.* Cambridge: Cambridge Univ. Press, 1994.

Battigelli, Anna. "Between the Glass and the Hand: The Eye in Margaret Cavendish's *Blazing World.*" *1650-1850: Ideas, Aesthetics, and Inquiries in the Early Modern Period* 2 (1995): 99-112.

———. "Political Thought/Political Action: Margaret Cavendish's Hobbesian Dilemma." In *Women Writers and the Early Modern British Political Tradition,* ed. Hilda Smith. 40-55. Cambridge: Cambridge Univ. Press, 1998.

Birch, Thomas. *The Court and Times of Charles the First.* London, 1848.

Bickley, Francis. *The Cavendish Family.* Boston: Houghton Mifflin, 1914.

Blaydes, Sophia. "The Duchess's Dilemma." *Bulletin of the West Virginia Association of College English Teachers* 4 (1977): 44-52.

———. "The Poetry of the Duchess of Newcastle: A Pyramid of Praise." *Bulletin of the West Virginia Association of College English Teachers* 6 (spring 1981): 26-34.

Bone, Quentin. *Henrietta Maria: Queen of the Cavaliers.* Urbana: Univ. of Illinois Press, 1972.

Bordinat, Philip. "The Duchess of Newcastle as a Literary Critic." *Bulletin of the West Virginia Association of College English Teachers* 5 (1979): 6-12.

Bowerbank, Sylvia. "The Spider's Delight: Margaret Cavendish and the 'Female' Imagination." *English Literary Renaissance* 14 (autumn 1984): 392-408.

Bremond, Henri. *A Literary History of Religious Thought in France from the Wars of Religion Down to Our Times.* 3 vols. Trans. K.L. Montgomery. London: Society for the Promoting of Christian Knowledge, 1928.

Brown, Keith. "The Artist of the *Leviathan* Title-Page." *British Library Journal* 4 (spring 1978): 24-36.

———. "Thomas Hobbes and the Title-Page of *Leviathan*." *Philosophy* 55 (1980): 410-11.

Brown, Sylvia. "Margaret Cavendish: Strategies Rhetorical and Philosophical against the Charge of Wantoness, Or Her Excuses for Writing so Much." *Critical Matrix: Princeton Working Papers in Women's Studies* 6 (1991): 20-45.

Butler, Martin. "Entertaining the Palatine Prince: Plays on Foreign Affairs 1635-1637." *English Literary Renaissance* 13 (1983): 319-44.

———. *Theatre and Crisis, 1632-1642.* Cambridge: Cambridge Univ. Press, 1984.

Butterfield, Herbert. *The Origins of Modern Science, 1300-1800.* New York: Free Press, 1957.

Cassirer, Ernst. *The Philosophy of the Enlightenment.* Trans. Fritz C. A. Koelln and James P. Pettegrove. Princeton, N.J.: Princeton Univ. Press, 1979.

———. *The Platonic Renaissance in England.* Trans. James P. Pettegrove. New York: Gordian, 1970.

Chernaik, Warren L. *The Poetry of Limitation: A Study of Edmund Waller.* New Haven, Conn.: Yale Univ. Press, 1968.

Chester, Joseph Lemuel. *The Marriage, Baptismal, and Burial Registers of the Collegiate Church or Abbey of St. Peter, Westminster.* London, 1876.

Clarendon, Edward. *The History of the Rebellion and Civil Wars in England.* Ed. W. Dunn Macray. 6 vols. Oxford: Clarendon Press, 1888.

———. *The Life of Edward Earl of Clarendon . . . Written by Himself.* 2 vols. Oxford: Oxford Univ. Press, 1857.

Clifford, James L. *From Puzzles to Portraits: Problems of a Literary Biographer.* Chapel Hill: Univ. of North Carolina Press, 1970.

Clucas, Stephen. "The Atomism of the Cavendish Circle: A Reappraisal." *The Seventeenth Century* 9 (autumn 1994): 247-73.

———. "Poetic Atomism in Seventeenth-Century England: Henry More, Thomas Traherne and 'Scientific Imagination.'" *Renaissance Studies* 5 (Sept. 1991): 327-40.

Clulee, Nicholas H. *John Dee's Natural Philosophy: Between Science and Religion.* London: Routledge, 1988.

Cottingham, John. *Descartes.* Oxford: Blackwell, 1986.

Cottingham, John, ed. *The Cambridge Companion to Descartes.* Cambridge: Cambridge Univ. Press, 1995.

Coudert, Allison, "A Cambridge Platonist's Kabbalist Nightmare." *Journal of the History of Ideas* 36 (1975): 633-52.

Dalziel, Margaret. "Richardson and Romance." *Australasian Universities Language and Literature Association* 33 (1970): 5-24.

Damasio, Antonio R. *Descartes' Error: Emotion, Reason, and the Human Brain.* New York: G.P. Putnam's Sons, 1994.

Dammers, Richard H. "Female Characterization in English Platonic Drama." *Res-*

toration and 18th Century Theatre Research, 2d ser. 11 (winter 1986): 34-41.

Dash, Irene G. "Single-Sex Retreats in Two Early Modern Dramas: *Love's Labor's Lost* and *The Convent of Pleasure.*" *Shakespeare Quarterly* 47 (1996): 387-95.

Davis, Natalie Zemon. "Gender and Genre: Women as Historical Writers, 1400-1820." In *Beyond Their Sex: Learned Women of the European Past,* ed. Patricia H. Labalme. 153-82. New York: New York Univ. Press, 1980.

Debus, Allen G. *The English Paracelsians.* London: Oldbourne, 1965.

de Mourgues, Odette. *Metaphysical Baroque and Précieux Poetry.* Oxford: Clarendon Press, 1973.

Dowlin, Cornell March. *Sir William Davenant's Gondibert, Its Preface, and Hobbes's Answer: A Study in English Neo-Classicism.* Philadelphia: Univ. of Pennsylvania Press, 1934.

Edel, Leon. *Literary Biography.* Garden City, N.Y.: Doubleday, 1959.

Epstein, William H., ed. *Contesting the Subject: Essays in the Postmodern Theory and Practice of Biography and Biographical Criticism.* West Lafayette, Ind., Purdue Univ. Press, 1991.

'Espinasse, Margaret. *Robert Hooke.* Berkeley: Univ. of California Press, 1956.

Ezell, Margaret J.M. *The Patriarch's Wife: Literary Evidence and the History of the Family.* Chapel Hill: Univ. of North Carolina Press, 1987.

————. "'To Be Your Daughter in Your Pen': The Social Functions of Literature in the Writings of Lady Elizabeth Brackley and Lady Jane Cavendish." *Huntington Library Quarterly* 51 (autumn 1988): 281-96.

Findley, Sandra, and Elaine Hobby. "Seventeenth Century Women's Autobiography." In *1642: Literature and Power in the Seventeenth Century. Proceedings of the Essex Conference on the Sociology of Literature,* ed. Francis Barker, et al., 11-36. Colchester: Univ. of Essex, 1981.

Firth, C.H. "Sir William Davenant and the Revival of the Drama During the Protectorate." *English Historical Review* 18 (1903): 319-21.

Fisher, N.R.R. "The Queenes Courte in her Councell Chamber at Westminster." *English Historical Review* 108 (1993): 314-37.

Fitzmaurice, James. "Fancy and the Family: Self-Characterizations of Margaret Cavendish." *Huntington Library Quarterly* 53 (summer 1990): 199-209.

————. "Margaret Cavendish on Her Own Writing: Evidence from Revision and Handmade Correction." *Papers of the Bibliographic Society of America* 85 (Sept. 1991): 297-307.

————. "Some Problems in Editing Margaret Cavendish." In *New Ways of Looking at Old Texts,* ed. W. Speed Hill. Binghamton, N.Y.: Medieval and Renaissance Texts and Studies, 1993.

————, ed. *Margaret Cavendish: Sociable Letters.* New York: Garland, 1997.

Fletcher, Jefferson Butler. "Précieuses at the Court of Charles I." *Journal of Comparataive Literature* 1 (1903): 120-53.

————. *The Religion of Beauty in Woman.* New York: Haskell House, 1966.

French, Peter J. *John Dee: The World of an Elizabethan Magus.* London: Routledge, 1972.

Gagen, Jean. "Honor and Fame in the Works of the Duchess of Newcastle." *Studies in Philology* 56 (July 1959): 519-38.

———. "Love and Honor in Dryden's Heroic Plays," *PMLA* 77 (1962): 208-20.

Gallagher, Catherine. "Embracing the Absolute: The Politics of the Female Subject in Seventeenth-Century England." *Genders* 1 (spring 1988): 24-39.

Gardiner, Samuel R., ed. *Documents Relating to the Proceedings against William Prynne.* London: Camden Society, 1877.

———. *History of the Great Civil War, 1642-1649.* 4 vols. London: Longmans, Green, 1901. Reprint, New York: AMS Press, 1965.

Gaukroger, Stephen. *Descartes: An Intellectual Biography.* Oxford: Clarendon Press, 1995.

Gelbart, Nina Rattner. "The Intellectual Development of Walter Charleton." *Ambix* 18, no. 3 (Nov. 1971): 149-68.

Giamatti, A. Bartlett. *Exile and Change in Renaissance Literature.* New Haven, Conn.: Yale Univ. Press, 1984.

Gilbert, Jack G. *Edmund Waller.* Boston: Twayne Publishers, 1979.

Gilde, Joseph M. "Shadwell and the Royal Society: Satire in *The Virtuoso. Studies in English Literature, 1500-1900* 10 (1970): 469-90.

Girouard, Mark. *Robert Smythson and the Elizabethan Country House.* New Haven, Conn.: Yale Univ. Press, 1983.

Goldsmith, Maurice, "Hobbes's Ambiguous Politics," *History of Political Thought* 11 (1990): 639-73.

Goulding, Richard W. *Bolsover Castle.* [Oxford], 1917.

———. *Catalogue of the Pictures Belonging to His Grace, the Duke of Portland, K.G.* Cambridge: Cambridge Univ. Press, 1936.

———. *Letters from the Originals at Welbeck Abbey.* London, 1909.

———. *Margaret (Lucas) Duchess of Newcastle.* Lincoln, Lincolnshire: Lincolnshire Chronicle, 1925.

Grant, Douglas. *Margaret the First: A Biography of Margaret Cavendish Duchess of Newcastle 1623-1673.* Toronto: Univ. of Toronto Press, 1957.

Greenleaf, W.H. *Order, Empiricism and Politics: Two Traditions of English Political Thought, 1500-1700.* Oxford: Oxford Univ. Press, 1964.

Grundy, Isobel, and Susan Wiseman, eds. *Women, Writing, History, 1640-1740.* London: B.T. Batsford, 1992.

Gunther, R.T. *Early Science in Oxford.* 15 vols. Oxford, 1923-67.

Hall, A.R. *The Scientific Revolution, 1500-1800: The Formation of the Modern Scientific Attitude.* London: Longmans, Green, 1954.

Hall, Marie Boas. *Promoting Experimental Learning: Experiment and the Royal Society, 1660-1727.* Cambridge: Cambridge Univ. Press, 1991.

Harbage, Alfred. *Cavalier Drama.* New York: Russell and Russell, 1964.

———. *Sir William Davenant: Poet Venturer, 1606-1668.* Philadelphia: Univ. of Pennsylvania Press, 1935.

Harrison, Charles Trawick. "The Ancient Atomists and English Literature of the Seventeenth Century." In *Harvard Studies in Classical Philology,* vol. 45, 1-80. Cambridge, Mass.: Harvard Univ. Press, 1934.

Harth, Erica. *Cartesian Women: Versions and Subversions of Rational Discourse in the Old Regime.* Ithaca: Cornell Univ. Press, 1992.

Healy, Thomas, and Jonathan Sawday, eds. *Literature and the English Civil War.* Cambridge: Cambridge Univ. Press, 1990.

Heinemann, Margot. *Puritanism and Theatre: Thomas Middleton and Opposition Drama under the Early Stuarts.* Cambridge: Cambridge Univ. Press, 1980.

Henrichs, T.A. "Language and Mind in Hobbes." *Yale French Studies* 49 (1973): 56-70.

Hervey, Helen. "Hobbes and Descartes in the Light of some Unpublished Letters of the Correspondence between Sir Charles Cavendish and Dr. John Pell." *Osiris* 10 (1952): 67-90.

Hibbert, Christopher. *Cavaliers and Roundheads: The English Civil War, 1642-1649.* New York: Scribner's, 1993.

Hill, Christopher. *The Intellectual Origins of the English Revolution.* Oxford: Oxford Univ. Press, 1991.

————. "William Harvey and the Idea of Monarchy." *Past and Present* 27 (1964): 54-72.

Hinman, Robert B. *Abraham Cowley's World of Order.* Cambridge, Mass.: Harvard Univ. Press, 1960.

Hirsch, David A. Hedrich. "Donne's Atomies and Anatomies: Deconstructed Bodies and the Resurrection of Atomic Theory." *Studies in English Literature, 1500-1900* 31 (winter 1991): 69-94.

Hiscock, Walter George. *John Evelyn and His Family Circle.* London: Routledge, 1955.

Hjort, Mette. *Rules and Conventions: Literature, Philosophy, Social Theory.* Baltimore: Johns Hopkins Univ. Press, 1992.

Hopkins, Lisa. "Judith Shakespeare's Reading: Teaching *The Concealed Fancies. Shakespeare Quarterly* 47 (1996): 396-406.

Houlahan, Mark. "*Leviathan* (1651): Thomas Hobbes and Protestant Apocalypse." *1650-1850: Ideas, Aesthetics, and Inquiries in the Early Modern Era* 2 (1996): 95-109.

Hüllen, Werner. "Style and Utopia. Sprat's Demand for a Plain Style, Reconsidered." In *Papers in the History of Linguistics: Proceedings of the Third International Conference on the History of the Language Sciences,* ed. Hans Aarsleff et al. Philadelphia: John Benjamins, 1987.

Hunter, J. Paul. "Robert Boyle and the Epistemology of the Novel." *Eighteenth-Century Fiction* 2 (1990): 275-91.

Hunter, Michael. *Establishing the New Science: The Experience of the Early Royal Society.* Woodbridge, Suffolk: Boydell, 1989.

————. *The Royal Society and its Fellows, 1660-1700: The Morphology of an Early Scientific Institution.* British Society for the History of Science, no. 4. Oxford: Alden Press, 1985.

————. *Science and the Shape of Orthodoxy: Intellectual Change in Late Seventeenth-Century Britain.* Woodbridge, Suffolk: Boydell, 1995.

————. *Science and Society in England.* Cambridge: Cambridge Univ. Press, 1981.

Hunter, Michael, and Simon Schaffer, eds. *Robert Hooke: New Studies.* Woodbridge, Suffolk: Boydell, 1989.

Hunter, Michael, and David Wootton, eds. *Atheism from the Reformation to the Enlightenment.* Oxford: Clarendon Press, 1992.

Italiano, Gloria. "Due Biografie Inglesi del XVII secolo: Margaret Newcastle e Lucy Hutchinson." *Paragone: Rivista Mensile di Arte Figurativa e Letteratura* 344 (1978): 60-73.

Jacob, James, and Timothy Raylor. "Opera and Obedience: Thomas Hobbes and *A Proposition for Advancement of Moralitie* by Sir William Davenant." *Seventeenth Century* 6, no. 2 (autumn 1991): 205-50.

Jacob, Margaret C. *The Cultural Meaning of the Scientific Revolution.* Philadelphia: Temple Univ. Press, 1988.

Jacquot, Jean. "Sir Charles Cavendish and His Learned Friends." *Annals of Science* 8 (1952): 13-27.

Johnson, Francis R. "Gresham College: Precursor of the Royal Society." *Journal of the History of Ideas* 1 (1940): 413-38.

Jones, Howard. *The Epicurean Tradition.* London: Routledge, 1992.

———. *Pierre Gassendi, 1592-1655: An Intellectual Biography.* Nieuwkoop, Netherlands: B. De Graaf, 1981.

Jones, Kathleen. *A Glorious Fame: The Life of Margaret Cavendish, Duchess of Newcastle, 1623-1673.* London: Bloomsbury, 1988.

Jones, Richard Foster. *Ancients and Moderns: A Study of the Rise of the Scientific Movement in Seventeenth-Century England.* New York: Dover, 1961.

———. "Science and Criticism in the Neo-Classical Age of English Literature." *Journal of the History of Ideas* 1 (1940): 381-412.

Joy, Lynn Sumida. *Gassendi the Atomist.* Cambridge: Cambridge Univ. Press, 1987.

Kargon, Robert Hugh. *Atomism in England from Hariot to Newton.* Oxford: Clarendon Press, 1966.

———. "Walter Charleton, Robert Boyle, and the Acceptance of Epicurean Atomism in England." *Isis* 55 (1964): 184-92.

Kashi, Prasad. "Margaret Cavendish's Blazing World: A Seventeenth-Century Utopia." In *Essays Presented to Amy G. Stock,* 58-67. ed. Kaul, R.K. Jaipur: Rajasthan Univ. Press, 1965.

Kelliher, Hilton. "Donne, Jonson, Richard Andrews and the Newcastle Manuscript." In *English Manuscript Studies 1100-1700,* ed. Peter Beal and Jeremy Griffiths. 134-73. Toronto: Univ. of Toronto Press, 1993.

Kenyon, John Philipps. *The Civil Wars in England.* New York: Knopf, 1988.

Khanna, Lee Cullen. "The Subject of Utopia: Margaret Cavendish and Her *Blazing-World.*" In *Utopian and Science Fiction by Women: Worlds of Difference,* ed. Jane L. Donawerth and Carol A. Kolmerten, 15-34. Syracuse, N.Y.: Syracuse Univ. Press, 1994.

Kors, Alan Charles, and Paul J. Korshin, eds. *Anticipations of the Enlightenment in England, France, and Germany.* Philadelphia: Univ. of Pennsylvania Press, 1987.

Kramer, Annette. "'Thus by Musick of a Ladyes Tongue': Margaret Cavendish's

Dramatic Innovations in Women's Education." *Women's History Review* 2 (1993): 57-80.

Kroll, Richard W.F. *The Material Word: Literate Culture in the Restoration and Early Eighteenth Century.* Baltimore: Johns Hopkins Univ. Press, 1991.

Laidler, Josephine, "A History of Pastoral Drama in England until 1700." *Englische Studien* 35 (1905): 193-259.

Lennon, Thomas M. *The Battle of the Gods and the Giants: The Legacies of Descartes and Gassendi, 1655-1715.* Princeton, N.J.: Princeton Univ. Press, 1993.

Lewalski, Barbara Kiefer. *Writing Women in Jacobean England.* Cambridge, Mass.: Harvard Univ. Press, 1993.

Lewis, C.S. *The Abolition of Man.* New York: Simon and Schuster, 1996.

Lindley, David, ed. *The Court Masque.* Manchester, Eng.: Manchester Univ. Press, 1984.

Lloyd, S.A. *Ideals as Interests in Hobbes's Leviathan: The Power of Mind over Matter.* Cambridge: Cambridge Univ. Press, 1992.

Longueville, Thomas. *The First Duke and Duchess of Newcastle-upon-Tyne.* London: Longmans, Green, 1910.

Loomie, Albert J., ed. *Ceremonies of Charles I: The Note Books of John Finet 1628-1641.* New York: Fordham Univ. Press, 1987.

Lynch, Kathleen M. "Conventions of Platonic Drama in the Heroic Plays of Orrery and Dryden." *PMLA* 44 (1929): 456-71.

———. *The Social Mode of Restoration Comedy.* New York: Octagon, 1926.

MacCarthy, Bridget G. *The Female Pen: Women Writers and Novelists, 1621-1818.* New York: New York Univ. Press, 1994.

MacDonald, Hugh, and Mary Hargreaves. *Thomas Hobbes: A Bibliography.* London: Bibliographical Society, 1952.

Macintosh, J.J. "Perception and Imagination in Descartes, Boyle and Hooke." *Canadian Journal of Philosophy* 13 (1983): 327-52.

Maclean, Gerald, ed. *Culture and Society in the Stuart Restoration: Literature, Drama, History.* Cambridge: Cambridge Univ. Press, 1995.

Macpherson, Crawford Brough. *The Political Theory of Possessive Individualism, Hobbes to Locke.* Oxford: Clarendon Press, 1962.

Madan, Falconer. *Oxford Books: A Bibliography of Printed Works Relating to the University and City of Oxford.* 3 vols. Oxford: Clarendon Press, 1912.

Mattes, Eleanor. "The 'Female Virtuoso' in Early Eighteenth-Century English Drama." *Women and Literature* 3 (1975): 3-9.

Mayo, Thomas Franklin. *Epicurus in England.* Dallas: Southwest Press, 1934.

McGuire, Mary Ann. "Margaret Cavendish, Duchess of Newcastle, on the Nature and Status of Women." *International Journal of Women's Studies* 2 (1978): 193-206.

Mell, Donald C., Theodore E.D. Braun, and Lucia M. Palmer. *Man, God, and Nature in the Enlightenment.* East Lansing, Mich.: Colleagues Press, 1988.

Mendelson, Sara Heller. *The Mental World of Stuart Women: Three Studies.* Amherst: Univ. of Massachusetts Press, 1987.

Merchant, Carolyn. *The Death of Nature: Women, Ecology, and the Scientific Revolution.* San Francisco: Harper and Row, 1980.

Meyer, Gerald Dennis. *The Scientific Lady in England, 1650-1760: An Account of Her Rise, with Emphasis on the Major Roles of the Telescope and Microscope.* Berkeley: Univ. of California Press, 1955.

Mintz, Samuel I. "The Duchess of Newcastle's Visit to the Royal Society." *Journal of English and Germanic Philology* 51 (1952): 168-76.

———. *The Hunting of Leviathan: Seventeenth-Century Reactions to the Materialism and Moral Philosophy of Thomas Hobbes.* Cambridge: Cambridge Univ. Press, 1962.

Morrison, Philip. "Beyond Atoms and the Void." *New Literary History* 23 (1992): 797-814.

Mulligan, Lotte. "Robert Hooke and Certain Knowledge." *Seventeenth Century* 7 (1992): 151-69.

Mulligan, Lotte, and Glenn Mulligan. "Reconstructing Restoration Science: Styles of Leadership and Social Composition of the Early Royal Society." *Social Studies of Science* 11 (1981): 327-64.

Nadelhaft, Jerome. "The Englishwoman's Sexual Civil War: Feminist Attitudes towards Men, Women, and Marriage 1650-1740." *Journal of the History of Ideas* 43 (Oct.-Dec. 1982): 555-79.

Nethercot, Arthur H. *Sir William Davenant: Poet Laureate and Playwright-Manager.* Chicago: Univ. of Chicago Press, 1938.

Nicolson, Marjorie Hope. *The Conway Letters: The Correspondence of Anne, Viscountess Conway, Henry More, and their Friends, 1642-1684.* London: Yale Univ. Press, 1930. Rev. ed., edited by Sarah Hutton, Oxford: Clarendon Press, 1992.

———. "The Early Stages of Cartesianism in England." *Studies in Philosophy* 28 (1929): 356-74.

———. *Mountain Gloom and Mountain Glory: The Development of the Aesthetics of the Infinite.* New York: Norton, 1959.

———. *Pepys's Diary and the New Science.* Charlottesville: Univ. Press of Virginia, 1965.

———. *Science and Imagination.* Ithaca, N.Y.: Cornell Univ. Press, 1962.

———. *Voyages to the Moon.* New York: Macmillan, 1960.

———. *A World in the Moon: A Study of the Changing Attitude toward the Moon in the Seventeenth and Eighteenth Centuries.* Northampton, Mass.: Department of Modern Languages of Smith College, [1936].

Norton, Mary. "'The Rising World of Waters Dark and Deep': Chaos Theory and *Paradise Lost.*" *Milton Studies* 32 (1995): 91-110.

Olney, James, ed. *Autobiography: Essays Theoretical and Critical.* Princeton, N.J.: Princeton Univ. Press, 1980.

Oman, Carola. *Henrietta Maria.* London: Hodder and Stoughton, 1936.

Orgel, Stephen. "Plato, the Magi, and Caroline Politics: A Reading of the Temple of Love." *Word and Image* 4, no. 3-4 (July-Dec. 1991): 663-77.

Orgel, Stephen, and Roy Strong. *Inigo Jones: The Theatre of the Stuart Court.* 2 vols. Berkeley: Univ. of California Press, 1973.

Osler, Margaret J., ed. *Atoms, Pneuma, and Tranquility.* Cambridge: Cambridge Univ. Press, 1991.

Pagden, Anthony, ed. *The Languages of Political Theory in Early-Modern Europe.* Cambridge: Cambridge Univ. Press, 1987.

Pagel, Walter. *Paracelsus: An Introduction to Philosophical Medicine in the Era of the Renaissance.* New York: S. Karger, 1958.

Paloma, Dolores. "Margaret Cavendish: Defining the Female Self." *Women's Studies: An Interdisciplinary Journal* 7 (1980): 55-66.

Patterson, Annabel. *Censorship and Interpretation: The Conditions of Writing and Reading in Early Modern England.* Madison: Univ. of Wisconsin Press, 1984.

Pearson, Jacqueline. *The Prostituted Muse: Images of Women and Women Dramatists, 1642-1737.* New York: St. Martin's, 1988.

Perry, Henry Ten Eyck. *The First Duchess of Newcastle and Her Husband as Figures in Literary History.* Boston: Ginn, 1918.

Petersson, Robert Torsten. *Sir Kenelm Digby: the Ornament of England, 1603-1665.* Cambridge, Mass.: Harvard Univ. Press, 1956.

Petrie, Charles, ed. *The Letters Speeches and Proclmations of King Charles I.* New York: Funk and Wagnalls, 1968.

Phillipson, Nicholas, and Quentin Skinner, eds. *Political Discourse in Early Modern Britain.* Cambridge: Cambridge Univ. Press, 1993.

Pocock, John Greville Agard, ed. *Politics, Language and Time.* New York: Atheneum, 1971.

———, ed. *The Varieties of British Political Thought, 1500-1800.* Cambridge: Cambridge Univ. Press, 1993.

Popkin, Richard H. *The History of Scepticism from Erasmus to Spinoza.* Berkeley: Univ. of California Press, 1979.

———. "Hobbes and Scepticism." In *History of Philosophy in the Making,* ed. Linus J. Thro. Washington, D.C.: Univ. Press of America, 1982.

Potter, Lois. *Secret Rites and Secret Writing: Royalist Literature, 1641-1660.* Cambridge: Cambridge Univ. Press, 1989.

Quinsey, Katherine M., ed. *Broken Boundaries: Women and Feminism in Restoration Drama.* Lexington: Univ. Press of Kentucky, 1996.

Randall, Dale B.J. *Winter Fruit: English Drama 1642-1660.* Lexington: Univ. Press of Kentucky, 1995.

Reik, Miriam M. *The Golden Lands of Thomas Hobbes.* Detroit: Wayne State Univ. Press, 1977.

Richards, Kenneth. "Queen Henrietta Maria as Patron of the Drama." *Studia Neophilologica* 42 (1970): 9-24.

Riggs, David. *Ben Jonson: A Life.* Cambridge, Mass.: Harvard Univ. Press, 1989.

Rogers, Graham Alan John, and Alan Ryan, eds. *Perspectives on Thomas Hobbes.* Oxford: Clarendon Press, 1988.

Rogers, John. *The Matter of Revolution: Science, Poetry, and Politics in the Age of Milton.* Ithaca: Cornell Univ. Press, 1996.

Rogow, Arnold A. *Thomas Hobbes: Radical in the Service of Reaction.* New York: Norton, 1986.

Rolleston, Humphrey. "Walter Charleton, D.M., F.R.C.P., F.R.S." *Bulletin of the History of Medicine* 8 (1940): 403-16.

Rose, Mary Beth, ed. *Women in the Middle Ages and the Renaissance: Literary and Historical Perspectives.* Syracuse, N.Y.: Syracuse Univ. Press, 1986.

Rosenthal, Laura J. *Playwrights and Plagiarists in Early Modern England: Gender, Authorship, Literary Property.* Ithaca, N.Y.: Cornell Univ. Press, 1996.

Rostenberg, Leona. "Robert Hooke: Restoration Bibliophile." *American Book Collector* 8, no. 4 (1987): 9-15.

Rubin, Davida. *Sir Kenelm Digby F.R.S. 1603-1665: A Bibliography Based on the Collection of K. Garth Huston, Sr., M.D.* San Francisco: Jeremy Norman, 1991.

Rushworth, John. *Historical Collections.* 8 vols. London, 1721- 1722.

Sarasohn, Lisa T. "A Science Turned Upside Down: Feminism and the Natural Philosophy of Margaret Cavendish." *Huntington Library Quarterly* 47 (autumn 1984): 289-307.

Sawday, Jonathan. "The Mint at Segovia: Digby, Hobbes, Charleton, and the Body as a Machine in the Seventeenth Century." *Prose Studies* 6 (1983): 21-35.

Schiebinger, Londa. "Margaret Cavendish, Duchess of Newcastle." In *Modern Women Philosophers, 1600-1900,* History of Women Philosophers, ed. Mary Ellen Waithe. Vol. 3, 1-20. Boston: Kluwer Academic Publishers, 1991.

———. *The Mind Has No Sex? Women in the Origins of Modern Science.* Cambridge, Mass.: Harvard Univ. Press, 1989.

Schochet, Gordon. *Patriarchalism in Political Thought: The Authoritarian Family and Political Speculation and Attitudes Especially in Seventeenth-Century England.* New York: Basic Books, 1975.

Schofield, Mary Ann, and Cecilia Macheski, eds. *Curtain Calls: British and American Women and the Theater, 1660-1820.* Athens: Ohio Univ. Press, 1991.

Schwoerer, Lois G. *Lady Rachel Russell: "One of the Best of Women."* Baltimore: Johns Hopkins Univ. Press, 1988.

Sensabaugh, G.F. "Love Ethics in Platonic Court Drama 1625-42." *Huntington Library Quarterly* 1 (1938): 277-304.

———. "Platonic Love and the Puritan Rebellion," *Studies in Philology* 37 (Jan. 1940): 457-81.

Shapin, Steven, and Simon Schaffer. *Leviathan and the Air-Pump: Hobbes, Boyle, and the Experimental Life.* Princeton, N.J.: Princeton Univ. Press, 1985.

Sharpe, Kevin. *Criticism and Compliment: The Politics of Literature in the England of Charles I.* Cambridge: Cambridge Univ. Press, 1987.

———. *The Personal Rule of Charles I.* New Haven, Conn.: Yale Univ. Press, 1992.

Sherman, Sandra. "Trembling Texts: Margaret Cavendish and the Dialectic of Authorship." *English Literary Renaissance* 24 (winter 1994): 184-210.

Siegel, Rudolph E. "Why Galen and Harvey Did Not Compare the Heart to a Water Pump." *American Journal of Cardiology* 20 (July 1967): 117-21.

Skinner, Quentin. *Reason and Rhetoric in the Philosophy of Hobbes.* Cambridge: Cambridge Univ. Press, 1996.

———. "Thomas Hobbes and His Disciples in France and England." *Comparative Studies in Society and History* 8, no. 2 (1965-66): 153-67.

———. "Thomas Hobbes and the Nature of the Early Royal Society." *Historical Journal* 12 (1969): 217-39.

Slaughter, Thomas P., ed. *Ideology and Politics on the Eve of Restoration: Newcastle's Advice to Charles II.* Philadelphia: American Philosophical Society, 1984.

Slomp, Gabriella. "Hobbes and the Equality of Women." *Political Studies* 42 (1994): 441-52.

Smith, Hilda L. *Reason's Disciples: Seventeenth-Century English Feminists.* Urbana: Univ. of Illinois Press, 1982.

———. "'Though it be the part of every good wife': Margaret Cavendish, Duchess of Newcastle." In *Women and History: Voices of Early Modern England,* ed. Valerie Frith, 119-44. Toronto: Coach House Press, 1995.

Smuts, Malcolm. *Court Culture and the Origins of a Royalist Tradition in Early Stuart England.* Philadelphia: Univ. of Pennsylvania Press, 1987.

———. "The Puritan Followers of Henrietta Maria." *EHR* 93 (1978): 26-45.

Sorell, Tom, ed. *The Cambridge Companion to Hobbes.* Cambridge: Cambridge Univ. Press, 1996.

Starkey, David, et al. *The English Court: from the Wars of the Roses to the Civil War.* London: Longman, 1987.

Stephen, Leslie. *English Literature and Society in the Eighteenth Century.* New York: Barnes and Noble, 1962.

———. *Hobbes.* Ann Arbor: Univ. of Michigan Press, 1961.

Stimpson, Dorothy. "Ballad of Gresham Colledge." *Isis* 18 (1932): 103-17.

Straznicky, Marta. "Reading the Stage: Margaret Cavendish and Commonwealth Closet Drama." *Criticism* 37 (summer 1995): 355-90.

Sullivan, Patricia A. "Female Writing beside the Rhetorical Tradition: Seventeenth Century British Biography and a Female Tradition in Rhetoric." *International Journal of Women's Studies* 3 (March/April 1980): 143-60.

Taylor, Charles. *Sources of the Self: The Making of the Modern Identity.* Cambridge, Mass.: Harvard Univ. Press, 1989.

Thomas, Keith. "Women and the Civil War Sects." *Past and Present* 13 (1958): 42-62.

Thomas, Peter William. *Sir John Berkenhead, 1617-1679: A Royalist Career in Politics and Polemics.* Oxford: Clarendon Press, 1969.

Thorpe, Clarence DeWitt. *The Aesthetic Theory of Thomas Hobbes.* New York: Russell and Russell, 1964.

Tieje, Arthur J. "The Expressed Aim of the Long Prose Fiction from 1579 to 1740." *Journal of English and Germanic Philology* 11 (1912): 402-32.

Trease, Geoffrey. *Portrait of a Cavalier: William Cavendish, First Duke of Newcastle.* New York: Taplinger, 1979.

Tricomini, Albert H. *Anticourt Drama in England, 1603-1642.* Charlottesville: Univ. Press of Virginia, 1989.

Trubowitz, Rachel. "The Reenchantment of Utopia and the Female Monarchical Self: Margaret Cavendish's *Blazing World. Tulsa Studies in Women's Literature* 11 (1992): 229-46.

Tuck, Richard. *Philosophy and Government 1572-1651.* Cambridge: Cambridge Univ. Press, 1993.

———. "Power and Authority in Seventeenth-Century England." *Historical Journal* 17 (1974): 43-61.

Turberville, Arthur Stanley. *A History of Welbeck Abbey and Its Owners.* 2 vols. London: Faber and Faber, 1938-39.

Turner, James. *The Dolphin's Skin: Six Studies in Eccentricity.* London: Cassell, 1956.

Underwood, E. Ashworth, ed. *Science Medicine and History: Essays on the Evolution of Scientific Thought and Medical Practice.* 2 vols. Oxford: Oxford Univ. Press, 1953.

Upham, Alfred. *The French Influence in English Literature from the Accession of Elizabeth to the Restoration.* New York: Octagon, 1965.

Van Leeuwen, Henry G. *The Problem of Certainty in English Thought, 1630-1690.* The Hague: Nijhoff, 1963.

Veevers, Erica. *Images of Love and Religion: Queen Henrietta Maria and Court Entertainments.* Cambridge: Cambridge Univ. Press, 1989.

Vincent, Leon H. *Hôtel De Rambouillet and the Précieuses.* Boston: Houghton Mifflin, 1900.

Webster, Charles. *From Paracelsus to Newton: Magic and the Making of Modern Science.* Cambridge: Cambridge Univ. Press, 1982.

West, David. "Lucretius and the Poetry of Argument." *Renaissance Studies* 5 (Sept. 1991): 242-49.

Westfall, Richard S. "Unpublished Boyle Papers Relating to the Scientific Method—II" *Annals of Science* 12 (1956): 103-17.

Whitelock, Bulstrode. *Memorials of the English Affairs from the Beginning of the Reign of Charles the First to the Happy Restoration of King Charles the Second.* 4 vols. Oxford, 1853.

Wiess, Samuel A. "Dating Mrs. Hutchinson's Translation of Lucretius." *Notes and Queries* 200 (1955): 109.

Williams, Robert W. "Pope and the 'Microscopic Eye.'" *Sydney Studies in English* 14 (1988-89): 21-37.

Wilputte, Earla A. "Margaret Cavendish's Imaginary Voyage to the Blazing World: Mapping a Feminine Discourse." In *Transatlantic Crossings: Eighteenth-Century Explorations,* ed. Donald Nichol, 109-17. St. John's, Newfoundland: Memorial Univ. of Newfoundland, 1995.

Wilson, Catherine. "Visual Surface and Visual Symbol: The Microscope and the Occult in Early Modern Science." *Journal of the History of Ideas* 49 (1988): 85-108.

Wilson, Katharina M., and Frank J. Warnke. *Women Writers of the Seventeenth Century.* Athens: Univ. of Georgia Press, 1989.

Woodfield, Richard. "Thomas Hobbes and the Formation of Aesthetics in England." *British Journal of Aesthetics* 20 (spring 1980): 146-52.

Woolf, Virginia. "The Duchess of Newcastle." In *The Common Reader.* 69-77. London: Harcourt Brace-Harvest, 1925.

Young, Bruce W. "Thomas Hobbes versus the Poets: Form, Expression, and Metaphor in Early Seventeenth-Century Poetry." *Encyclia* 63 (1986): 151-62.

Index

air pump, 90

Aristophanes: *The Frogs*, 102

Ars Poetica (Horace), 36

atomism, 9, 12, 38, 98; varieties of, 45; reception in England, 49-51, 60; M.C.'s exploration of, 39-61; and epistemological uncertainty, 52-58; M.C.'s rejection as a theory of matter, 62

Aubrey, John: quoted, 46, 68

Bacon, Francis: quoted, 92, 103

Berkshire, Thomas Howard, first earl of: quoted, 69

Birch, Thomas: quoted, 110-11

Blazing World (Cavendish), 28, 80-83, 103-13, quoted, 80-82, 103-9

Bolsover Castle, 3, 88, 148 n 41

Bone, Quentin, 134 n 1, quoted, 18, 22

Bowerbank, Sylvia: quoted, 154 n 52

Boyle, Robert, 51, 60; experimental program of, 90, 101, 102, 111

Brackley, Elizabeth: as playwright, 25-26; *The Concealed Fansyes*, 139 n 50

Browne, Elizabeth, 35

Browne, Richard, 35, 120

Butler, Martin, 135 n 7, 136 n 11, 137 n 26, quoted, 12

Butler, Mary. *See* Cavendish, Mary, duchess of Devonshire

cabala, 107-8

Caroline drama, 12, 16, 32, 115

Cartwright, William: *The Royall Slave*, 137 n 25, 139 n 47, quoted, 137 n 25

Cavendish, Charles: tutors M.C., 46-48; travels to London with M.C., 3, 48, 65; and Hobbes, 47, 64; *Letters*, quoted, 47

Cavendish, Henry, second duke of Newcastle, 15

Cavendish, Jane. *See* Cheyne, Jane

Cavendish, Margaret, duchess of Newcastle: date of birth, 2, 117-18; childhood, 2, 7; early education, 2; joins court of Henrietta Maria, 2, 11-24; and Platonic love doctrine, 11-38, 88; exposed to Henrietta Maria's proselytizing efforts, 11, 16-19; experience of war, 2, 8, 41-45, 60, 76-78; experience of exile, 1-3, 5, 7, 22-23, 35, 38, 40, 45; courted by W.C., 2-3, 11-12, 22-24, 119-20; illness at court, 23; marriage, 1, 3, 11, 35, 39-41, 46, 60, 120; mother dies, 41, 44, 45; ill health of, 43-44, 86, 87, 120; plays of, 11-38; tutored by Charles Cavendish and W.C., 1, 39, 46-48, 141 n 18, 153 n 36; reading of, 141 n 17, 146 n 16, 148 n 35; writing habits of, 1, 2, 7, 8-10, 86, 88, 114, 120; handwriting of, 119; travels to London with Charles Cavendish, 3, 48, 65; meets with Committee on Compounding, 48, 76-77, 133 n 6; first publishes, 3, 48; imports atomism to England, 39-61; religious skepticism of, 11, 54-55, 59, 72, 80, 101, 110; epistemological skepticism of, 37, 38, 48-49, 52-58, 70, 73-78, 82, 85-95, 104-13; rejects atomism, 62; and Descartes, 3, 8, 9, 10, 45-50, 72, 98, 100, 104; returns from exile, 85-89; retires to Welbeck Abbey, 88; politics of, 55-84; and Thomas Hobbes, 62-84; anxiety toward printed word, 8, 31-32, 37, 67, 72-73, 78-80; anxiety toward spoken word,

26-27, 33-34, 78; and Erastianism, 69-84; natural philosophy of, 98-102; and mechanism, 93, 96, 97, 98-102, 114; critiques Royal Society's experimental program and Robert Hooke's *Micrographia*, 38, 53, 85-113; and rationalism, 12, 85-113; attends meeting of the Royal Society, 5, 110-13; death of, 5, 114; burial of, 5, 115; monument erected in honor of, 5, 115; character of, 5-7, 21, 32, 44. Works: *Blazing World*, 28, 80-83, 103-13, quoted, 80-82, 103-9; *Grounds of Natural Philosophy*, 114; *The Lady Contemplation*, 27-31, quoted, 16, 27-30; *Letters*, 22-24, 119-32, 138 n 43, quoted, 23, 33, 38, 85, 116; *Life of . . . William Cavendishe*, 4, 31-32, 67, 71-72, quoted, 1, 19, 31-32, 71-72, 87, 88, 114, 148 n 34, 150 nn 8, 9; *Love's Adventures*, 26, 27, 33, quoted, 33; *Nature's Pictures*, 25, 73-78, 114, quoted, 8, 68, 73-78, 119; *Observations upon Experimental Philosophy*, 9, 90-113, quoted, 9, 55, 93-98, 111; *Orations*, 78-80, 114, quoted, 55, 72-73, 78-79; *Philosophical and Physical Opinions*, 88-89, 98, quoted, 8, 62, 65, 68, 70-71, 88-89, 100, 101, 116, 142 n 18, 145 n 2, 153 n 36, 156 n 1; *Philosophical Letters*, quoted, 72, 83, 98, 99, 100-101; *Philosophicall Fancies*, 4, 48-49, 50, quoted, 142 n 26; *Playes*, 25, 65, prefatory matter quoted, 25; *Plays, Never Before Printed*, 25, 114, prefatory matter quoted, 32; *Poems and Fancies*, 4, 48, 50-61, quoted, 47-48, 51-54, 57, 58-59, 84, 117-18, 138 n 41, 143 n 26; *Poems, or, Several Fancies in Verse*, 114; *The Presence*, 16, 34-38, 157 n 5, quoted, 34-37; *Sociable Letters*, 25, 86-88, 149 n 2, quoted, 44, 72, 73, 78, 79-80, 86-88, 135 n 4, 148 n 34, 149 n 2; "A True Relation," 23-24, 41, 116, quoted, 2, 7, 12, 19, 21-22, 24, 41, 44-45, 133 n 6; *The World's Olio*, 24, 48-49, 55-60, 114, quoted, 24-25, 46, 55-60, 69-70, 71, 110, 143 n 27;

Youth's Glory and Death's Banquet, 33-34, quoted, 33-34, 142 n 19
Cavendish, Mary, duchess of Devonshire, 134 n 15
Cavendish, William, first duke of Newcastle: date of birth, 146 n 11; abandons war effort, 2-3, 22; proscribed and banished, 3; arrives in Paris, 2, 22; courtship of M.C., 23; love poems to M.C., 120; M.C.'s description of, 32; Parisian salon of, 1, 39, 45-46, 49, 65; and Platonism, 16; and Hobbes, 64-65; lives on credit, 41; on M.C.'s education, 46, 153 n 36; anxiety toward the printed word, 37, 67; political theory of, 63, 71; collaborates with M.C., 25-26, 77-78; on cost of publishing his work, 25; concerned about M.C.'s health, 43-44; ill health of, 141 n 10; returns from exile, 87-88; excluded from king's inner circle, 4, 87; retires to Welbeck Abbey, 4, 88; created duke of Newcastle, 4, 151 n 24; attitude toward new science, 150 n 11; patronizes Thomas Shadwell, 115; collects *Letters and Poems*, 116; and *Blazing World*, quoted, 103-4; and *Nature's Pictures*, quoted, 25; and *Philosophical and Physical Opinions*, quoted, 46, 150 n 11. Works: *Advice*, 83, 87, 108, quoted, 16, 67, 148 n 34; "The Beggars' Marriage," 77; "Letter of Instruction," quoted, 72; *Letters*, quoted, 25; *La Methode Nouvelle . . . de Dresser les Chevaux*, 25; "The Philosopher's Complaint," 77-78, quoted, 77
Cavendish, William, second earl of Devonshire. *See* Devonshire, William Cavendish, second earl of
Chaplain, Elizabeth (maid to M.C.), 6, 150 n 4
Charles I, 13-14, 31, 87, quoted, 14, 87
Charles II, 16, 71-72, 87, 151 n 24
Charleton, Walter, 110; friendship with M.C., 6; and atomism, 46, 49, 55, 56, 60; and Paracelsianism, 98; translates

Life of . . . W.C., 114. Works: *Darknes of Atheism Dispelled by the Light of Nature*, 49, quoted, 49; *Epicurus's Morals*, 49; *Letters*, quoted, 55-56, 141 n 17; *Physiologia Epicuro-Gassendo-Charltoniana*, 49, quoted, 50

Chester, Joseph Lemuel, 117-18

Cheyne, Jane (née Cavendish): as playwright, 25-26; *The Concealed Fansyes*, 139 n 50

Clarendon, Edward Hyde, first earl of: quoted, 47, 142 n 24

Clucas, Stephen: quoted, 141 n 15

Colchester, siege of, 42-43

Collection of Private Devotions (Cosin), 15

Committee on Compounding, 48, 76-77, 133 n 6

Condren, Conal: quoted, 67

Cosin, John: 32, 136 n 15; *Collection of Private Devotions* (1627), 15

court culture, 13-19, 21-25, 37

Cowley, Abraham, 66

cross-dressing: M.C.'s, 5, 134 n 11; in plays, 26, 33

Damasio, Antonio: quoted, 153 n 43

Davenant, William, 63, 83; on poetry, 66-67; *Preface to Gondibert*, 47, quoted, 66-67; *The Temple of Love*, quoted, 17

Davys, John, 14

deduction. *See* rationalism

Delicious Entertainments of the Soule (de Sales), 15

De Rerum Natura (Lucretius): quoted, 40

Descartes, René: M.C.'s reading of, 3, 8, 9, 10; and Newcastle salon, 45-50; M.C.'s response to, 72, 98, 100, 104; *Les passions de L'Ame*, 47

Devonshire, William Cavendish, second earl of, 64, 66

Digby, Kenelm, 6, 46; *The Private Memoirs of Sir Kenelm Digby*, 16

Dryden, John: *Aureng-Zebe*, quoted, 144 n 45

Duarti, Eleanor, 86

Edel, Leon: quoted, 6

empiricism. *See* experimentalism

Epicurean atomism. *See* atomism

Epicurus, 40, 50, 60. *See also* Lucretius

Erastianism, 69-84

Evelyn, John, 15, 35; on siege of Colchester, quoted, 42; and atomism, 46, 49, 60; on M.C.'s marriage, 140 n 60; "Ballad," quoted, 5, 112; *Diary*, quoted, 4, 15, 42, 49, 112, 140 n 60; *An Essay on . . . Lucretius*, 49, quoted, 50-51

Evelyn, Mary, 4-6, quoted, 4, 6

experimentalism, 85-113

Ezell, Margaret, 139 n 50, quoted, 26

Fairfax, Thomas: siege of Colchester, 42, 43, quoted, 43

Fanshawe, Anne: quoted, 21

Fitzmaurice, James: quoted, 31, 150 n 5, 155 n 53

Gagen, Jean: quoted, 155 n 53

Gallagher, Catherine: quoted, 109-10

Gassendi, Pierre: M.C.'s reading of, 3, 8, 9; and atomism, 38, 45-47, 49, 50, 56, 60, 143 n 32

Gelbart, Nina: quoted, 45, 98

Gerarde, John, 98

Glanvill, Joseph, 6; *Plus Ultra*, 103; *The Vanity of Dogmatizing*, quoted, 103

Godwin, Francis: *The Man in the Moone*, 53, 58, 145 n 46

Gonsague-Nevers, Marie-Louise de, 120

Goulding, Richard, 117, 120, quoted, 117

Grant, Douglas, 117, 134 n 15, quoted, 149 n 1, 150 n 4

Green, Mary Anne Everett, 134 n 1

Grounds of Natural Philosophy (Cavendish), 114

Gunther, R.T.: quoted, 91

Hall, A.R.: quoted, 142 n 21

Hall, Marie Boas: quoted, 89, 91

Harbage, Alfred: quoted, 32

Harrison, Charles Trawick: quoted, 143 n 30

Harvey, William, 93

Harwood, John T.: quoted, 90-91

Henrietta Maria, 85, 88, 117, 119, 134 n 1;

influence on M.C., 11-38; and
Catholicism, 11, 15, 17, 18, 80-81;
theatrical activity of, 13-18, 136 nn 10,
11; and court culture, 13-19, 21, 24,
137 n 26, 139 n 47; wartime activity
of, 11, 18-19, 22; displeased with
W.C.'s courtship of M.L., 23, 120;
Letters, quoted, 18-19
Histriomastix (Prynne), 17
Hobbes, Thomas, 46, 47, 98; influence on
M.C., 7, 8, 9, 10, 12, 57, 62-84; and
Devonshires, 64; and W.C., 3, 64-65,
146 nn 11, 13; and Descartes, 47; and
Erastianism, 69-84; and experimental-
ism, 90, 102, 104. Works: "Answer to
the Preface to Gondibert," 66; *The Art
of Rhetoric*, quoted, 80; "Autobiogra-
phy," quoted, 65, 68, 69; "Consider-
ations on the Reputation . . . of
Thomas Hobbes," quoted, 90;
Elements of Law, 65, 69; *Letters*, 64, 65-
66; *Leviathan*, 47, 63, 65, quoted, 63-
64, 83; *Of Liberty and Necessity*, 65; *A
Minute or First Draught of the
Optiques*, 65, quoted, 146 n 15
Hollar, Wenceslas, 63
Hooke, Robert, 53; M.C.'s reading of, 9;
Micrographia, 89-113, quoted, 91-92,
95, 96, 109, 152 n 27, 153 n 42
Horace: *Ars Poetica*, quoted, 36
Hôtel Rambouillet, 16
Howard, Thomas, first earl of Berkshire:
quoted, 69
Howell, James, 16, 137 n 20, quoted, 16
Hutchinson, Lucy, 4, 50, 145 n 2, quoted,
50, 144 n 34
Hyde, Edward, first earl of Clarendon:
quoted, 47, 142 n 24

induction. *See* experimentalism

Jacquot, Jean: quoted, 142 n 21
James, William: quoted, 114
Job, Book of, 45, 70, 147 n 27
Johnson, Samuel, 59
Jones, Howard, 144 n 34, quoted, 50, 143
nn 30, 32
Jones, Inigo: and Henrietta Maria, 16-17;

Salmacida Spolia, 18; *The Temple of
Love*, 17
Jones, Kathleen, 117
Jones, Richard Foster: quoted, 103

Kargon, Robert: quoted, 45, 56, 143 n 33
Kepler, Johannes, 53
Khanna, Lee Cullen: quoted, 154 n 52
Killigrew, Mary (née Lucas; M.C.'s sister),
3, 41-43

Lady Contemplation, The (Cavendish),
27-31, quoted, 16, 27-30
Letters (Cavendish), 22-24, 119-32, 138 n
43, quoted, 23, 33, 38, 85, 116
*Letters and Poems in Honour of . . .
Margaret . . . Cavendish*, 116
Leviathan (Hobbes), 47, 63, 65, quoted,
63-64, 83
Lewis, C.S., 98
Life of . . . William Cavendishe
(Cavendish), 4, 31-32, 67, 71-72,
quoted, 1, 19, 31-32, 71-72, 87, 88,
114, 148 n 34, 150 nn 8, 9
Lisle, George, 42
Love's Adventures (Cavendish), 26, 27, 33,
quoted, 33
Lucas, Anne (M.C.'s sister), 20, 86
Lucas, Charles (M.C.'s brother), 3, 42, 43,
76-77
Lucas, Elizabeth (née Leighton; M.C.'s
mother): as a mother, 2; attacked in
Colchester, 20; persuades M.C. to stay
at court, 22; wartime experience of,
41; on marriage, 41, 119, 135 n 2;
handwriting of, 119; death of, 3, 41-
43; grave desecrated, 42; remembered
by M.C., 41, 44-45; *Letters*, quoted, 41
Lucas, John (M.C.'s brother), 23; stores
arms for the king, 2, 20
Lucas, Thomas (M.C.'s father), 2, 117
Lucas home: plundered, 2, 20, 42-45, 138
n 37
Lucretius, 46, 57; *De Rerum Natura*, 40,
49, 50, quoted, 40
Lyttelton, Charles: quoted, 5

MacCarthy, B.G.: quoted, 150 n 5

Mackworth, Francis, 31
Makin, Bathsua, 4, quoted, 4
Man in the Moone, The (Godwin), 53, 58, quoted, 145 n 46
Marston Moor, 22
masques, 16; M.C.'s reading of, 12
Mayerne, Theodore, 98; on M.C.'s health, 43-44; *Letters*, quoted, 43-44
mechanism, 93, 96-102, 114
Medici, Marie de, 16
Mendelson, Sara, 117
Merchant, Carolyn, 152 n 30
Mercurius Aulicus, 20, 139 n 47, quoted, 138 nn 28, 33
Mercurius Rusticus, 20, 138 n 37, quoted, 20
Meyer, Gerald Dennis: quoted, 152 n 26
Milton, John, 51
Mintz, Samuel: quoted, 70, 147 n 28
Montagu, Walter, 12, 16; *The Shepheard's Paradise*, 12, 17-18, 138 n 27
More, Henry, 9, 72, 98, 101, 156 n 66; *Antidote Against Atheism*, 99
Motteville, Francoise de, 19

Nature's Pictures (Cavendish), 25, 73-78, 114, quoted, 8, 68, 73-78, 119
Newcastle, duchess of. *See* Cavendish, Margaret, duchess of Newcastle
Newcastle, first duke of. *See* Cavendish, William, first duke of Newcastle
Newton, Isaac, 51, 60
Nicolson, Marjorie: quoted, 53, 155 n 63
Norton, Mary, 144 n 35

Observations upon Experimental Philosophy (Cavendish), 9, 90-113, quoted, 9, 55, 93-98, 111
Oman, Carola: quoted, 22, 135 n 5
optical instruments, 53, 90-113
Orations (Cavendish), 78-80, 114, quoted, 55, 72-73, 78-79
Osborne, Dorothy, 4; *Letters*, quoted, 4

Paloma, Dolores: quoted, 155 n 54
Panzani, Gregorio, 135 n 7
Paracelsianism, 98-102
Paracelsus: quoted, 99

Payne, Linda: quoted, 139 n 56, 155 n 54
Peacock, John: quoted, 14-15, 17, 137 n 22
Pearson, Jacqueline: quoted, 139 n 51
Pepys, Samuel: reaction to M.C., 4, 5; on M.C.'s visit to the Royal Society, 111-12; *Diary*, quoted, 4, 5, 111, 112, 156 n 66
Petty, William: quoted, 46
Philips, Katherine, 4, 134 n 15
Philosophical and Physical Opinions (Cavendish), 88-89, 98, quoted, 8, 62, 65, 68, 70-71, 88-89, 100, 101, 116, 142 n 18, 145 n 2, 153 n 36, 156 n 1
Philosophical Letters (Cavendish), quoted, 72, 83, 98, 99, 100-101
Philosophicall Fancies (Cavendish), 4, 48-49, 50, quoted, 142 n 26
Platonism: in Caroline drama, 16; and court culture, 13-19; M.C.'s Platonic idealism, 8, 11-38, 88; Henrietta Maria's use of Platonic love doctrine, 13-19; M.C.'s use of Platonic love doctrine, 12, 23-38, 135 n 4; and pastoral romance, 12, 29-31, 88; in *The Lady Contemplation*, 27-31; in *Love's Adventures*, 26-27, 33; in *The Presence*, 34-38; in *Youth's Glory and Death's Banquet*, 33-34
Playes (Cavendish), 25, 65, prefatory matter quoted, 25
Plays, Never Before Printed (Cavendish), 25, 114, prefatory matter quoted, 32
Poems and Fancies (Cavendish), 4, 48, 50-61, quoted, 47-48, 51-54, 57, 58-59, 84, 117-18, 138 n 41, 143 n 26
Poems, or, Several Fancies in Verse (Cavendish), 114
Potter, Lois, 139 n 47
Power, Henry: *Experimental Philosophy*, 90, quoted, 103
Presence, The (Cavendish), 16, 34-38, 157 n 5, quoted, 34-37
Private Memoirs of Sir Kenelm Digby, 16
Prynne, William: 17, 137 n 26; *Censure of Mr. Cozens*, 136 n 15; *Histriomastix*, 17; *The Popish Royall Favourite*, quoted, 138 n 26

Pye, Catherine (née Lucas; M.C.'s sister), 22, 86
Pym, John, 138 n 28

rationalism, 12, 85-113
Reik, Miriam: quoted, 47
Rich, Mary, countess of Warwick: quoted, 12
Riggs, David: quoted, 147 n 21
Rogers, John, 144 n 35, quoted, 145 n 2
Rogow, Arnold: quoted, 145 n 6, 146 nn 11, 13
Rosenthal, Laura: quoted, 140 n 59
Royal Society, 5, 9, 56, 88-113, 116; experimental program of, 89-93; M.C. attends meeting, 110-13
Rubens, Peter Paul, 3
Rushworth, John, 31
Ryan, Alan: quoted, 69
Ryves, Bruno, 138 n 37

Sales, Francis de, Saint: *Delicious Entertainments of the Soule*, 15; *A Devoute Life*, quoted, 15
Salvetti, Amerigo: quoted, 14
Sarasohn, Lisa: quoted, 55
Schaffer, Simon, 90, 111, quoted, 90, 152 n 25
Sensabaugh, G.F.: quoted, 15
Shadwell, Thomas: *The Virtuoso*, quoted, 115
Shapin, Steven, 90, 111, quoted, 90, 152 n 25
Sharpe, Kevin, 135 n 7, 137 n 26, quoted, 13-14
Shepheard's Paradise, The (Montagu), 12, 17-18, 138 n 27
Sherman, Sandra: quoted, 155 n 52
Skinner, Quentin, 146 n 9, quoted, 64, 89
Smith, Hilda: quoted, 149 n 43
Smuts, Malcolm, 135 n 7, 137 n 26, quoted, 17
Sociable Letters (Cavendish), 25, 86-88, 149 n 2, quoted, 44, 72, 73, 78, 79-80, 86-88, 135 n 4, 148 n 34, 149 n 2
Somerset House, 17, 81

Sprat, Thomas: *History of the Royal Society*, 89, 90, quoted, 89, 151 n 12
Stanley, Thomas: *History of Philosophy*, 49-50, 102
Straznicky, Marta: quoted, 140 n 56
Swift, Jonathan, 58
Sylvester, Joshua: translation of Du Bartas' *Divine Weeks*, quoted, 142 n 19

Taylor, Charles: quoted, 114
Temple, William, 4
Temple of Love, The (Davenant and Jones): quoted, 17
Thomas, Peter William: quoted, 17, 139 n 47
Topp, Elizabeth. *See* Chaplain, Elizabeth
Trubowitz, Rachel: quoted, 154 n 52
"True Relation, A" (Cavendish), 23-24, 41, 116, quoted, 2, 7, 12, 19, 21-22, 24, 41, 44-45, 133 n 6

Urfé, Honoré d': *L'Astrée*, 16

Van Diepenbeeck, Abraham, 148 n 40
Van Helmont, Jan Baptista, 9, 72, 98-99
Veevers, Erica, 134 n 1, 136 n 11, quoted, 16, 17
Virtuoso, The (Shadwell): quoted, 115
Vladislav VII, 120

Waller, Edmund, 46, 66
Waller, Richard: *The Life of Dr. Robert Hooke*, quoted, 53
Warwick, countess of. *See* Rich, Mary
Welbeck Abbey, 3, 4, 88, 148 n 41
Wilkins, John: *Discovery of a World in the Moone*, 53
Wood, Anthony, 117
Woolf, Virginia: quoted, 48
World's Olio, The (Cavendish), 24, 48-49, 55-60, 114, quoted, 24-25, 46, 55-60, 69-70, 71, 110, 143 n 27

Youth's Glory and Death's Banquet (Cavendish), 33-34, quoted, 33-34, 142 n 19